W9-AXJ-926

the year of DRINKING ADVENTUROUSLY

52 WAYS TO GET OUT OF YOUR COMFORT ZONE

JEFF CIOLETTI

THE

YEAR OF DRINKING ADVENTUROUSLY

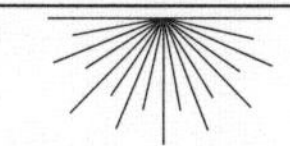

52 WAYS TO GET OUT OF YOUR COMFORT ZONE

By

JEFF CIOLETTI

Turner Publishing

Turner Publishing Company
424 Church Street • Suite 2240 • Nashville, Tennessee 37219
445 Park Avenue • 9th Floor • New York, New York 10022
www.turnerpublishing.com

The Year of Drinking Adventurously

Cover design: Maddie Cothren
Book design: Nathalie Ouederni

Library of Congress Cataloging-in-Publication Data

Cioletti, Jeff.
The year of drinking adventurously : 52 weeks, 52 ways to get out of your comfort zone / by Jeff Cioletti.
pages cm
1. Alcoholic beverages--History. 2. Drinking of alcoholic beverages. I. Title.
TP520.C56 2015
641.2'1--dc23
2015009483

[9781681621029]

Printed in the United States of America
15 16 17 18 19 20 10 9 8 7 6 5 4 3 2 1

For my wife, Craige

CONTENTS

COCKTAILING ADVENTUROUSLY

INTRODUCTION

CHEERS TO THE YEAR

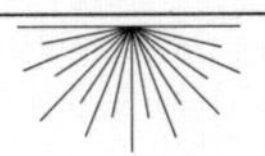

Few words in the English language are as loaded as the word comfort. We seek it in our relationships, our jobs, and, in a more literal sense, our furniture, our vehicles, and the seats we choose on a plane. That's all, undeniably, important and positive stuff. But there's also a dark side to striving for comfort. It may be cozy like a warm blanket, but it's also the refuge of the intimidated—those who fear the unknown. I'm not judging or pointing fingers; it's a notion that exists in all of us to a certain extent, and it manifests in some more than others.

Who hasn't, on at least a few occasions, been told to get out of their comfort zone by a professor, a parent, a partner, a boss, or an annoying platitude hanging on the wall of the boss's office?

Eye-roll-inducing motivational posters notwithstanding, getting a little helpful nudge beyond the realm of the familiar once in a while is a critical catalyst for personal growth and one of the keys to living a healthy and fulfilling life.

Injecting a little adventure into your existence doesn't have to mean jumping off a bridge with an elastic harness strapped to your leg or tumbling out of a plane with nothing between you and the cold, hard ground eight thousand feet below. While bungee jumpers and skydivers are fully deserving of our utmost respect and admiration, most of us will live out our days perfectly content having never experienced the physical free fall. It's the tiny, individual components of our everyday routines that offer the best untapped opportunities for our own adventurous leaps—the films we watch, the books we read, the roads we drive, the food we eat and, of course, the beverages we drink.

If you haven't figured it out already, the next few hundred pages will be making a case for that last one. Otherwise, my friend, you've probably picked up the wrong book. Thanks for stopping by!

Let's face it, going to a bar or browsing the aisles at a liquor store can be an overwhelming experience. There are more beverage options today than there were at any other point in the history of alcohol consumption and settling on one is the very definition of daunting. The great twentieth-century philosophers collectively known as Devo once said something about us really wanting freedom from choice.

How many times have you or someone you know sat on a stool, stared blankly at the magnificent array of artfully designed glass containers or tap handles on the bar and then, when pressed to make a decision, sheepishly uttered something like "vodka tonic?"

There's nothing inherently shameful in that. We all retreat behind what we know. And if you've got a regular go-to drink that you love, by all means keep on loving it. But also ask yourself why you love it. Is it because (a) You've tried everything else there is to try and, yep, it's the best; (b) You don't put much thought into something that, for you, is nothing more than an alcohol delivery system; or (c) It's just easier to default to the approachably familiar.

If you answered A, there's a 99.99 percent chance that you're lying. If you'd tried everything under the sun, you wouldn't be reading this because the human liver couldn't handle it and corpses can't read. If you answered B, you also wouldn't be reading this right now because a person indifferent about what and how one drinks wouldn't have picked up a book about imbibing adventurously in the first place. I would wager that most of you fall into the C category.

The reason I'm betting on approachable familiarity is that a dozen or so years ago, that would have been my response. I'd even admit to having been a B in those days as well.

It wasn't until I joined the editorial staff of a beverage magazine in early 2003 that I had even an inkling of what to order beyond what social convention had conditioned me to consume. In college, it was whatever the cheapest beer was—$2 a pitcher at a bar or $8.99 for a case of twenty-four at a retail store. Beer was something that was not meant to taste good, and for nearly the first decade of my legal adult drinking, I believed that.

Around the same time I discovered, on a spring break trip to London, what we call "hard" cider. The moment I got home, I didn't hesitate to integrate it into my admittedly limited drinking repertoire. The sweeter it was, the better. And that was a good thing, because in the 1990s, that was pretty much all one could get on this side of the pond—cloyingly sugary offerings that may or may not have been fermented from actual, harvested-from-the-tree apples. This was, I must point out, a good fifteen years before the start of the true cider revolution in North America (which you'll read a bit about on some of the pages that follow). That meant that even this iteration of oppressively sweet alcoholic sugar water was relegated to inauthentic Irish and English pubs. Once I left my college town and those places proved fewer and farther between, it was time to adopt a new drink to order in "grown-up" bars. Hello, gin and tonic. Don't get me wrong; gin is an absolutely wonderful spirit, as you'll read in week twenty-eight. But when you're a broke twenty-five-year-old scrounging enough pennies for a night out in Manhattan, as I was, you barely can afford well drinks. So I always hoped against hope that the cheap gin, whose dominant botanical tasted remarkably like battery acid, would be diluted enough to make it semipotable but not so diluted that it failed in its mission as an alcohol delivery system (there's that B again).

Immersing myself in the beverage market, in a strictly journalistic sense, was akin to exploring a previously undiscovered planet. I was, up to that time, ignorant and rather indifferent toward the breadth of categories, styles, and brands of beverage alcohol available to the American consumer. Within my first six months, I was intrigued. By the end of year one, I was in love. By the time the second year had ended, I was rhapsodically passionate.

While I don't expect everyone who reads this to reach that destination, I do hope that you're all at least inspired. Among the fifty-two chapters—each a different drink for a different week of the year—you'll discover at least a handful of beer, spirits, ciders, or wines that might find their way into your personal imbibing rotation.

Think of this as a sort of Drinking Diversity Manifesto. Nearly three-quarters of legal-drinking-age alcohol consumers fall under the header of cross-category drinker—or the less cumbersome "cross-drinker" (there's even a team of folks in North Carolina who launched CrossDrinker.com to celebrate this phenomenon). Drinkers who fit this profile like to dabble in each of the major adult beverage categories—beer, wine, spirits, saké, cider—even when they vocally identify primarily as a drinker of one over the other. If you're a dyed-in-the-wool craft beer geek and rarely venture out of the pint glass, you may, for instance, be tempted to get better acquainted with saké. White wine may be your regular go-to, but perhaps you'll be inspired to invite a Berliner Weisse into your sipping vessel. Or, if you think you've tried it all and are ready for the indescribable and incomparable, it's time to exclaim "Ganbei!" and down a cup of baijiu. On the other hand, you could just be that vodka tonic person who's ready to throw caution to the wind and say, "Hit me with your best shot, barkeep!"

I'm going to warn you right now. You're not going to like every drink in this book. In fact, it's likely you will downright loathe some of them. With about 80 percent of the beverages herein, it's about taste, particularly the wonder of flavors unexplored. The rest? Well, let's just say it's more about the journey and leave it at that.

And there has been no better time, in the history of fermentation and distillation, to embark on that journey. We are in the midst of a revolution that spans most adult-beverage categories. Drinkers the world over are embracing the artisanal, from beers that eschew industrial-strength efficiencies in favor of hand-crafted integrity and diversity of flavor experience, to spirits that spend more time resting in oak barrels than the average US president stays in office. This back-to-basics orientation is making us think more about the history, heritage, and story behind what's in our glass.

Since this is a full year we're talking about, I've loosely structured things to begin the first week of January and conclude the final week of December. The emphasis is on "loosely." Some chapters or "weeks," for the sake of cohesive organization, correspond with seasons or specific holidays. If it's the middle of March, there will be a focus on Irish whiskey in the spirit of St. Patrick's Day. There are also a host of not-so-universally celebrated observances that are specific to particular beverages. Yes, there actually is a National Moonshine Day. I did not make up any of these! However, you can enjoy any of the drinks detailed between the covers at any point during the year, whenever the mood strikes you.

I do advise, though, that you take the yearlong challenge week by week. No bingeing please! Some of this stuff is pretty damned strong and best experienced in moderation. If you're looking for fifty-two quick and easy ways to get tanked, then close this book right now and either move out of the frat house or consider a twelve-step program.

Besides, the drinks you're about to discover are much more enjoyable if you take your time and savor the experience. And be sure to stick around during the closing credits because the back of the book features some terrific cocktail recipes based on many of the beverages you'll encounter throughout this year.

Still with me? Splendid! Then without further ado, I wish you Godspeed as you embark on The Year of Drinking Adventurously.

WEEKS 1–52

WHISKEY WEEKS

Overwhelming barely begins to cover the vast array of choices available to adult drinkers today. Just as overwhelming is knowing where to start. Since the year is just beginning and it's likely very cold outside, what better way to warm up than with a glass of whiskey? Perhaps you've yet to break the seal on that bottle of Scotch someone gave you over the holidays. Now's your chance. If you can find a working fireplace in front of which to sip it, even better.

Over these first four weeks in the depths of winter, we're going to be diving headlong into whisk(e)y. That's not a typo. That's a conscious decision to be as inclusive as possible and respect the two prominent spellings of the word, neither of which is wrong. The Scots, who arguably are responsible for the worldwide culture surrounding the spirit, spell it sans e, as do the Japanese and most Canadians. The Irish, however, leave the e intact. The Americans tend to default to using that extra letter, but there are some in the bourbon realm for whom the y alone is sufficient.

There may only be two acceptable variations in its spelling, but the distinctions in ingredients, production methods, aroma, flavor profiles, and drinking rituals are far more numerous.

But before we talk about any of those, let's start at the very beginning. The word whisky derives from the Gaelic word uisge/uisce—the former spelling being Irish Gaelic and the latter Scottish—meaning "water of life" (a phrase that recurs throughout this book, as most international cultures have their own respective distillates to which they apply the term).

Since those days in the late Middle Ages when distilling began in earnest, whiskey gradually has become a global phenomenon. And, like anything fashionable, it's inevitable that it will fall out of fashion. Such was the fate of whiskey in the 1970s and 1980s, when the bottom fell out and distilleries from Kentucky to Kilmarnock shuttered, seemingly forever.

Thankfully, a confluence of factors, from the rise of the Internet and social media, to the foodie movement, have helped usher in the twenty-first-century whiskey renaissance.

Drinkers have become more whiskey-literate as they've been able to find each other on Twitter and Facebook, share their passions, and learn from each other. They've also been able to engage with the distillers of those beverages like never before.

And, as they've sought out top-notch culinary creations with the finest ingredients and chefs' artistic flair, so too have they been exploring spirits that provide a complementary experience. Barbecue, for example, has become haute cuisine in the past decade. It's done wonders for the whiskey that pairs best with it: bourbon.

The beverage has reclaimed its rightful place in the spotlight, and hopefully this time around it stays there. Perhaps you can be a part of making sure that happens. With that in mind, think of the next few weeks as a rudimentary primer to help make the venerable, age-old spirit part of your drinking adventure.

Week 1.

From the Highlands to the Islands

The Search for Scotch

Fair warning: There is no fathomable way the topic of Scotch whisky can be done justice in only a handful of pages. There are few potables that ignite so much passion and even fewer that can be as polarizing. Even to call a product "Scotch" does the entire craft and heritage of whisky distilling within Scotland a tremendous disservice. Writing this is a fool's errand, an exercise in alienation. There's the double-pronged risk of alienating the novices and infuriating the connoisseurs. But that being said, please keep reading.

We'll tackle the most basic of the basics first: single malt versus blended.

The "single" in single malt signifies that the whisky is produced from malted barley (and water, of course) from a single distillery. This shouldn't be confused with single-grain whisky, which also has a presence in Scotland. Like single malt, single-grain products are crafted at a solitary distillery, but they include whole grains, sometimes combined with other cereals (barley could be comingled with wheat or spelt, for instance).

Hold on. Let's back up a second. It's no wonder most people find fine whiskies intimidating when terms like "malt" are thrown around freely and assumed to be widely understood. Most have encountered the word in some context (milkshakes, perhaps), but when it relates to grain, malted grains are those that have been steeped in water and allowed to germinate. They're then dried in kilns, converting starches to fermentable sugars. Unmalted grains don't go through that process.

Now, on to blended whiskies.

Blending is essentially combining whiskies from multiple distilleries to create a desirable flavor profile that's consistent bottle to bottle. Most of the time the exact components of that blend and their precise proportions are a religiously guarded secret spanning generations, known only to the master distiller—distillery underlings worked from recipes instructing them to mix X percentage of unmarked bottle No. 1, Y percentage of unmarked bottle No. 2, Z percentage of unmarked bottle No. 3, etc. They were completely in the dark about which specific whiskies were in each of those bottles until the master distiller retired and passed on the knowledge to one lucky successor. How anyone ever manages to keep it straight is nothing short of miraculous; some blends are known to include in the neighborhood of forty different whiskies.

Things get a little more intricate underneath the blended umbrella. There are "blended malt whiskies"—also known by the more archaic title of "vatted" whiskies—which essentially combine a minimum of two (but usually more) single malts to achieve a certain taste and aroma profile. Then, there's "blended grain" whisky, which marries the unmalted grain whiskies of multiple producers. Finally, there's simply "blended" whisky, which can merge any proportion of malt and grain whiskies from various distilleries. The dominant, mass-marketed brands fall into that category.

Blends still account for the lion's share of the Scotch category—in the neighborhood of 85 to 90 percent of its volume—and the sheer number of them is partly to blame for the bad rap they sometimes get. When there are that many products, a lot of them are not going to be very good. Indeed, vast arrays of subpar Scotches exist, thanks to the corner-cutting comingling of cheaper grains, as well as inadequate maturation. (The golden-brownish color typical of whiskey, when aged properly, comes from the wood in which it's matured. Some lesser brands have been known to add caramel coloring to simulate that.) There are some fine blended expressions out there with quite lengthy maturation periods. The Pot Still, the iconic Glasgow whisky bar that boasts some six hundred different bottles, has a few on its list that fetch upwards of $40 a glass—and connoisseurs are willing to pay it.

But despite blends' continued volume dominance, that's not where all of the momentum and excitement lie in today's market. The spotlight belongs to single malts.

The advent of social media gets a good chunk of the credit for helping to foster that dynamic by creating a better-educated whisky drinker. Before the masses were tweeting to their hearts' content, there were few who identified as "whisky geeks." Sure, there were connoisseurs (and maybe a handful of snobs as well), but the Twitters, Facebooks, and Instagrams of the world have enabled drinkers to unite around a shared passion and spread knowledge about historical details and tasting nuances previously considered too esoteric to be inclusive. Such digital platforms have enhanced even the most casual of drinkers' vocabularies exponentially, enabling them to distinguish among the main whisky-producing regions, as nebulous (and sometimes confusing) as those can be. Ready for a brief geography lesson? Here goes:

HIGHLANDS

It's the largest slice of Scotland, beginning just north of Edinburgh and Glasgow and spanning all the way to the northernmost tip of the Scottish mainland. Given that huge expanse, good luck trying to get someone to explain the "quintessential" characteristics of a Highland malt. Most distillers and aficionados will agree that Highlands are "bold" and "rugged," have a bit of bite, and are slightly rough around the edges—although those traits could easily be used to describe the area's sloping terrain, as well as its inhabitants. However, since each distillery and each expression bottled by individual distilleries is different, that's about as common as it gets. Some classic Highland single malts include:

- ARDMORE
- DALWHINNIE
- GLENGOYNE
- GLENMORANGIE
- LOCH LOMOND
- OBAN
- TOMATIN
- TULLIBARDINE

SPEYSIDE

Technically, the Speyside region is in the Highlands, but it's a distilling tradition unto itself. The area offers a perfect confluence of factors that are conducive to whiskey making: a barley-friendly climate, fertile soil, and the cool, pristine water from its namesake, the River Spey. It's a relatively small sliver in the northeast, but it's the region with the highest concentration of distilleries—about half of Scotland's output originates there. That also means that there are wild variations. Broadly speaking, however, experienced tasters will often note "mildly sweet," "fruity," and "grassy" notes. Other predominate descriptors of regional offerings include "nutty" and "sulphury." The regional output is sometimes divided between "light Speyside" and "heavy Speyside" malts.

It's hard to select just a handful of distilleries to mention because there's some pretty world-class stuff in the Speyside camp, but here's a very abridged short list:

- ABERLOUR
- CARDHU
- CRAGGANMORE
- GLEN GRANT
- GLENFARCLAS (Interestingly, its label says "Highland" malt, but that's just for historical purposes; Glenfarclas very much identifies as a Speyside malt)
- GLENFIDDICH
- GLENLIVET
- GLENROTHES
- KNOCKANDO
- THE MACALLAN

ISLAY

The island off the southwest coast gets its own designation, even though there's a quasi-style labeled "Islands" encompassing the distilling activities on the other water-surrounded land masses. Islay (pronounced Eye-la) single malts are easiest to spot because they tend to be the smokiest of the lot. That's thanks to the heavy dose of peat smoking the malt undergoes. The island itself is pretty peat-rich to begin with and a lot of that seeps into the water as well. The lines have blurred a bit among the regions and a number of Highland and Speyside producers are releasing peaty versions of their own—but even then it's easy to distinguish those from a true Islay. A friend of mine encapsulated the style best when we were kicking back with a few glasses of an eighteen-year-old Islay: "It's like kissing a supermodel who smokes." Here are a few of the stars who walk the runway:

- ARDBEG
- BRUICHLADDICH
- BOWMORE
- CAOL ILA
- LAPHROAIG
- LAGAVULIN

ISLANDS

Any whisky produced on an island other than Islay gets grouped under this heading, which isn't really an official region to begin with. The malts are so diverse that the only element that they really have in common is that they're produced in distilleries that people need to cross a lengthy bridge or ride a ferry to visit. The maritime air might impart a bit of saltiness to the water with which these are produced, but beyond that they really defy categorization, drawing upon the best elements of many of the other regions. There's often a touch—sometimes a downright punch—of peatiness, similar to the Islay whiskies, but it's certainly not a defining characteristic. The loose confederation of whiskies of this ilk, along with their respective island homes:

- ARRAN (Isle of Arran; a relative newcomer, founded in 1993)
- SCAPA (Mainland of Orkney Islands)
- TALISKER (Isle of Skye; the pronounced hit of peat will make one swear it's an Islay)
- TOBERMORY (Isle of Mull)

LOWLANDS

There are only a relative few distilleries producing in the Lowland region, south of the Highlands and encompassing Scotland's two biggest cities, Glasgow and Edinburgh. Again, painting in extremely broad strokes, Lowland malts are among the lightest and softest of Scotches. While even the other non-Islay producers often incorporate some subtle degree of peat, Lowland's peat factor is usually nonexistent or undetectable. Highland and Speyside lovers have been known, on occasion, to turn their noses up at Lowland malts, but they are fine whiskies in their own right and a good introduction to single malts for newbies. Lowland brands include:

- ANNANDALE (perhaps a sign of reinvigoration for the Lowland region, Annandale shut down in the early 1920s, only to be reopened ninety years later)
- AUCHENTOSHAN (the rare Scotch whisky distilled three times versus the traditional two)
- GLENKINCHIE

CAMPBELTOWN

It's barely a style since there are only three actual producers left and it's often not even considered a whisky region given the fact that this diminutive area on the southern tip of the Kintyre peninsula west of the Lowlands saw its once-thriving distilling industry evaporate. The Scotch Whisky Association, the trade body that giveth and taketh in Scotland's distilling industry, recently restored Campbeltown's regional status. The Campbeltown triumvirate:

- GLENGYLE (KILKERRAN)
- GLEN SCOTIA
- SPRINGBANK

The real growth for Scotch whisky has been just about anywhere but Scotland. The United States, Western Europe, and Singapore have been its biggest export markets in recent years, and the beverage has drawn an increasing number of drinker pilgrimages to Scotland.

On a recent visit of my own, the contrast between the old and the new couldn't have been starker. Tomatin Distillery, whose classic but modern operation embodies a juxtaposition between history and the future, served as the perfect case study. In the early 2000s, the blend-to-single-malt ratio was about a 90–10 split. Now, it's more in the 65–35 range and still narrowing.[1] A decade ago, if Scotch whisky aficionados wanted to get their hands on a single malt from Tomatin and other distillers of its ilk, they'd be lucky to be able to get a five-year-old and a ten- or twelve-year-old version. Now, the boom in demand has helped usher in a golden age of innovation, with new expressions debuting constantly. And that doesn't just mean rolling out barrels that have been tucked away in warehouses and aging for decades—eighteen-year-old, twenty-six-year-old, thirty-year-old, and the like—but, say, an eleven-, twelve-, fourteen-, or sixteen-year-old aged in sherry or oak casks bottled at 46 percent or 57 percent alcohol by volume. (Sherry-barrel aging, by the way, brings a particularly sublime dimension to the whisky.)

A whisky matured for thirty years might seem old to most, but it's a mere infant compared with some of the more extreme expressions. The gift shop at the Speyside distillery, Glenfarclas, for instance, stocks a sixty-year-old. (The stated age reflects the time in the barrel; once it goes in a bottle it stops maturing.)

The real high rollers with money to burn would probably not even bat an eye at the price tag: £14,500, or, when the exchange rate is in America's favor, a cool $22,000. And even that's peanuts when measured against the six-figure sums many ultra-rare bottlings from a number of distilleries have fetched at auctions.

Given all of the focus on single malts and the heavy emphasis on heritage that accompanies them, it's easy to forget that there really wasn't much of a single-malt category before about thirty-five years ago. Distillers' whisky output had been primarily for blending purposes.

That's why most of the Scotches that are the closest things to household names—beyond the aficionado's household, mind you—are blends. Dewar's? Blend. Chivas Regal? Ditto. Famous Grouse? That, too. Johnnie Walker? You can see where this is going.

Johnnie Walker provides a good illustration of how blending works. The Cardhu Distillery, which makes some very fine single malts, has a great deal of paraphernalia related to Mr. Walker adorning its visitors' center near Archiestown, Scotland. And why wouldn't it, since they're both owned by global spirits, beer, and wine conglomerate Diageo? Cardhu serves as the de facto "Johnnie Walker experience" for tourists. Of course, that means that one of the most frequently asked questions tour guides must field is "So, this is where you distill Johnnie Walker, right?"

They always have to explain that Johnnie Walker's range, be it Red, Black, Gold, or Blue, isn't distilled anywhere. The single-malt and grain components of the blend are distilled all over Scotland, but the product we know as Johnnie Walker doesn't have a distillery.

Though blends historically have dominated, there are those distilleries that have, through the ages, sustained themselves with their single-malt business. Glenfarclas is one of those that have always bucked the trend. Only about 5 percent of its output has been allocated to blended whisky, a ratio that has more or less held steady since long before the single-malt surge.[2] The independent distiller is known for having one of the broadest ranges of maturation levels—ten, twelve, fifteen, seventeen, twenty-one, and twenty-five-year-old are just a few—and has remained fairly stable since the pre-boom days of the 1970s.

Before I had embarked on any serious distillery-hopping through Scotland, I had always been under the impression that the modern stewards of the respective traditions would be teeming with geocentric hubris; in the world I dreamed up, a Speyside purveyor would talk smack about a Highland producer, who'd in turn taunt an Islay icon, who'd bad-mouth the other islands (I guess I watched too much professional wrestling in my formative years). But in reality, most of the whisky makers from one tip of Scotland to another have developed spirits that exhibit some flavor and mouthfeel elements more commonly associated with whiskies produced outside their individual regions. Smoky, peaty whiskies, for instance, are synonymous with Islay, but it's not out of the ordinary to find hints of peat in Speyside creations.

"[The Scotch Whisky Industry] settled on regionalization as the big differentiator of whisky flavor; that's always worked, up to a point," Andy Cant, distillery manager at Cardhu, explains as he guides me through a tasting. "But there are exceptions to the rule; there are always subcategories."[3]

Cant should know. Cardhu's parent owns about a third of the distilleries across the majority of Scotland's whisky regions. Consolidation has been the governing dynamic for the industry for nearly as long as there has been an industry.

A legal industry, that is.

It's true that whisky distilling in Scotland dates back to the time of Columbus, but for around two centuries of its early history, most of the producers ran illicit operations. In the mid-seventeenth century, distillers started getting taxed through the nose, and few could afford to stay in business. But that didn't stop the four hundred or so clandestine producers that kept the Scotch tradition going through the first two decades of the nineteenth century. In 1823, Parliament passed the Excise Act, which made the tax structure far less draconian and encouraged makers to legalize by 1824.

A tale the Cardhu team likes to tell involves a woman who very well could be considered the mother of modern distilling, Helen Cumming. She was the primary distiller at the illegal facility she and her whisky-smuggler husband, John Cumming, set up. Pre-Excise Act, when government officers would drop by unannounced to investigate, she enthusiastically invited them inside. She'd slyly wave a flag, alerting other distillers and giving them enough time to hide all traces of whisky making from the excise officers. The distillery was able to produce on the up-and-up come 1824. In 1893, Helen's daughter-in-law, Elizabeth Cumming, sold the business to the Walker family—as in Johnnie Walker.[4]

Such under-cover-of-night exploits that characterized the development of the modern Scotch industry aren't too dissimilar to the romanticized history of moonshining in America.

A spirit as exalted as Scotch has been among elite connoisseurs is as rooted in the nefarious activities of outlaws as its far less prestigious Appalachian cousin.

There's also a link with the products coming out of Kentucky. Scotch whisky producers often mature their spirits in used bourbon barrels—bourbon producers, which you'll get to know better in the next week, can only use their barrels once; Scotch makers face no such restriction. Such cooperation speaks to the kinship that whiskey makers share across the continents, as distinct as their flavors and traditions may be.

Week 2

Capturing the American Spirit

Bourbon (with a Splash of Rye)

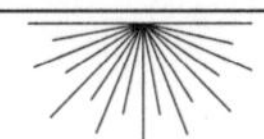

There are few noncomedies made in the 1980s that are as quotable as David Lynch's *Blue Velvet*. Especially for those of us who write about beverages, there are some lines that are downright iconic. The one everyone knows is the depraved, laughing gas–huffing maniac Frank Booth's (Dennis Hopper) decree on what constitutes a bad beer (Heineken) and a good beer (Pabst Blue Ribbon). But the one that's cited far less frequently and usually only by devout Lynchians involves his angry demand for bourbon.

And that sums up the state of bourbon whisky circa 1986. Its consumption had plummeted dramatically. The only people who admitted to drinking it were your dad, your grandpa, liver-compromised drunks, and sadistic movie villains.

Admittedly, that's a bit of hyperbolic indulgence on my part, but you get the idea. It was a dark time for America's native spirit. The free fall started at the tail end of the 1960s and continued into the 1990s. Then, finally, the trend started to reverse itself. But why?

The renaissance was the result of a confluence of a number of factors, none of which took hold overnight.

Somewhat paradoxically, one of the reasons Americans left the category was ultimately a major factor in bringing them back. In the 1960s and 1970s, spirits such as vodka, tequila, and rum started to come into vogue and the always-rebellious baby boomers started retreating to these products. At the same time, overall spirits consumption was declining as American wines started coming into their own and beer behemoths like Anheuser-Busch, under the leadership of August Busch III, entered a period of aggressive growth, further drawing US drinkers away from the spirits category.

That wasn't going to last forever, of course, especially since what was being marketed as "beer" was a pale, flavorless, commoditized version of a once-great drink, ripe for a revolution. That revolution happened in the form of what we now call "craft beer," which, in the grander beverage scheme of things, falls under the "premiumization" umbrella. Consumers started trading up to new flavor experiences and generally higher-end products. It seemed to parallel the foodie revolution in most major metro markets as well.

Drinkers demanded more from their vodkas and the super- and ultrapremium segments were born with carefully crafted grain-neutral spirits distilled six or seven times for ultimate smoothness. Imbibers weren't just asking for martinis, cosmos, or vodka tonics anymore; they were ordering Grey Goose martinis, Ciroc cosmopolitans, and Belvedere and tonics.

A disproportionate number of multimedia talking heads credit *Sex and the City* for the rise of cocktail culture in the early 2000s, primarily the cosmos and the faux-tinis served in the conical, stemmed glass. Its influence has been overstated, but on some level, the show served to demystify more sophisticated drinking experiences for its general audience, helping to open minds for greater things to come.

With drinkers' appetites whetted for some of the finer tipples—what industry analysts like to call "affordable luxuries"—consumers wanted to see to which other beverages they could trade up. That's when they started rediscovering whiskey, particularly those on the higher end of the market. Vodka growth started to slow by the beginning of the second decade of the new millennium and by 2014, whiskey overtook vodka as the most lucrative distilled spirits segment.

The cable TV-incubated pop cultural zeitgeist reared its head again some three years after Carrie Bradshaw and crew's small-screen exploits came to an end. Next it was Don Draper and company, making classic whiskey-based cocktails cool again. *Mad Men*, like its more feminine New York–based predecessor, tends to get a little more credit than it deserves—after all, only about four or five million people watched the AMC show each week, about a quarter of the audience that its network-mate *The Walking Dead* draws—but there's no denying that it has played some small role. There would possibly be far fewer millennials ordering Old-Fashioneds and Manhattans if they hadn't spent any time with the ad team at Sterling Cooper (and all of its other iterations).

Not to bore you with more statistics than you can stomach, but there's some fascinating intel to be gleaned from the numbers. Simmons Market Research Bureau conducted a study, contrasting bourbon attitudes in 2012 with those in 2004. In nearly every legal-drinking-age demographic (with the exception of the sixty-five plus demo), the number of Americans who describe themselves as bourbon drinkers increased by a few percentage points.

The foodie movement has had a bit to do with bourbon's rebirth, as has been the case with just about every better beverage segment. The culinary adventurer's quest for authenticity played right into bourbon's hands, for what is more authentic than America's native spirit, whose own story is virtually the story of the nation itself.

So, what exactly makes bourbon bourbon? First, it's supposed to be distilled in the United States. The rest of the world generally plays ball with this guideline and won't label something bourbon unless it actually is produced stateside. Of course, that's not always the case. Word to the wise when traveling abroad: Accept no substitutes.

Secondly, at least 51 percent of its mash must be corn. Corn has such a stigma when it's used as a beer adjunct, thinning the flavor and body and all, but with bourbon it's one of the key components that give it its unique flavor.

When the distillation process is complete, it cannot be more than one hundred sixty proof (80 percent alcohol by volume—ABV for short). Before it goes into the barrel for aging, it can't be more than one hundred twenty-five proof (62.5 percent ABV).

Now, about those barrels: The oak must be charred on the inside (critical for the color and flavor; it imparts a slight smokiness and caramalizes sugars in wood for deeper sweetness). It's quite a sight to visit a cooperage and witness the flames rise high from the oak barrels. It's a fairly ancient, yet absolutely perfect, technology that requires no improving. But with barrels being so sturdy, surely distillers can buy as many as they need and keep aging future batches in them? Absolutely wrong! The cooperage may be used once and only once. Sound like a waste? Head over to the garden center at Home Depot and take a closer look at the pots in which the shrubbery's planted. They're just charred-oak barrels cut in half.

An even more robust aftermarket has emerged in the past half-decade or so as more and more craft brewers have decided to add a bit of bourbon's flavor complexity to beer.

What's more, if the distillers want to label it "straight bourbon," it has to spend at least two years in the barrel. Many Kentucky-based distillers are likely to tell you that they tend to let it sit there twice that time.

Other terms to watch out for: "small batch" and "single barrel." Small batch generally involves comingling the contents of a small number of barrels; so, whatever is in the bottle of small-batch bourbon you're drinking comes from just those barrels. Now, "small" is a very relative, extremely nebulous word in this context. It could be just a handful of barrels we're talking about or it could be fifty.

Single barrel is just as it sounds: The contents of the bottle came out of one barrel and were not combined with the contents of any other. One of the better-known single-barrel bourbons is Blanton's, produced at the Buffalo Trace distillery—now a unit of the Sazerac Company—in Frankfort, Kentucky. The brand is iconic for the horse-and-jockey figurine topping its bottle stopper.

Oh, and one thing about Kentucky: limestone's pretty ubiquitous throughout the Bluegrass State. Along most highways you'll spot plenty of the stuff construction crews blasted through to build those roads—and the water is filtered through it, adding more location-specific nuances to the spirit. That's one of the main reasons why the vast majority of the nation's bourbon—about 95 percent at last count—continues to be produced in Kentucky.

However, there's one aspect of bourbon that might not be nearly as ubiquitous as one might think: actual distilling. Kentucky's bourbon country is famous, but there are only a handful of operating distilleries owned by an even smaller handful of parent companies—that is, facilities performing all of the steps necessary in making the stuff before the liquid enters the barrel. Many times bourbons matured in Kentucky by Kentucky-based brand owners aren't even born in the states. They're often distilled by an Indiana-based producer and sold by the barrel to those brand-owning companies in Kentucky and elsewhere. The most common term for the distillery-less distillers is non-distiller producer, NDP for short.

NDPs range from marketers that buy the whiskey fully aged, bottle it, and slap their own label on it, to those that buy it fresh off the still and perform their own blending, maturation, and finishing. Many bourbon enthusiasts criticize the former type, mostly in the interest of transparency. It's not atypical for an independent bottler that plays little or no role in the actual production process to cook up a folksy backstory for marketing purposes.

Some NDPs are independent bottlers that had distilled in previous generations, but ceased production when the market declined in the 1970s and 1980s. The Willett Distillery in Bardstown, Kentucky, for instance, produced whiskey from 1935 until the early 1980s. In 1984, it rebranded itself as Kentucky Bourbon Distillers (KBD) and continued to bottle whatever it had left in its barrels. When that stock ran low, it began to purchase its spirits from other producers.

But as bourbon bounced back, KBD revived the Willett name, and in 2012 began distilling on-site again with brand-new equipment.

The bourbon resurgence also has drawn a great deal of investment from large, multinational spirits marketers. Diageo, the world's largest, recently constructed a $115 million distillery in Shelby County, Kentucky, to produce its Bulleit brand, which, for the first two decades of its existence, has been an NDP product.

However, since it takes a great deal of time for bourbon to reach full maturation, a number of these new operations remain years away from releasing products crafted entirely at their own facilities.

How does one tell an NDP's bourbon from one produced entirely in-house? It's helpful to read labels very carefully. Sometimes the package reads "aged and bottled" at such-and-such distillery or sometimes just "bottled." If you're a purist who values an entirely single-distillery corn-to-glass bourbon, keep an eye out for the words "distilled, bottled, and aged by" somewhere on the bottle. Sometimes, though, it's better just to sip a bourbon blindly; you like what you like, and you shouldn't let ambiguous provenance bias you against an otherwise well-crafted and delicious spirit.

If you were to poll your circle of friends, you'd very likely find an astonishingly high number within your social network who'd say they just can't stand bourbon (or any other whiskey for that matter). There's absolutely no shame in that. Just take it from a guy in whose blood bourbon flows: Fred Noe, third-generation Jim Beam distiller and grandson of Mr. Beam himself.

"The first time I ever drank it, I took a big drink of it straight and it wasn't a pleasurable experience," Noe tells me. "I think a lot of people drink too much too fast, and that's why they get turned off of bourbon."[5]

Old Hollywood horse operas never did the whiskey any favors.

"You see the cowboys bellying up to the bar, 'Gimme a shot of whiskey!' and they pour and knock it back," Noe recalls. "It's not the way to enjoy bourbon. You've got to sip it and savor it, not just throw it back."

And there's no shame in not wanting to drink it neat. Even a pro like Noe—again, bourbon in his blood—had to take some baby steps before he started enjoying it straight.

"I first started drinking it with Sprite," he admits, "then I got to water. And now I drink it pretty neat, maybe with a splash of water or with a cube or two of ice."

REDISCOVERING RYE

As it turns out, bourbon was only the beginning. Its rebirth has served as the harbinger of greater things in the world of whiskey. Bourbon helped open the eyes of the American consumer to the wonders of rye. It makes sense because there's more that unites than divides the two styles. Remove bourbon's "made in America" requirement, replace the 51 percent corn minimum with a 51 percent rye minimum, and that's the whiskey in a nutshell. Forty-nine percent of a bourbon's grain bill very well could be rye, while the same proportion of a rye brand's recipe actually might be corn. The frontier between the two is a meager two percentage points.

However, when a distiller sets out to make a rye, they're going to make a rye and are usually not content with the bare minimum. Some boast 75 percent or even 100 percent of the grain that gives the whiskey, like it gives the bread, its distinctly spicy flavor.

"Rye and bourbon are kissing cousins," says Dave Pickerell, an icon in the whiskey world who spent fourteen years as master distiller of Maker's Mark before he went on to work with some forty-five distillers in twenty-five states. [6]

A past chair of the Kentucky Distillers Association, Pickerell was one of the first to see the rye resurgence coming. And he's been instrumental in helping make it happen. In 2001, The Distilled Spirits Council of the United States (DISCUS), the trade group that represents the nation's producers and brand owners, and the Wine and Spirits Wholesalers of America, the association representing distributors, teamed up with the folks who run George Washington's home, Mount Vernon, to recommence production of the first president's distilling activities. Washington had a working rye distillery, which continued producing for a decade and a half after his death. In 2007, after an eight-year excavation and reconstruction project, Pickerell oversaw the first batches of George Washington Rye in nearly 200 years.

Pickerell also played a central role in launching WhistlePig 100 percent rye, which initially was distilled in Canada, but finished at WhistlePig's home base in Vermont. WhistlePig opened its own single-estate farm distillery there in 2015, running all stages of the process from one site. He's also master distiller of Upstate New York's Hillrock Estate Distillery, which produces, among other whiskeys, a double-cask rye.

"That's what I left Maker's Mark to do," reveals Pickerell, "to bring to market the best tasting rye whiskey that had ever graced the American palate."

Those palates, it seems, are catching up. In 2006, the entire rye segment stood at one hundred fifty thousand cases annually, with virtually no money being spent on marketing. Today, a single brand—Bulleit Rye—is responsible for that much volume.

Hopefully the rye and bourbon surge is here to stay and the range of choices available remains robust. But let's not worry about the future. The time to enjoy it is right now. Here are a few places to start, including products from both distillers proper and NDPs (I remain neutral on the matter; if it's good, it's good):

KENTUCKY BOURBON

- BUFFALO TRACE (THE SAZERAC COMPANY): Great neat, on the rocks, or in Old-Fashioneds and mint juleps, Buffalo Trace is quite affordable (usually around $27 per 750 milliliter (mL) bottle) for a whiskey of its quality.
- MAKER'S MARK (BEAM SUNTORY): Its signature boxish bottle with a long neck and red wax closure is hard to miss.
- ELIJAH CRAIG 12 (HEAVEN HILL DISTILLERY): The small-batch bourbon, aged for twelve years, is named for a late eighteenth/early nineteenth-century distilling pioneer. There's also an eighteen-year-old single-barrel variant.
- KNOB CREEK (BEAM SUNTORY): The small-batch bourbon is aged for nine years, bottled at one hundred proof or 50 percent alcohol by volume (ABV), and is quite robust in flavor.
- BLANTON'S (THE SAZERAC COMPANY): Look for this single-barrel bourbon's bottle shape that's best described as a 3-D octagon, topped with one of eight different horse-and-jockey bottle stoppers, marked with either a B, L, A, N, T, O, N, or S.
- WILLETT POT STILL RESERVE (WILLETT DISTILLERY/KENTUCKY BOURBON DISTILLERS LTD.): Since we're on the subject of crazy bottle shapes, there's no mistaking this single-barrel offering; it's shaped like an actual pot still with a stout base and a really long neck.
- JIM BEAM SIGNATURE CRAFT SINGLE BARREL (BEAM SUNTORY): The most recognizable name in bourbon recently unveiled its ultrapremium Signature Craft line, which also features a twelve-year-old small batch, as well as a whiskey finished in Spanish brandy barrels.

Bourbon from Beyond Kentucky

- HUDSON BABY BOURBON (TUTHILLTOWN SPIRITS/ WILLIAM GRANT & SONS): In 2005 Tuthilltown Spirits became the first distillery to produce in the state of New York since Prohibition. Its world-famous Baby Bourbon is 100 percent corn-based and aged in barrels a fraction the size of standard bourbon cooperage so there's more liquid-wood contact in a shorter period of time. Though matured for under four years, Baby Bourbon tastes much older. Though Tuthilltown sold its Hudson whiskey line to Scotland-based William Grant & Sons in 2010, it continues to produce the line at its Gardiner, NY distillery.

- HILLROCK SOLERA AGED BOURBON (HILLROCK ESTATE DISTILLERY): Another highly respected Upstate New York distiller, Hillrock applied a different solution to the aging-whiskey-without-the-years conundrum. The Solera method, traditionally used in sherry production, involves stacking barrels of varying age in a pyramid formation and continuously comingling the young with the old. The youngest is on top and the oldest is on the bottom. When a fraction of the liquid in the oldest is removed, it's replenished with a portion of the next youngest, and so on.

Rye Whiskey

- WOODFORD RESERVE KENTUCKY STRAIGHT RYE WHISKEY (BROWN-FORMAN): Woodford has been known for its world-class small-batch bourbon, but the subsequent rye resurgence is not lost on brand owner Brown-Forman (better known as the company that owns Jack Daniel's). The master distiller spent about a decade perfecting the recipe before it released the 53 percent rye whiskey in 2015.

- BULLEIT RYE (DIAGEO): Like Woodford, Bulleit built a following as a bourbon. It was a natural progression, as Bulleit bourbon was known for its relatively high rye content of 28 percent. Bulleit Rye ups that to 95 percent.

- ➳ WHISTLEPIG STRAIGHT RYE WHISKEY (WHISTLEPIG): The 100 percent rye is aged for at least ten years and bottled at one hundred proof. It's garnered much acclaim since its 2010 release.

- ➳ RYEMAGEDDON (CORSAIR ARTISAN DISTILLERY): From one of the most innovative distillers in the country comes a blend of malted rye and chocolate rye whose name pretty much says it all.

Week 3

NORTHERN EXPOSURE

CANADIAN WHISKY

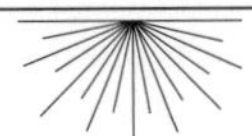

Every whiskey-making tradition in every whiskey-making region has suffered from one misunderstanding or another throughout the course of distilling history, but few have been misunderstood as much as the products hailing from the country with which the United States shares its northernmost border. Chalk it up to mediocre journalism, uneven marketing, or plain old overshadowing from the activities of a more populous neighbor—whatever the reason, there's no arguing with the fact that Canada has, time and again, gotten the shaft. That ends now.

Ottawa's Davin de Kergommeaux has made a career out of separating the facts from the fiction of Canadian whisky (and there are a lot of the latter). One of the biggest myths is that America's Prohibition is what made Canadian whisky (no e, thank you very much) come into its own. In fact, Canada's whisky market suffered severe damage from those fourteen dark years its neighbor to the south shoved down North American drinkers' throats. Since the end of the Civil War, the United States had been the world's largest market for Canadian whisky. So, guess what happens when, after more than a half-century of gangbusters business, your biggest customer can no longer buy your products by rule of law?

Here, de Kergommeaux says, is what: "Sales plummeted about 90 percent during Prohibition." [7]

There certainly was plenty of the spirit being smuggled below the border during the 1920s and early 1930s, but much of that actually was coming from Scotland and Ireland. It was landing in Canada (legal), where American bootleggers would grab it and sneak it to the states (not legal). Even one of the most iconic Canuck brands took a fairly colossal hit during that period.

"Canadian Club makes much of their Prohibition sales," de Kergommeaux points out, "but what they say is that by the end of Prohibition, there was more whisky evaporating in their warehouses than crossing the border."

The author of *Canadian Whisky: The Portable Expert*, trained sommelier, and certified "Malt Maniac" (his words), de Kergommeaux is perhaps the greatest evangelist the Great White North has for its distilling traditions. And those traditions are vast. So vast that the greatest faux pas one can commit is to refer to Canadian as a "style" of whisky. That's like saying "American craft" is a style of beer. The country boasts a distilling heritage that spans some two hundred fifty years and there likely is at least that number of different flavors and techniques to emerge over that time. There are a few characteristics common across many of those, however. First, a drinker wouldn't be wrong to detect some vanilla notes. That, as in anything aged in a barrel, is the wood at work. Hints of toffee and butterscotch wouldn't be out of place either. The finish can exhibit a pleasant sort of bitterness; call it a grapefruity bite. It's a palate-cleansing finale for a complex beverage.

But before you reach the parting note, there's also a generous helping of peppery spice, thanks in no small part to the healthy dose of rye, characteristic in many of the country's whiskies. In fact, Canada's spirit from time to time has been referred to as "rye whiskey," whether or not it actually contained any of the grain. Historically, so much of it had been used up north that "rye" and "Canadian whisky" often were used interchangeably. As noted earlier, in order for American ryes to be labeled as such, just over half of their base must be that grain. There is no such minimum requirement for Canadian whisky.

"Rye does not produce very much alcohol," de Kergommeaux says. "So, in the states, you have to have 51 percent rye to taste it, but it only contributes about 6 percent toward the alcohol—corn does 14, 15, 16 percent of it."

The rye has far more influence on the final product in Canada due to one key distinction in the production process: Canadians blend their cereals when they're in spirit form (usually post-maturation, but, on a few occasions, before they hit the barrel), but American producers typically blend them at the grain level. The governing rationale behind blending at the spirit level is that it's considered a more precise process than at the grain stage. That way, the producers can use enzymes specific to rye with a batch of rye, those associated with wheat with a batch of wheat, and so on. [8]

As for the types of barrels in which Canadian whisky is aged—those can be as varied at the whiskies themselves. You recall that bourbon may be aged only in previously unused charred oak casks. Canadian brands use plenty of brand-new virgin oak, and they've also been known to mature in barrels that have been used once or multiple times before. It's not uncommon to age the spirit in a cask that was once home to an American bourbon or a 100 percent rye. It all depends on the distiller's desired flavor profile. Whiskies maturing in virgin oak have a tendency to extract much of their flavor from the wood, imparting those pronounced vanilla notes, as well as some hints of toffee, caramel, and butterscotch characteristic of the finest bourbons.

But sometimes it's too much of a good thing. "Those flavors overwrite all of the hundreds of other flavors that are also found in the oak," de Kergommeaux explains.

The whisky makers who want to direct a little more of the spotlight on those notes for a particular offering would opt for used barrels.

"By going to a used barrel," de Kergommeaux adds, "we're able to pull out the other flavors and emphasize the secondary and tertiary flavors that are found in the oak staves."

The Lot No. 40 brand, for instance, is very wood-forward; the drinker immediately can taste the influence of the virgin oak in a glass. By contrast, a few sips of a product like J.P. Wiser's 18 Years Old reveals no virgin oak character, as there's none used in its maturation.

But we're getting ahead of ourselves a bit. Those two represent opposite extremes in Canadian flavor and are best appreciated in the correct context. Folks new to Canada's spirited tradition might not even know where to start to get a sense of everything the country has to offer. Fortunately, de Kergommeaux, foremost authority on the subject that he is, has been generous enough to curate a small tasting flight for us as a kind of primer on the breadth and diversity of the Canadian sensory experience. Some of the brands in the sample are quite recognizable—household names even—and are rather easy to come by. Chances are many already have had these in some form, not even realizing they're part of the two-and-a-half-century north-of-the-border heritage. The whiskies are best tasted in the following order:

1. GIBSON'S FINEST 12 YEAR-OLD

Gibson's is a prime example of a standard yet well-crafted Canadian whisky, with hints of the treasure-trove of notes that make Canadian whisky distinct: the spice, the toffee, and the mildly bitter finish. It's a fairly mainstream option that benefits a great deal from the dozen years it spends in barrels formerly occupied by bourbon.

2. CROWN ROYAL

This was what I was talking about when I wrote "household name." Crown Royal is pretty ubiquitous. It's also the textbook case of the art of blending some fifty different whiskies aged in a wide variety of barrels. There's an elegance in that intricate symphony; don't let its reasonable price tag or the fact that it's often doused with Coca-Cola or ginger ale fool you. Stick with the entry level Crown Royal for this round.

3. CANADIAN CLUB 100 PERCENT RYE

Here's another trademark that shares Crown Royal's ubiquity. Each benefits from multimillion-dollar marketing campaigns and highly developed distribution networks. It makes sense since Crown's parent company is the world's largest spirits marketer, Diageo, while Canadian Club belongs to the number three conglomerate, Beam Suntory. There are several bottlings that bear the Canadian Club label—from a crowd-pleasing six-year-old, to special reserves and sherry-cask-aged varieties—but the 100 percent rye offers the best sense of what a Canadian whisky composed of rye and only rye tastes like. It also provides a good baseline to help you detect the grain's signature spiciness in blends that combine it with other cereals. "This is a whisky that is very fruity, has lots of spice, is very robust, and is bottled at 40 percent ABV, so it's not going to burn, and it's not going to frighten people," offers de Kergommeaux. "They'll take the second sip." It's also priced approachably—around $27.99 a bottle in most markets—so drinkers needn't fret about investing in a little tasting experiment.

4. FORTY CREEK DOUBLE BARREL RESERVE

It's time now to kick things up a notch. Forty Creek shares a lot of the characteristics of Gibson's twelve, but cranked up to eleven on the flavor scale. It showcases some really heavy vanilla, which is further accentuated by its rich mouth feel. It sports a bit of a roasted aroma as well, with light nutty touches. It just blankets the tongue.

5. LOT NO. 40

Here's another one that's 100 percent rye—90 percent rye grain and 10 percent malted rye to be exact—aged in new wood, giving tasters a sense of how brand-new oak interacts with a spirit that's already rather robust from the get-go, swinging from earthy, to fruity, to spicy in a single sip.

That's as good a cross-section as you're going to get, but it barely scratches the surface of the complexities that wait in a glass of whisky produced from Atlantic to Pacific Canada. Use each of those five as a conduit into a much larger world.

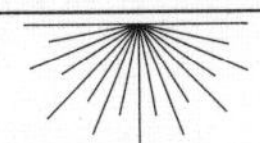

Land of Rising Prominence

Japanese Whisky

Three guesses where the best whiskey in the world is produced. If you said Scotland, Ireland, or even Kentucky, you'd be dead wrong. Get ready for this. The 2015 edition of the *Whisky Bible*, which, as its title suggests, is the go-to source for the venerable distilled spirit, for the first time named a brand produced in Japan the absolute hands-down greatest on the planet. The tipple in question was Yamazaki Single Malt Sherry Cask 2013 bottling, from Japanese spirits giant Suntory, now Beam Suntory following its 2014 acquisition of US-based Beam, Inc.

The *Whisky Bible*'s editor and internationally renowned authority on the subject, Jim Murray, gave it a staggering 97.5 points out of a possible 100, lavishing it with superlatives and calling it "near incredible genius."[9]

Naturally, that's a purely subjective rating, but it is a highly educated one. And there's now no disputing the fact that Japan's whiskey-making activity is right up there with, and in some cases surpasses, that of the Scottish tradition that inspired it.

It certainly wasn't the first time that expressions crafted six thousand miles east of Scotland made the grade. As far back as 2001, Whisky Magazine deemed a Japanese brand "Best of the Best."

As far as whisky distilling goes, the Japanese are relative newcomers. Scottish, Irish, and even American participation in the craft stretches back multiple centuries, while Japan, commercially speaking, has only been at it for ninety years (noncommercial whisky distilling started in the second half of the nineteenth century). And during its industry's first few decades, it was largely consumed only on its own turf (Don't forget there was a big war happening for a few years while Japanese whisky was still in its infancy and that obviously hindered its expansion). It wasn't an overnight sensation in its home country, either. It wasn't until the 1960s that the spirit had gained serious traction there.

At that time, it was primarily light, blended whisky served mizuwari—literally, "mixed with water"—we're not talking a drop of the stuff to open up the flavor, but about a two-to-one water-to-whisky ratio. And plenty of ice.

"The warm, humid climate and the culture of drinking alongside food meant that mizuwari was the perfect serve, and it drove sales well into the 1970s,"[10] says Jake Mountain, chief blogger and all-around content guy for online whisky retailer Master of Malt.

And then, a dynamic common across just about every classic beverage category (and a recurring theme in this book) started to rear its ugly head: Younger consumers started to dismiss the drinks of their elders as monumentally unhip. That's not to say a small connoisseur segment of single-malt aficionados didn't emerge—as had happened around the same time in Scotland—but it wasn't enough to fully sustain the industry on the home islands. That's when distillers started to look westward for export opportunities.

"By the time the rest of the world really took notice, including the awards' bodies, Japan had been producing some top whiskies for decades and the expressions winning these awards had also been around for years," notes Mountain.

The Scots shouldn't get too jealous that Japan's getting a lot of the attention now. They should view Japan's distinction as a proud parent would watching a son or daughter graduate an Ivy League medical school. After all, it's Scotch whisky with which the Japanese version has its closest kinship. Suntory's inaugural master distiller Masataka Taketsuru learned his craft in Scotland, initially at Speyside's Longmorn Distillery and later Campbeltown's Hazelton Distillery, and brought his newfound expertise home. He also brought with him a new wife, one Jessie Roberta "Rita" Cowan, in whose family home Taketsuru lived during his studies.[11]

That's why Japanese whisky brands' flavor profile and taxonomy—"single malt," etc.—have so much in common with their Scottish predecessors. It's also why the Japanese, when using the Western alphabet, leave out the letter e from the word—common practice in Scotland but not so common in Ireland or the United States.

However, despite all of the similarities in flavor and heritage, the Japanese, without a doubt, have cut the cord and made whisky their own. Indeed, there are plenty of ways the two traditions diverge. For one thing, when Taketsuru was discovering the craft among the Scots, he was immersed in what was, at the time, primarily folk tradition. Taketsuru was more science-minded in his pursuits and sought to understand why certain aspects of the production process yielded the results they did.

Additionally, the notion of blending differs significantly in Japan. Where Scotch distillers were able to pick and choose among whiskies from hundreds of generations-old distilleries—each specializing in its own unique style, influenced by its own local resources and terroir—to fine-tune the flavor profiles they desired, the Japanese didn't have that luxury. They had to figure out how to create a variety of styles within a single distillery, more or less simulating the multiple-distillery concept. In the early years, even as more distilleries started to pop up, no companies were trading their whiskies. Even today, a visit to a Japanese distillery would reveal stills of different shapes and sizes, each designed to achieve specific character nuances.

The trained taster likely would detect fewer malty notes and greater clarity of flavor—often deeper in the fragrant, floral realm—than in Scotch whisky, primarily due to Japanese producers' use of much clearer wort—the liquid that contains all of the malt sugars to be converted to alcohol during the fermentation process (fermentation precedes distilling).

Japan has been known to use maturation casks unique to the country as well. While the distillers do still use the same types of cooperage favored by their Scottish brethren—used sherry and bourbon barrels, as well as European and American oak—they're also aging their products in the country's native Mizunara oak. That's been known to impart some notes of sandalwood and incense. A few are getting more innovative and even more culture-specific and maturing in vessels like plum wine casks.

And, when it comes to yeast—remember, those are the microorganisms that work their magic to turn sugar into alcohol—Japanese are far more protective of the strains they use. "Whilst most Scottish distilleries are all using dried distiller's yeast," Mountain says, "much more research has gone into this area in Japan and different strains are used and protected within companies."

Admittedly, identifying, in practice, distinctions between Scotch and Japanese styles is above the pay grade of most adult drinkers (my hand is raised) and, at the end of the day, there's more that unites than divides them.

It's par for the course for the respective local markets of the major whiskey-making countries to be highly consolidated, and it's no different in Japan. Beam Suntory is the dominant player, followed by Nikka Whisky Distilling Company. There are nine distilleries currently producing, owned by an even smaller number of parent companies:

BEAM SUNTORY (FORMERLY SUNTORY)

Yamazaki: Best known for its Yamazaki single-malt line, the most popular being the twelve-year-old, aged in Japanese white oak barrels. The more expensive eighteen-year-old brings more complex aromas and a lingering finish. As noted, it was the special release 2013 Single Malt Sherry Cask that Jim Murray's "Whisky Bible" named the best in the world.

Hakushu: Smoky and fruity notes characterize Hakushu's twelve-year-old single-malt expression; the eighteen-year-old reveals a bit of citrus with a sweet finish. It also markets a twenty-five-year-old, as well as a Distiller's Reserve series and other limited releases, like one amped-up with peat smokiness (much like Islay single malts) and another aged in sherry casks.

NIKKA WHISKY DISTILLING COMPANY

Though he started his career working for Suntory, industry pioneer Taketsuru struck out on his own and founded what would become Nikka. Nikka owns the Yoichi and Miyagikyo distillery.

Yoichi: Ten-, twelve-, fifteen-, and twenty-year-old single malts are among the core products that bear the Yoichi label; the fifteen has a particularly sweet nose. Yoichi also produces, in a nod to the founder, Taketsuru, a line of blended whiskies.

Miyagikyo: The twelve-year-old offers a bit of vanilla and a little peat; Miyagikyo fifteen has a hint of nuttiness.

FUJI GOTEMBA

Owned by Japanese beer and soft drink giant Kirin, Fuji Gotemba's brands bear the "Kirin Whisky" label, including Tarujyuku 50°, a fifty–fifty malt/grain whisky blend, as well as Kirin Blender's Choice single grain and Fuji Sanroku eighteen-year-old single malt.

SHINSHU

Located on the southern island of Kyushu, known for its concentration of shochu distilleries, it markets single malts and blends under the Mars Whisky brand.

EIGASHIMA SHUZO DISTILLERY

Eigashima is another distiller that began as a producer of shochu, as well as saké. Now it's known for its White Oak whisky line, which includes its standard product, White Oak Akashi Blended, as well as a few limited single malts as young as three years old and as mature as fifteen.

CHICHIBU DISTILLERY

Chichibu is among the new kids on the block; it's only been up and running since 2008, but it's got quite the cult following. Its initial offering was called, appropriately enough, The First—distilled in 2008 and bottled in 2011. It also has a range of single-cask specials, including those with graduating levels of peatiness. Naturally, at this stage, its products are all fairly young. It'll be a few years before we see a twelve-year-old.

MIYASHITA SHOZU

As far as whisky is concerned, Miyashita is the true baby of the bunch, releasing its first expression, a three-year-old, in 2015. But it's far from an infant when it comes to other alcohols. The whisky bottling coincided with its one-hundredth anniversary as a saké brewery.

***

The number of operating whisky distilleries with actual products on the market may be small enough to count on two hands, but the breadth of flavor experiences they offer are too many to tally: Some are smoky, others are fruity or spicy, and a few beyond those aged in ex-sherry casks undoubtedly would reveal notes of that Spanish fortified wine—and many more may exhibit any combination of those characteristics. Some might like one expression more than another, others might like none at all. But one thing everyone can agree on is that Japanese whisky is having its moment and the whole world is noticing.

Week 5

The World's Most Popular Spirit No One's Ever Heard Of

Baijiu

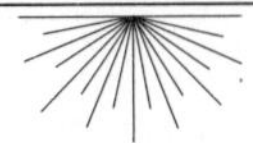

China never ceases to intrigue the West. Just think about the American movie business, for instance. Blockbuster studios increasingly are tweaking their franchises to incorporate more overt Chinese or Sino-friendly content to get wider distribution in the world's most populous country—which makes perfect sense when many big tent-pole summer flicks often post higher grosses in China than in their home market.

That dynamic is not what one would call reciprocal, however. In many ways, the United States needs China more than China needs the United States. And that's why much of what the Chinese drink, beyond the brands American companies export there, are largely a mystery to us. How many stateside drinkers, for example, have heard of Snow lager? It happens to be the number one beer brand in the world[12], but at least 99 percent of it is sold in China.

It should therefore come as no surprise that the largest spirit category in the world (nearly one-third of global spirits volume), baijiu, is something that the majority of Westerners haven't even heard of, much less even know how to pronounce ("by-jo"). Slowly but surely, however, China's national drink is finding its way across America through a network of importers and distributors targeting drinkers of single-malt whiskies and high-end Cognacs.

CENTURIES OF TRADITION

Baijiu's documented history reaches back six centuries, though some scholars claim that the seeds for baijiu-producing culture were planted as long as two to four millennia ago. (Would you expect anything more recent from such an ancient civilization?) Sorghum is the predominant go-to grain from which it's distilled but, depending on the region, rice, glutinous (aka "sticky") rice, corn, wheat, or other starchy fermentable grains may be used. It's usually a combination of any number of those.

The word loosely translates to "white liquor" and it's occasionally erroneously called "white wine." Distilled and bottled at an average of 40-plus percent alcohol (usually more than 50 percent but generally not exceeding 60 percent), this is certainly no wine.

I love a good ritual when I drink, and baijiu does not disappoint. Traditionally, the host pours it into tiny, half-ounce, stemmed glasses. When two drinkers toast, each one tries to outdo the other in humility, each lowering her cup so the other person's is raised above it. It's a show of respect with each participant essentially telling the other, "I hold you in high regard."

"In China, everyone wants to be humble,"[13] explains Yuan Liu, senior vice president of business development at baijiu importer CNS enterprises, as he demonstrates the tradition over baijiu cocktails and neat pours at the Beverly Hills location of high-end, Michelin-starred Chinese eatery Hakkasan.

Once one person lowers her glass, her companion will, in turn, lower his. "They'll think, 'okay, I'm the guest, so I actually lower my glass,'" Liu continues. A sort of game of one-upmanship—or, in this case, "one-downmanship" ensues until they're clinking below the table's surface (talk about drinking a person under the table!). Eventually, someone has to put a stop to it and often, one person will make an executive decision and lift the other person's glass, thus seizing victory in this humble game.

There's a bit more to the ritual. One's left hand typically covers one's glass; in Chinese and Buddhist tradition, the left hand symbolizes compassion. It should obscure the right hand, which tends to signify more nefarious personal attributes.

"Drink the whole thing and then show the empty glass, basically saying 'I drank everything,'" Liu says. "It's a sign of trust. It's saying I drank everything you gave me."

More often than not, Chinese drinkers consume baijiu with food. It's perfectly fine to sip it on its own, but the notion of drinking sans meal is relatively new to China's populace. Bars, as we know them, didn't really exist there until about the early 1990s. Most alcohol consumption outside the home took place in restaurants.

The culinary aspect of China's drinking culture brings up one very important question: what on earth does it taste like? There is, unfortunately, no easy answer to that. Keep in mind that there are some ten thousand baijiu distilleries in its home country, meaning there's a lot of variation in both flavor and quality.

The closest comparison is to say it tastes similar to nothing you've ever had before. There really is nothing to compare it with; it's its own animal.

"I always tell people to forget about how we understand drinks in the Western world," Liu notes, "because we're looking for specific tastes—'I'm tasting chocolate, caramel . . .' You kind of have to put that aside a little."

And don't get too theatrical with the act of smelling it. In other words, don't treat it like wine, with all of the deep, heavy sniffing. The aroma will come to you and your restraint will be rewarded.

The most striking element about it is that the alcohol surprisingly doesn't overwhelm all of the other flavor complexity. Normally when a spirit's ABV clocks in at 40 percent—let alone 50 or 55 percent—the nose gets a hit of the alcohol burn before clearing the way for the other aromatic characteristics. Especially with premium-grade baijiu, that nostril-searing sensation rarely manifests. That doesn't, however, mean it's free of any other complications. Chief among those is the fact that a drinker, even a seasoned appreciator of whiskey, wine, beer—what have you—who savors and dutifully jots down flavor impressions, likely will be at a loss to convey what it tastes like in evocative terms. During the Hakkasan happy hour, the closest I got was, "This one reminds me of, I don't know, a sour pineapple?" or "Wow, I'm getting notes of soy sauce and vinegar? No, wait, that's not quite right." These are flavors unto themselves and one tastes radically different from the next.

It is, therefore, immensely difficult to apply any sort of taxonomy to neatly categorize the thousands of expressions a consumer is likely to experience. Marketers will, however, paint them with the broadest of strokes, especially with regard to their olfactory dynamics.

There are five basic aroma types:

- COMPLEX AROMA: It's just as it sounds. There's a lot going on and this particular type of baijiu tends to have a long finish.
- STRONG AROMA: Floral, fruity notes tend to dominate strong-aroma baijiu, which are fermented in aged cellars. Strong-aroma baijiu is the common style in the Sichuan province.
- MILD/LIGHT AROMA: Baijiu of this ilk tends to be more neutral flavor, not unlike vodka, but not very much like it at the same time.
- RICE AROMA: These are on the smoother, sweeter side and are typical in the south of China.
- OTHER AROMA: Those falling under this heading tend to incorporate hybrid fermentation and distilling processes or a combination of different raw materials. Some of their character might suggest elements from other categories or create entirely new aromas.

To fully experience any of those aromas, baijiu is best enjoyed at room temperature. Chilling it is perfectly acceptable—especially in the summer—but many of the flavor characteristics are lost to the cold. There's also a fairly practical reason: chilling it will cause the alcohol to be suppressed in one's system, whereas one is more likely to exhale much of the vapor when consumed at room temperature (unless that room is a walk-in freezer, of course).

Some claim that one doesn't get drunk as quickly from baijiu as one would from other spirits, even those of a lower proof, and that partially may be due to breathing out more of the vaporized alcohol.

"There's a saying in China," Liu reveals. "When you drink baijiu, your feet will get drunk but your head doesn't get drunk."

But I wouldn't recommend testing that assertion. The liquid's still, on average, 20 percent stronger than vodka, gin, and most midrange whiskeys. So, keep your calculator handy and plan your drinking session accordingly.

Neat is the preferred method of baijiu consumption, as it has been for centuries, but the spirit has not been immune to the cocktail revolution. Its aggressive flavor may cause bartenders to shy away from mixing it, but those who do have been able to craft some truly one-of-a-kind creations.

It's fitting that Hakkasan, which, for the most part, is among the pioneers to even carry baijiu on-premise in North America, has been able to get fairly innovative on the mixology front when many of its peers have shied away from the devilishly tricky-to-mix Chinese liquor. One of Hakkasan's concoctions is the pink-hued Eastern Elixir, which marries the base spirit with Aperol (the popular Italian aperitif), grapefruit juice, tarragon, lemon juice, and coffee syrup. You'd think that with that many ingredients, any base spirit would be completely masked, right? Wrong. Amazingly, the baijiu asserts itself enough that there's never any doubt about what's the star of this show.

TAKE IT SLOW

I'd be remiss if I didn't go into at least some detail about the method of production, since it differs so greatly from other distilled potables. Baijiu, especially the products on the premium end of the market, take a long time to make. Really long. And I'm not just talking about the aging process. Before the spirit even makes it to the maturation containers, it undergoes some of the lengthiest fermentation and distillation processes in the known alcohol world. It can take up to six months to make just the low-end baijius. For a number of the premium products, the process of harvesting, fermentation, distillation, and the repetition of those latter two steps (often multiple go-rounds, as many as nine for some brands) may take as long as five years. Now, you're probably thinking, "So what? I have plenty of bottles of twelve-year-old and eighteen-year-old Scotch, and even straight bourbon that costs about $30 for a 750 mL bottle typically is aged for two to four years (and ten-plus years for the pricier stuff)". Yes, but that's the aging process. When I say baijiu could take up to five years to produce, I mean five years before it even enters the aging receptacle. To be sure, that's not the norm—five years for the combined production and aging regimen is more typical—but it's certainly not uncommon.

And in the nearly six months it takes to make some of the cheaper brands, bottles of gin and vodka already will have been distributed and consumed three or four times over.

"That's why it's so expensive," says Liu. "It's such an arduous process."

And, despite quantum leaps in production technology, many aspects of the craft remain tied to methods that are hundreds of years old. Chief among those and the key element that sets it apart from other spirits is the traditional fermentation pit—basically a hole that's dug in the ground, about ten feet deep, eight feet long, and eight feet wide. That's where the magic happens.

The artisans harvest the grains, blend them to achieve the correct proportions for the desired flavor profile, and then steam them to soften the grain mixture. Next they'll take a locally cultivated yeast culture, pulverize it, and combine it with the grain mix. At that moment, the yeast begins to convert the starches into ethanol.

It's then placed in the pit and covered with mud. That's not just any mud, mind you, it's mud from that pit. And, oh, if dirt could talk! The pit has been used so many times over so many years—indeed, centuries in some cases—that it's a multigenerational breeding ground for microorganisms that all play a role in shaping baijiu's character.

Possibly the wildest (pun sort of intended) aspect of the production method is how the yeast strains (and other microscopic critters) are cultivated. The makers take a block of wheat, cut it into smaller brick-shaped pieces, and leave it in a dark room to attract all sorts of microorganisms from its surrounding environment—in essence, creating an ecosystem all for the purpose of crafting the perfect spirit. "It's man and nature working together," says Liu.

The fermentation process ranges between sixty and one hundred twenty days—five to ten times longer than an average beer and part of the reason overall production takes so long. The protracted schedule largely is designed to ensure all of the impurities are extracted from the grains.

Once that's complete, the distillers put the mash in large porous vessels, under which they boil water to steam out the ethanol—the fermented grains are actually in solid form prior to boiling, and steaming is the only way to extract the alcohol.

Distillation ensues.

Once the production team completes the requisite number of fermentation/distillation rounds—again, it could be as many as nine or as few as one—it's time to deposit the spirit into the terracotta aging jars. Unlike barrels used for maturing whiskey, rum, and other brown spirits, these particular vessels do not impart any color or introduce any new flavors to the finished product (as is the case with vanilla and caramel notes that charred oak barrels bring to bourbon). For the most part, it's a continuation of the filtration process, jettisoning undesirable aromas over time and generally letting it mellow. It often subtly augments the texture, giving it a slight viscosity, but that's about it.

Here's the utterly mind-blowing part. A person drinking a glass of that smooth, complex, mildly viscous liquid in 2015 may very well be tasting ever-so-nuanced notes from 1615. Credit that to the circle of life. After fermentation, spent grain goes back into the pits to feed future iterations. And, in many places, that cycle has been dutifully repeated for several centuries.

"It's how people used to look at life," says Liu. "They see life as a continuous process; it takes and gives at the same time. As soon as it takes something, it gives back. Otherwise life would cease to exist."

That philosophy suffused daily Chinese life for centuries.

To make baijiu a part of your daily life, there are a few brands you're likely to encounter:

- **KWEICHOW MOUTAI (KWEICHOW MOUTAI COMPANY, LTD.):** Moutai, named after the town of the same name in the Kweichow province, is the most popular spirit in China (making it one of the most popular in the world, by default). Recognizable by its opaque white bottle with red and gold label, Moutai is the baijiu of choice for sealing business deals and diplomatic meetings. The spirit is 50 percent sorghum and 50 percent wheat.

- **SHUI JING FANG (DIAGEO):** Global spirits giant Diageo recently bought a majority stake in the brand and has begun marketing it under the name Wellbay. It comes from what's believed to be the oldest distillery in China, dating back six hundred years. Shui Jing Fang consists of 36 percent sorghum; the remaining 64 percent is a mix of rice, wheat, glutinous rice, and corn. If you buy the brand at retail, you're not going to want to throw the package out. The cardboard box for the striking 375 mL glass bottle comes with a wooden base on which to mount the bottle—instant conversation piece when friends come over.

- **MIANZHU DAQU (JIAN NAN CHUN GROUP):** The city of Mianzhu boasts some three thousand to four thousand years of alcohol-beverage-making history so the distillers of Mianzhu Daqu are pretty good at what they do. Sorghum makes up half of its grain content; the other half is a mix of glutinous rice, regular rice, wheat, and corn.

Despite the fact that baijiu has been part of the day-to-day routines of China's population for all of those centuries, there's no legal, protected appellation of origin for it. There's nothing barring a distiller from making it in any other part of the world, though few do, in the strictest traditional sense (and good luck digging those fermentation pits and letting the microfauna cavort for four or five years before it's even ready).

Here in the states, however, there just happens to be a little craft distillery in the greater Portland, Oregon, area (where else?) that commercially produces the spirit. Vinn Distillery's version doesn't have the same complex grain bill that many of its Chinese predecessors have—Vinn Baijiu is entirely rice-based—but it is rooted in generations of tradition extending back to the old country.

It's likely that more North American producers will try to put their own spin on the tradition, considering how rapidly China is advancing on the world stage. Baijiu awareness among Western cultures is pretty close to zero right now, but check back in the not-too-distant future. The landscape will have changed dramatically, mark my words.

Week 6

The Lighter Side of Chinese Imbibing

Huangjiu

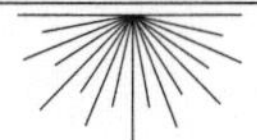

Maybe after a week of drinking your way across China (from your arm chair or otherwise), you feel like you've already had a bit too much to drink, and you just can't do another one hundred six proof distilled spirit. That's okay, the billions of gallons of baijiu in the world aren't going anywhere and will be there waiting for you when you're ready. And, luckily, the Chinese drinking culture isn't always about the hard stuff. That's where huangjiu ("wong-jo") comes in.

Huangjiu, which means "yellow wine" or sometimes "yellow liquor," technically isn't a wine and definitely isn't a liquor. It's one of those words that get a little lost in translation, similar to the way baijiu is often mistakenly called "white wine."

It doesn't go through the distillation process, so that does make it closer to a wine, but, like Japan's saké, it really is its own thing. And that thing, like saké, does involve rice. However, like baijiu, other cereals—rice, millet, wheat, etc.—get in on the action as well. The beverage is usually below 20 percent alcohol by volume and, despite its translation, it isn't always yellowish in color.

More often than not it's primarily used as a cooking ingredient in the states, which is fine for the cheaper ones. But there's so much diversity and complexity among the, shall we say, "better" ones, that using them solely for culinary purposes does them a tremendous disservice. At least taste them first!

Warm is the preferred way to drink Chinese rice wines—not scalding hot, but say, 120 degrees Fahrenheit. The conventional wisdom is that it enhances the aroma, but it's not uncommon to drink it straight, on the rocks, or mixed in a cocktail. There's also a sizable contingent of people in China who swear by it for purported medicinal properties. There may not be any scientific basis to that, but it's hard to debate that it warms the innards on a nippy day—not to suggest that it's only drunk in the winter because that's hardly the case.

Some can be clear, while others might be beige, yellowish brown, or reddish brown, and each will fall into one of five categories on the dry/sweet spectrum:

Dry: Unfermented sugar content maxes out at 1 percent and therefore lives up to its dry classification.

Semidry: The residual sugar concentration is between 1 and 3 percent.

Semisweet: The sugar content is between 3 and 10 percent. Huangjius of this type are not meant to be stored for long periods of time.

Sweet: Hope you have a sweet tooth. The sugar content ranges between 10 percent and 20 percent.

Extrasweet: Might as well call it "dessert;" it's at least 20 percent sugar.

Not to further complicate things, but under the huangjiu umbrella, there are several distinct types. Think of it this way, you don't walk into a restaurant or bar and say, "I'd like a glass of wine." You specify whether you want a white or red and, more specifically, a Cabernet, Merlot, Chardonnay, Sauvignon Blanc—you get the picture. In China, Huangjiu is just as generic and vague as "wine" is for the rest of the world.

Mijiu: Sometimes "Mijiu" is used interchangeably with huangjiu, but there are distinctions. Where Huangjiu translates to "yellow wine," "mijiu" translates to "rice wine." Mijiu could be considered a cousin of Japanese sake (though more dessert-like in nature because it's got a pronounced sweetness).

Fujian glutinous rice wine: Producers add various Chinese medicinal herbs to glutinous ("sticky") rice and a distilled rice wine of low alcohol content.

Huadiao jiu: The 16 percent alcohol huangjiu is sometimes called nu'er hong, which means "daughter red," and there's a pretty intriguing story behind that nomenclature. In Shaoxing, there was a tradition of burying a vessel of the beverage underground when someone gave birth to a daughter; it would stay there for many years until the daughter was ready to be married. And speaking of Shaoxing . . .

Shaoxing wine is among the easiest styles to find (relatively speaking, of course) on US soil. Unfortunately, the most readily available variety comes in an olive-oil type bottle whose label reads "Shaoxing Cooking Wine," frequently with added salt. Your best bet is to find a liquor store in or near a major city's Chinatown (New York and San Francisco in particular) or one of the more traditional restaurants in those enclaves (the ones whose menus play up more obscure regional dishes and not "American Chinese" like chop suey and General Tso's chicken). The popular Sichuan restaurant Joe's Shanghai in Manhattan offers it by the bottle for $25. Historians have traced rice wine making in the Shaoxing region back more than two and a half millennia. Shaoxing wine is typically the higher-end version, whose yeast gives it a reddish tint. Think of it as the super-reserve huangjiu, sometimes aged for as many as four or five decades.

Though baijiu and huangjiu are radically different in flavor, consistency, and alcohol content, there is one significant aspect they have in common: tasters are at a complete loss for words when trying to draw comparisons for either. The closest any Westerner gets with the descriptive language is "sherry-like," due to some earthy components the two share. But that verbiage still doesn't even touch it. Best to just sample it. We often get so bogged down trying to assign labels to the indescribable that we forget to figure out whether we actually like something or not.

Week 7

Valentine's Day Just Got Hotter

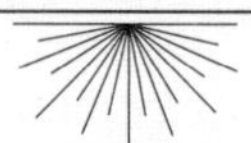

Since the seventh week of the year is right around a certain cupid-centric holiday, what better way to spice things up in the romance department than with chili peppers?

In the (seemingly) eternal beer versus wine war for the hearts and minds of foodies everywhere, one of the more entertaining battles royal to emerge is the dinner pairing that pits grain against grape in a multicourse gastronomic smackdown. Usually a wine sommelier and brewmaster or Cicerone (the dominant server certification in beer) make their cases for why their respective fermented beverages are best in a culinary context. More often than not, beer wins—for no other reason than the fact that, among mainstream diners, it enters the fray as the underdog everyone tends to underestimate. Little do they know, the scrappy little beverage could already have an unfair advantage built-in: If anything remotely spicy is on the menu, wine automatically forfeits. Even the most unflappable of wine experts will concede this fact.

But beer can be quite the ungracious winner. Case in point: the rise in the popularity of chili-pepper brews. It's as though beer is rubbing its superiority in wine's face, reminding its grape-derived frenemy how much of a colossal failure it is in the capsaicin realm. Kind of a dick move, no?

As tragic as it is that there will never be a Caliente Chianti (kidding), it doesn't diminish the reality that hot pepper beers have evolved into quite a tasty little subgenre. No mean feat considering how dangerously close to the edge of gimmick they already walk.

I remember in the early 2000s, when I was just discovering the depth and range of beers that were becoming available to the American consumer, I was at the National Beer Wholesalers Association (NBWA) convention in Las Vegas when I encountered a brand called Cave Creek Chili Beer. It's a brand that's been the target of much derision from the craft beer world, primarily because it doesn't really take any risks to break away from the gravitational pull of gimmickery. It takes a very inoffensive (read: bland) pale lager and infuses it with peppers. While not particularly nuanced or complex, it at least accomplishes what it sets out to do: brew a beer with a spicy kick.

Since then, brewers have been increasingly conscious of the gimmick threshold and have been extremely wary about crossing it. At the same time, they've been eager to take the chili concept much further than letting a few peppers steep in a throwaway pilsner. Whether their ultimate results have been successful are a source of great debate, but there's no denying they've at least been try to bring their A games.

Their hard work often has been rewarded, as hot pepper beers increasingly have been medaling in major competitions like the World Beer Cup and the Great American Beer Festival. However, given their usually experimental nature, their availability tends to be fleeting.

— SRIRACHA STOUT —

There's one brewery in particular whose very mission of late seems to be to continuously blur the gimmick line in just about everything it produces: Rogue. In the past handful of years alone, the Oregon operation has released everything from a maple-bacon-doughnut-flavored ale to an oddity made with yeast harvested from brewmaster John Maier's beard. Following those concoctions, its Sriracha Stout seems mainstream and tame by comparison. Packaged in a 750 mL red glass bottle that meticulously replicates the Vietnamese Huy Fong rooster sauce's famous container, it combines the roasty maltiness of a stout with the slow burn of a hearty Asian meal.

It's far from Rogue's first foray into pepperdom; its Chipotle Ale combined the namesake ingredient with homegrown hops and malts in a deep amber brew. Rogue, which also produces spirits, has distilled

Chipotle Ale, as well as giving a searing jolt to a much stronger beverage.

— FADE TO BLACK, VOL. 3: CHILI PEPPER PORTER —

Left Hand Brewing Company's Fade to Black series has long been the Longmont, Colorado, brewery's canvas for works of experimental art. For Vol. 3, it took dried ancho, smoked Serrano, and brown chipotle peppers and infused them in a dark mahogany, medium-bodied porter. The resulting brew balances the vegetal, peppery heat with a subtle smokiness, making it a good companion for rich stews of assorted wild game.

— BALLAST POINT PEPPER SERIES —

Ballast Point Brewing Company definitely benefits from being located a mere twenty miles from the Mexican border. The San Diego operation has produced draught-only chili offshoots of brands in its regular portfolio. Its traditional American pale ale gets a Serrano twist; its smoky lager, Smoke Screen, rises to new heights with added jalapeño; Sculpin IPA, which enjoys a bit of a nationwide cult following on its own without any peppery additions, welcomes a generous helping of spicy heat from ghost peppers, often considered the hottest of the hot; and Ballast Point's Wahoo Wheat goes Southeast Asian with the addition of Thai chili, lime, and ginger.

— ALASKAN JALAPEÑO IMPERIAL IPA —

Part of Juneau-based Alaskan Brewing Company's limited-edition Pilot Series, Jalapeño Imperial IPA treats its namesake ingredient as if it were one of the four hops in the recipe. They're used during both the brewing and fermentation process—the latter of which gives it an added hot pepper aroma. It's hop and heat-forward and makes a nice flavor partner for everything from fish and chips to bacon cheeseburgers.

— BILLY'S CHILIES —

Boulder, Colorado's, Twisted Pine Brewing Company takes an unfiltered wheat beer and amps it up with Serrano, habanero, jalapeño, Anaheim, and Fresno peppers. Despite the gang of five dominant flavor agents, the kick is more complex than tongue-frying and actually makes for a drinkable, approachable brew, with a sessionable alcohol content of 5.2 percent that goes well with fish tacos. For early drinkers, skip the mimosa and drink it with a breakfast burrito. Twisted Pine also produced a limited-edition offering that turned up the heat a bit, adding those crazy ghost peppers to the other five.

— ROCK BOTTOM — THREE PEPPER ALE

Beer geeks far too often turn their noses up at Rock Bottom brewpubs because it's a chain. Keep in mind, though, that the chain wouldn't be as monumentally successful as it is if it wasn't churning out good beer. And it's got the awards to prove it. Its Three Pepper Ale, a fairly easy-drinking pale ale with a pronounced, but not overpowering, jalapeño kick took the silver in the "field beer" category (those that incorporate vegetables into their recipes) of the 2014 Great American Beer Festival.

Week 8

BEER RYE-VOLUTION

Brewing with Rye

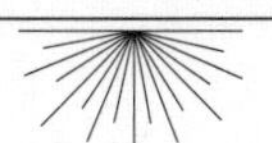

Here's a simple truth to which most people don't give much thought: whiskey, in its most basic, stripped-down form, is really just distilled beer. That's especially accurate when it's Scotch, which is barley-malt-based. It even applies to bourbon, which, by definition, has to be made predominantly of corn. Sure, craft beer purists tend to turn their noses up at brews containing corn, as it's somewhat unfairly come to be perceived as a cheap, flavor-weakening adjunct, thanks to its pervasive use among macro-megabrewers. But most of them would admit, albeit grudgingly, that it's still beer.

There's no such ambivalence when it comes to rye. In fact, an ancillary benefit of whiskey's rye-naissance has been a corresponding surge among brewers incorporating it into their recipes. It marks a bit of a return to America's roots, as it was fairly common for brewers to supplement barley malt and other grains with rye during colonial times. It was more about what was available to them at the time, rather than a particular flavor profile they were pursuing.

The Founding Fathers were known to be pretty good brewers in their own right and at least one in particular, Thomas Jefferson, reportedly used a generous helping of rye. Since Jefferson and many of his beer-loving peers went on to hold the nation's highest office, what better time to reflect on rye's reemergence in brewing than President's Day week?

It's actually pretty tricky business getting the grain balance right. While there are 100 percent rye whiskeys, there are no 100 percent rye beers. With the latter beverage, "less is more" seems to be the governing philosophy. Barley malt dominates, while rye accounts for around 10 percent, at most 20 percent, of the grain bill. (The German Roggenbier style—roggen means rye—was popular in the Middle Ages and revived by some German brewers in the twentieth century; it traditionally included substantially more rye, usually 50 percent barley malt, 25 percent wheat, and 25 percent rye.[14])

The best way to envision the flavor impact rye has on a beer without even drinking it is to imagine replacing the bread on a Reuben sandwich with anything but rye. Not quite the same without that tart little jolt, is it?

I like to think of the rye grain as an emotional child. It's at its best when it's playing well with others, not screaming for attention. It's also a great enhancer of already-stellar-on-their-own styles.

The hops that dominate India Pale Ales already are quite well known for certain spicy characteristics, so it's no surprise that brewers have found considerable success adding a complementary bite courtesy of rye.

— THOMAS JEFFERSON'S TAVERN ALE —

Yards Brewing Company's home base is the city where the Declaration of Independence was signed, which qualifies it more than most to make a product line called Ales of the Revolution—beers loosely based on the Founding Fathers' recipes. Yards brewmaster Tom Kehoe worked with Philadelphia's City Tavern—an iconic landmark dating back to pre-Revolutionary times—to develop Thomas Jefferson's Tavern Ale, a strong, golden ale that includes rye, honey, and wheat. The hefty 8 percent ABV ale pairs well with fatty dishes like roast duck.

— BITTERSWEET LENNY'S R.I.P.A. —

In 2006, Shmaltz Brewing Company, founded by Jeremy Cowan and known for its offbeat and mildly irreverent He'Brew beer range, honored comic legend Lenny Bruce with Bittersweet Lenny's R.I.P.A. for the fortieth anniversary of his death. The 10 percent ABV brew falls in the realm of double IPA, brewed with, as Shmaltz likes to point out, "an obscene amount of malts and hops." Bittersweet Lenny's proved so popular that it moved into Shmaltz's year-round lineup.

BRONX RYE PALE ALE

When the Bronx Brewery (based in the New York City borough of the same name), launched in 2011, right out of the gate its pale ale was a solid representation of one of the most brewed styles in America. But that didn't mean the brewers were content to just leave it alone. In addition to a limited-edition barrel-aged version, Bronx released a spiced-up riff, nearly a quarter of whose grain bill is malted and flaked rye. Even with that hefty dose, it's still remarkably balanced, letting the floral hops, biscuity barley malt, and the special guest-star grain evenly assert themselves on the palate at varying intervals.

RUTHLESS RYE

My fanciful imagination painted a scenario in which the Sierra Nevada team sat in a command center straight out of the Truman Show omnisciently observing the hit-and-miss efforts of smaller, less-seasoned producers as they stumbled their way through rye brewing. Then, in 2012, the Sierra crew emerged from its heavenly seclusion with Ruthless Rye IPA in tow, declaring, "This, my friends, is how it is done." The reality wasn't quite like that, but that's kind of the impact the award-winning rye made when it arrived for the first time that year. When it comes to balance, Sierra cracked the code with its equal parts citrus hop bitterness/fresh-ground pepper spiciness creation. It took the gold at the 2012 World Beer Cup for good reason.

EMBRR RYE PORTER

Pale ales and IPAs have been a frequent canvas on which to experiment with rye, but they're far from being the only options, or even the best for that matter. Dark, roasted malt beers are just crying out for a bit of spice, and more than a few brewers have been happy to oblige. In 2014, Ithaca Brewing Company, based in the oasis of Upstate New York academia that's home to Cornell University and the college that took its name from the town, produces Embrr rye porter with some chocolate malt, roasted barley, and both malted and flaked rye. It's the perfect warmer for the region's punishing winters.

X-1 CHOCOLATE IMPERIAL RYE PORTER

This one's as gloriously kitchen-sinky as it sounds—and it won a silver medal at the 2012 World Beer Cup for its trouble. Brewed by Bel Air, Maryland's DuClaw Brewing Company, each sip of this robust porter reveals alternating notes of chocolate, rye, and coffee. DuClaw adds real chocolate in the brewing process, imparting a bittersweet, silky smoothness. X-1 debuted in 2010 as the first of its experimental eXile series. This one has very limited availability, but if you're lucky you might find bars hording it in their cellars.

BELL'S RYE STOUT

Another rye that's been seduced by the dark side, Rye Stout's availability is a little more fleeting; it's a specialty fall/winter seasonal available every other year. But it's worth the wait, especially from a brewery known for taking the stout style to uncharted territory. The rye flavor is delicately balanced by those roasted coffee notes. It's like a warm blanket by the fireside. And keeping warm in the winter is something the Kalamazoo, Michigan, brewery knows a thing or two about. They don't call the state's lower peninsula "the Mitten" for nothing.

***

Rye ales are terrific for their own sake, but their appeal speaks to something far greater than any one beverage. They're a symbol of the close kinship between beer and whiskey. If there's ever been a case to be made for becoming a cross drinker, it's the intercategory versatility of this classic grain.

Week 9

Staring Down the Barrel

Remember how bourbon barrels, in order for what's inside them to be called "bourbon," must only be used once? Sounds like a huge waste of wood, right? Not really. Like syndicated TV reruns, there's a huge aftermarket for these preowned wooden lovelies. For starters, they can ship them across the border to Canada or across the pond to Scotland—neither Canadian nor Scotch whisky have any restrictions against maturing in previously filled cooperage.

These days, though, bourbon producers aren't limited to looking for customers within the spirits world.

One of the most enduring trends to emerge from the craft brewing world during the past ten to fifteen years has been barrel aging, most commonly in bourbon cooperage, though often in Scotch and other nonbourbon American whiskeys as well.

Filling wood barrels with beer is far from a new concept. Obviously, back in the day, wood was the only option for aging and storage vessels, long before stainless steel got into the game. Aging happened more or less by accident during long-distance journeys on primitive transportation technologies.

But the one thing progress took away was character that the wood imparted to the beer. Modern brewers have brought that flavor back and introduced some other nuances a barrel's previous inhabitants leave behind.

Even the tiniest breweries these days, those that barely have room for a fermenting tank, manage to squeeze a couple of barrels into their space to add a spirited dimension to anything from a basic pale ale to a boozy Russian Imperial Stout.

Barrel-aged brews rarely account for a sizable portion of a brewery's volume, given how long and inefficient the process is (the breweries would go bankrupt otherwise). But those (roughly) thirty-one-gallon oak containers are the vessels that frequently let the brewing team have the most fun.

Barrel-aged brews have been a bit of a double-edged sword. The residual bourbon (or other spirit, sometimes wine) can hide a lot of the flaws. The more time it spends in the whiskey-saturated wood, the more mistakes it masks. That's a very cynical view, I know, but I do think there's a tendency—albeit, a minor one—to use the barrel as a crutch.

But the ones that have it down to an art and science have produced some of the finest fermented elixirs to grace a bottle or keg.

As we'll note during sour beer week, barrels play a pivotal role in achieving the desired tartness. We're not talking about those here. We'll be sticking with mostly whiskey-barrel aging, sans sour notes.

BOURBON COUNTY STOUT

Barrel aging has actually become the legacy for Goose Island Beer Company, one that even an acquisition by a mega-multinational couldn't erase. Beer geeks may have been up in arms back in 2011 when Anheuser-Busch InBev bought the Chicago brewing institution, raging against the machine, promising they'd never sip another glass of the now-tainted product of a "sellout." But that hasn't stopped these same people from indulging in a snifter or two of the brewery's iconic Bourbon County Stout in all its glorious vintages whenever they get their hands on it. Goose Island is widely credited as the brewery that put whiskey-barrel aging on the beer map. In 1992, then-brewmaster Greg Hall was about to produce Goose Island's one-thousandth batch and wanted to experiment a bit. So, he took the strongest, densest stout he could make and poured it into some bourbon barrels. A legend was born.

KENTUCKY BREAKFAST STOUT

Founders Brewing Company's Kentucky Breakfast Stout, a bourbon-soaked, oak-enhanced version of its coffee-laden Breakfast Stout, has reached similar heights in the craft beer community, with bursting-at-the-seams, standing-room-only crowds anytime a local watering hole adds it to the chalkboard tap listing. In late 2014, the Grand Rapids, Michigan, operation announced that Spain's Mahou San Miguel Group bought a 30 percent stake (A-B InBev made a similar investment a few years before, buying Goose Island outright). A few cried foul, but even if the European conglomerate scoops up the remaining 70 percent, no one's going to be turning down a glass of KBS (as it's known among the devout). Who wouldn't want to sip a stout that's sort of a cold toddy—reminiscent of a cup of coffee with a shot of bourbon in it. KBS registers a hefty 11.2 percent alcohol by volume.

CURIEUX

Portland, Maine's, Allagash Brewing Company was New England's first dedicated Belgian-style brewery and in the two decades since it opened its doors, founder Rob Tod has continued to keep it close to its Belgo roots. Curieux takes a classic Belgian-style tripel ale and ages it in Jim Beam barrels for eight weeks. The bourbon-matured beer then gets blended back with a little bit of fresh tripel. Lots of vanilla notes in this 11 percent alcohol-by-volume dark-golden-hued brew.

SCHLAFLY BOURBON BARREL AGED IMPERIAL STOUT

St. Louis–based Schlafly gets a couple of shout-outs in these pages; and why not, they make damned fine beer. One of the finest among them is its Bourbon Barrel Aged Imperial Stout, which pours a deep black and boasts a delicate balance between a big hit of malt sweetness and a goodly amount of hop bitterness. This is another one above the 11 percent alcohol mark.

THE ABYSS

Deschutes Brewery in Bend, Oregon, founded in 1988, has become one of the largest craft brewers in the country, producing some three hundred thousand barrels of beer a year. A small portion of that volume belongs to The Abyss, a pitch-black imperial stout that gets a fresh reserve release each year. In addition to sundry dark malts (and a couple of paler ones), Deschutes brews The Abyss with blackstrap molasses, brewer's licorice, vanilla beans, and cherry bark. Twenty-eight percent of the final product sits in bourbon barrels, Oregon oak, and pinot noir casks for six months. No two vintages are alike, and it's one of those brews that demands a side-by-side vertical tasting to compare and contrast.

WELL BUILT ESB

Colorado's Breckenridge Brewery runs a fairly innovative barrel program with rotating in-and-out releases. The hop bite in its English-inspired Extra Special Bitter gets some enhancement from its home state's Stranahan's Whiskey Distillery. The one-off (Sorry, all gone!) Well Built spent six months in the Stranahan's barrels and is then bottled as a 7.8 percent ABV.

INNIS & GUNN

We can't talk about barrel-aged beers without mentioning the Scottish brewery that built much of its identity around the technique—and quite by accident. The story the Edinburgh-based operation tells involves not a desire to create a brew enhanced by whisky, but the other way around. A Scotch distiller was looking to season its casks with some of Innis & Gunn's beer. The brewery developed a custom-made recipe, aged it in the barrels for about a month, dumped it out, and then refilled the casks with whisky. Although the beer never was intended to be sold, some had tried it and discovered how much the wood had transformed the brew. Now, in addition to its original oak-aged beer, Innis & Gunn produces Toasted Oak IPA and even a rum-aged offering. It also markets a revolving roster of limited editions that includes everything from a beer aged in Highland and Islay malt whisky casks to those matured in Canadian cherrywood and Irish whiskey barrels.

Barrel aging is so pervasive that it's really hard to do it justice with such a limited tasting flight. But the ones mentioned run both light and dark, offering a sense of the delicate interplay of wood and whiskey across a spectrum of already flavorful beer styles. The Brewers Association, the trade organization representing America's small craft brewers, likes to tout the fact that the average American lives within ten miles of one of the country's 5,000-ish breweries. Next time you get a chance, visit the ones nearest you, poke your head around, and look for a collection of wooden casks. There's about a 50 or 60 percent chance that the facility has at least a few pieces of slightly damp old-school cooperage whose contents patiently wait to reach full maturity. If that's the case, try to become best friends with the brewery. You're not going to want to miss it when the very limited quantities reach their intended draught lines or fill their even fewer-and-further-between bottles.

BELLE EPOQUE REDUX

TWENTY-FIRST-CENTURY ABSINTHE

The good news is that there's now an actual official holiday for one of the most mythical and misunderstood spirits in the history of alcohol. March 5, which occurs during the tenth week of the year, is National Absinthe Day.

Now for the potentially bad news: After you read this, you may be extremely disappointed. Such is the nature of myth; the reality doesn't quite live up to the hype.

That is essentially what defines absinthe in the United States. There had been something of a cult surrounding the anise-flavored spirit for most of the past century. Travelers visiting a small handful of European countries would "smuggle" bottles back to America to share with friends eager to sample the nectar of the forbidden fruit. And by forbidden, I mean it was, until 2007, completely illegal both in the United States and many places abroad, owing mainly to colossal misunderstanding and alarmist propaganda.

The ill will stems from wormwood, one of the herbal ingredients in absinthe. Within the wormwood there's a chemical compound called thujone, which many claimed had hallucinogenic properties. That's why it had been banned in the United States, as well as in numerous other countries, since before the First World War.

That's not to say thujone is 100 percent harmless. But the thujone concentration is usually a maximum of ten parts per million (the European Union caps the safe level at thirty-five parts per million), which means a drinker would have to down bottle after bottle before encountering any adverse effects.[15] Trouble is, that consumer would be long dead from alcohol poisoning before even coming close to finding out how much is too much thujone.

Oh, and by the way, the stuff is present in vermouth, which anyone who's ever had a martini knows has been legal since the enactment of the Twenty-First Amendment.

As the implementation and ultimate repeal of Prohibition in the 1920s and early 1930s taught us, nothing makes people want something more than telling them they can't have it. And, with the little-p prohibition of absinthe lasting nearly seven times longer than big-p Prohibition, there's a lot of pent-up desire to reconcile.

When I first tried absinthe in the late 1990s, it was still not legally available in this country. A friend had spirited (pun intended) a bottle of what he called "evil green" from his recent trip to Prague. A group of us huddled in a small kitchen as he poured samples of this one hundred thirty-proof illicit liquid. But hold your horses, he said. No consumption would commence before we observed the proper ritual: Place one cube of sugar on a spoon, grab a Zippo lighter, set the cube aflame, stir the caramelized sweetener into the glass of evil green, sip, and, finally, await the oncoming hallucinations. And then . . . well, nothing. That's because there aren't any to be had. The belief in such reality-warping attributes was the result of nothing more than the fearmongering that had gotten the stuff banned in the first place. And we all bought into it, foolish consumers that we are.

It didn't help that silly films like Moulin Rouge furthered that misconception as Ewan McGregor and his artsy cohorts in late nineteenth-century Paris (aka La Belle Epoque) drank heartily and beheld the presence of the "green fairy" that magically flew from the bottle's label, and looked and sounded suspiciously like Kylie Minogue.

About a half decade after the Baz Luhrman musical transplanted late twentieth-century rock and pop songs to La Belle Epoque, absinthe was once again legal in the United States, as well as most of Europe. And since then, the myth has been in the process of dying a slow but long-overdue death.

One of the first US-based companies to market an American-made absinthe was the Alameda, California, artisanal spirits producer St. George Spirits, a pioneer in the now-exploding craft distilling movement. St. George opened its doors in 1982, long before the term "craft beer," let alone "craft spirits," entered the lexicon. St. George had been dabbling with absinthe distilling since about 1996, more than a decade before it was legal to sell it. The operative word is "sell," as it was perfectly legal for distillers to make it, they just couldn't make it available to the public. "I played around with it because I'd never tried it and I thought it would be a really interesting spirit, so for years before it was legal here in the states, I had been playing with it,"[16] recalls St. George Spirits master distiller Lance Winters. It turned out to be an incredibly smart move, as it enabled the St. George team to hone the recipe over the course of nearly a dozen years. It was ready for prime time and hit the ground running when the United States finally lifted the ban in 2007. It's still fairly mind-boggling that it took a supposedly modern-minded society like the United States until the latter half of the first decade of the twenty-first century to lift the prohibition on a spirit that posed no more of a threat to the American public than the thousands of other perfectly legal adult beverages.

"For something like that to become legal, it costs a lot of money to change the law," offers Winters. "You have to lobby, and lobbyists are pretty expensive. And then you're dealing with almost a century of misconception about a product."

Even in legalization's aftermath, that misconception persists, which can be either a blessing or a curse, depending on whom you ask.

Winters vividly recalls December 21, 2007, the day St. George started selling its absinthe to the public. Or, more specifically, he remembers the conversations he had with eager purchasers.

"We had a line out the front door of the distillery that zigzagged through our parking lot and out the gate," he says. "When I asked people why they were so excited about absinthe, they said, 'I can legally buy something I can hallucinate with.' I said, 'I hate to disappoint you, but I'd rather disappoint you before you fork over the money for a bottle of this stuff. You're not going to hallucinate. It's not a hallucinogenic product. That's all propaganda that came from an absence of the product being out there.'"

It was, therefore, the absence of absinthe that fed the myth. Say that five times fast.

It goes without saying that large quantities of any alcohol probably would make even the most unimaginative drinker see things that aren't there, be they green fairies, orange elephants, or, say, the ghost of Toulouse Lautrec. So, remember that, on average, a glass of absinthe neat has about 50 percent more alcohol than the same size serving of whiskey, vodka, rum, tequila, or gin. Calibrate accordingly and consume responsibly.

There are, of course, other right ways and wrong ways to consume absinthe that have less to do with alcohol concentration and more to do with ceremony, enjoyment, and not being a complete jackass. First, about those flaming, sweet little cubes: don't bother. The primary reason people started stirring semicaramelized sugar into their drink was that there were a lot of less-than-stellar absinthes on the market in the spirit's heyday. Also, what does burning a white substance on a spoon evoke? (Hint: Trainspotting) And we wonder why legalization had some drinkers eager to start hallucinating.

There's much debate over whether straight-up sugar without the fire has any place in a glass of absinthe.

"I hate putting sugar in mine," says Winters. "I feel like it destroys the very clean characteristics of it and ends up leaving this cloying sweetness in the finish."

That's mostly a matter of personal preference though. There are elegant-looking, specially slotted Victorian-era spoons on the market designed to allow water to drip onto the sugar and then flow through the openings into the glass. The water typically drips from a specially designed fountain. That fountain actually is something that Winters can endorse.

"It's aesthetically pleasing, and it's a beautiful thing to do," he offers. "And adding a little water to a spirit that's one hundred twenty proof is a responsible thing to do. *That* I'm totally down with."

I'm going to go with Winters on that one. Sugar's fine if it's part of a cocktail. It's obviously a critical component of an Old-Fashioned, of which I've had more than a few (hundred) in my time. But when I'm drinking whiskey neat, I'm certainly not putting any sweetener in it. A drop of water or a cube of ice on occasion, but never sugar. Water can open up many of the caramel and vanilla aromas in a good bourbon and it can do the same for the anise and fennel notes in a good absinthe. Sugar just makes it something else.

Ritual should be a part of every imbibing occasion. It's a key component of drinking adventurously. It's about slowing down, being in the moment, and just generally enjoying life. It's not about getting tanked, which is why I favor ditching any silverware-singeing allusions to the drug trade and any misguided hope of hallucination and take the same care in celebrating absinthe that the distillers took in crafting it.

And it doesn't have to be a pricey affair. Now that the spirit is legal in the United States, some of the best absinthes are easy to procure from American producers.

St. George Absinthe Vert (St. George Spirits): As Winters noted, his distillery's brand is marketed as the first legal absinthe released after the US ban was lifted in 2007. The one-hundred-twenty-proof beverage starts as brandy and is then infused with wormwood, star anise, and fennel. The makers distill that combination before performing a secondary infusion of mint, tarragon, opal basil, lemon balm (aka Melissa), hyssop, meadowsweet, and stinging nettles. That secondary infusion gives the spirit its green hue.

Vieux Carré (Philadelphia Distilling): Philadelphia, like St. George, is a distillery known primarily for its gin (more on that in week twenty-four). In 2008, it launched Vieux Carré, which it touts as the first legal absinthe from an East Coast distiller. It's also one hundred twenty proof and has pronounced licorice and anise flavors.

Absinthe Blanche (Copper and Kings American Brandy Company): Louisville, Kentucky's, Copper and Kings forgoes the secondary infusion, resulting in a clear spirit that's one hundred thirty-five proof. Copper and Kings also makes three other flavored absinthe varieties: lavender, citrus, and ginger.

Doc's Absinthe (Doc's All Natural Spirits): South Africa-raised New York city distiller Kevin Herson started making absinthe in his Harlem basement in 2012 before moving to a facility in Brooklyn. Doc's flagship product is a one hundred twenty-two proof spirit with a malted barley and spelt base and ten botanicals.

WEEK 11

EIRE WE GO AGAIN

IRISH WHISKEY

If you felt like something was missing from our whiskey excursion at the beginning of the year, you were right. I hadn't forgotten about the Irish distilling tradition; I was just saving it for the St. Patrick's Day festivities going on this week.

The current whiskey renaissance has been especially kind to Ireland, as Irish whiskey imports in the United States have been growing faster than any other style. The one caveat, mind you, is that it's also a relatively small segment, so the double-digit volume growth it's been enjoying has been off a much tinier base than some of its other counterparts, like bourbon and Scotch.

Still, a double-digit year-on-year percent increase is impressive in its own right. Jameson's doing most of the heavy lifting, of course. This hugely popular Irish brand is the hands-down leader in the segment—the tsunami that's causing the rising tide that lifts all boats. And those boats are more than happy to have the help.

Being owned by Pernod Ricard, the second largest spirits marketer on the planet, has had its advantages for Jameson and, by extension, the category at large. Pernod Ricard (which also owns a number of other well-regarded Irish whiskeys) knows how to market its brands and, seeing the direction the overall whiskey market was heading, knew to put a hefty budget behind the product with resources the much smaller brands' owners could only dream of possessing.

Just like bourbon and other styles, Irish whiskey had suffered a period of decline through most of the twentieth century; the vast majority of distilleries shuttered, and only a handful were still producing on the Emerald Isle. The pendulum started to swing in the other direction just prior to the turn of the millennium, and Irish whiskey started growing again.

Very broadly speaking, Irish is considered to be among the smoother, slightly sweeter, easier drinking whiskeys, approachable enough that it should attract vodka drinkers who might be ready to transition to something with more flavor (or with flavor, period, since vodka, by definition, is supposed to be flavorless).

The most significant facet that makes Irish whiskey distinct from Scotch is that Irish is usually distilled three times, while Scotch usually goes through only two distillations. I say "usually" in both cases because there are notable exceptions to the rule in both Scotland and Ireland: The Lowland malt Auchentoshan goes through three rounds of distillation. The distillery says the drinker detects pronounced fruit and citrus notes because all of the impurities of the liquid are distilled away. Other Scotch distillers wouldn't necessarily consider them to be impurities, as the fewer distillations means the spirit retains more of the characteristics of the grain. There were a few other Lowland producers that thrice-distilled, but those either have ceased operations or shifted to double distilling entirely.

Conversely, some distilleries in Ireland have been releasing double-distilled whiskeys that are a little closer in profile to their Scotch brethren.

Beam Suntory, the current name of the entity that emerged in 2014 when Japan's Suntory (known for the whiskey brand of the same name, as well as the Yamazaki range) acquired Beam, Inc. (owner of its namesake, Jim Beam, as well as iconic bourbons like Maker's Mark and Scotch brands such as Laphroaig and Bowmore), has in its portfolio a couple of Irish whiskey brands that buck the thrice-distilled convention: Kilbeggan and 2 Gingers, the latter of which it purchased from its creator, Minnesota bar owner and entrepreneur Kieran Folliard.

But most of what we'll be discussing this week will be of the triple-distilled tradition.

The notion that Irish has the most significant growth rate among whiskeys (again, off a very small base) usually floors most drinkers, especially those who know their way around a dram. Surely bourbon must be climbing faster. But bourbon, rye, and Scotch, one could argue, are the whiskey drinker's whiskeys. Irish, on the other hand, is the "everything else" drinker's whiskey. It's the bridge that connects a person who customarily consumes vodka cocktails to this previously unexplored realm (for them) of more flavorfully complex spirits.

They might not be ready to drink a single-malt Scotch, bourbon, or rye neat or on the rocks, but they're willing to check out what this Jameson thing is all about.

But that admittedly oversimplified dynamic has been a colossal boon for producers and marketers of Irish whiskey, and not just for Jameson.

One way of looking at the Irish resurgence is that it's reclaiming its birthright.

Many modern drinkers don't realize that Irish whiskey once was the envy of the world before Scotch eclipsed it. In fact, in the nineteenth and early twentieth century, Irish distillers didn't think much of what the Scots were cranking out. They certainly didn't see it as any credible form of competition. It was a Tortoise and the Hare scenario in its purest form. Scotch producers had introduced column distilling, which enabled them to make grain whiskies, those composed of cereals other than malted barley (corn, wheat, etc.). Prior to the introduction of column stills, all whiskey making had been performed solely in pot stills (think giant kettles). The bottom of the still is heated, the liquid boils, and the vapors rise to the neck at the top. The vapors channel to a condenser that cools it, turning it back to a liquid with a more concentrated alcohol content. However, pot stills only allow for one batch at a time.

After that, the stills need to be cleaned before rebooting the whole process.

Column stills, on the other hand, allow for continuous distillation, enabling far greater output in a much shorter period of time. It also produces a distillate with an even higher concentration of alcohol.[17] Column stills, therefore, became a far more efficient and economical option.

The Irish continued using pot stills for quite some time, which created the opportunity for the Scots to get much cheaper whisky to the market much more quickly. The column still also made for a purer spirit. But that's not necessarily a good thing. Pot stills collect other nonalcohol elements in the vapor that adds flavor and character to the spirit, with variations from batch to batch. Modern connoisseurs have come to embrace those little inconsistencies, and it's a major factor in single-malt Scotch's renaissance, as well as the rise of artisanal distilling.

It was pot stills that made Irish offerings among the most prized in the spirits world. One style in particular emerged about two centuries ago that many considered to be the finest of the finest: pure pot still whiskey. Similar to a single-malt Scotch, pure pot still Irish whiskey came from one distillery. But a significant point of distinction was that pure pot stills combined malted and unmalted barley. And the flavor is what really put Ireland on the spirits map. What's most remarkable is that the style was a creation of necessity. It was a response to, you guessed it, taxation. Producers at the time faced a stiff levy on malt. Instead of ponying up and potentially bankrupting their operations, they started experimenting with unmalted barley—immune to the tax—and developed the pure pot still variety. It consisted primarily of a ratio of 60 percent unmalted barley to 40 percent malted, but that varied from time to time.

"It became hugely popular in the nineteenth century and the beginning of the twentieth century, and it's what made Ireland world famous for distilling whiskey,"[18] says internationally renowned expert on the subject and founder of the Ireland Whiskey Trail, Heidi Donelon. "Toward the second half of the nineteenth century, Irish whiskey was regarded as the best in the world and Dublin whiskey was regarded as the best of Irish whiskey. Dublin pot still whiskey was regarded as the best of the best."

Think French wine three to four decades ago. At that time, vintners in Old World France felt untouchable. "They weren't worried about California, Chile, Australia," Donelon observes. "They weren't worried about any of these countries for their wines because they regarded their own wine as the best. The Irish one hundred years ago were very much in the same situation."

Unfortunately, the style was all but abandoned in an effort to play catch-up with the Scots. "From the 1960s, the Irish realized that if they didn't start producing blended whiskeys, they were finished," Donelon reveals. "At that stage Irish whiskey was really, really struggling. All of these brands we know today, like Jameson, would have been pot still whiskeys right up until the 1960s."

Up until just a few years ago, there were only two brands of the pot still variety left in all of Ireland: Redbreast and Green Spot.

But, thanks to the recent surge in the country's distilled output, as well as the overarching spirits premiumization or "trading up" trend, the window for pot still whiskeys has opened once again.

Admittedly, the trading-up phenomenon that precipitated the single-malt Scotch land grab, as well as what's created a market for such higher-end brands as Grey Goose vodka and Patrón tequila, lagged a bit in Ireland. But it's finally catching up and the pure pot still style has been reborn—except they've ditched the "pure." The resurgent segment's new moniker is "single pot still" (including the word "single" certainly is no coincidence). We can either blame or thank America for the name change. The US Food and Drug Administration wouldn't approve the "pure" label, as regulators believe it connotes something healthful. The upside of that is the new name comes with a new lease on life. And connoisseurs are just completely gaga over it.

Fruity notes, such as hints of black currant, typically come through in the single pot stills, as does an underlying spiciness, depending on the length of the maturation period. At a tasting that Donelon once conducted, a participant described the flavor as "ginger on steroids." So, yes, very interesting stuff indeed.

"People love the idea that they're drinking something relatively unknown," Donelon says.

But what of those who have yet to get on board with the spirit. Whiskey in general, let alone one from a particular region, still puts off more people than it should, especially those who think they won't like it, having not tried much beyond the rotgut stuff they may have binged on in college. In the right context, Ireland's greatest liquid export could be what finally breaks them of their biases. For those skittish newbies, I have only one word: chocolate. "Get yourself a nice piece of dark chocolate," Donelon advises. "Have a little bit of chocolate, take a sip of whiskey, and take a second bite of chocolate."

It's a fairly logical pairing as cocoa often is one of the notes that subtly expresses itself in a good glass of Irish. There's also a candied orange peel nuance that might manifest in a glass as well. That harmonizes quite well with chocolate.

"The discovery is unbelievable for a lot of people," Donelon asserts.

Here are a few to discover:

SINGLE POT STILL

Redbreast 12 (Pernod Ricard): There's no better entrée to single pot still style than the twelve-year-old Redbreast. It's full-bodied and complex with a spicy aroma and hints of red fruits. For more of a challenge, work up to the fifteen-year-old, also aged in a combination of American bourbon and Spanish Oloroso sherry casks. A step up from there is the twenty-one-year-old.

Powers John's Lane 12-Year-Old (Pernod Ricard): Named for the long-since-shuttered Powers distillery, the twelve-year-old whiskey has notes of leather, tobacco, and that distinct spiciness typical of the style.

OTHER IRISH STYLES

Kilbeggan (Beam Suntory): The blend, produced in a nearly two-centuries-old pot still, is twice-distilled, which puts it more in a league with Scotch. However, it still exhibits a lot of the signature sweetness and smoothness typical of Irish whiskey.

Teeling Single Malt (Teeling Distillery): Yes, single malt is more closely associated with Scotch, but it does exist in Irish whiskey. But never mind the fact that it's from a single distillery; the real attraction is its barrel finish. It combines spirits finished in a combination of red and white wine, Madeira, sherry, and port casks. Another element it shares with Scotch: it's double-distilled.

Greenore 8-Year Small-Batch Single Grain (Beam Suntory): The eight-year-old Greenore is noteworthy because it's one of the few single-grain Irish whiskeys on the market.

Single grains are made from cereals other than malted barley—in this case, corn, which might attract a few bourbon aficionados. If that's not enough, it's aged in ex-bourbon barrels.

Week 12

Keeping It Real:

Cask-Conditioned Ales

Perhaps the greatest tragedy facing worldwide imbibing is the gradual demise of the institution that is the British pub. When American travelers head across the pond, the local watering hole/social center/neighborhood living room is among the first places to which they make a beeline as soon as their passports are stamped at immigration. Little do they realize that if they were to return exactly a year later, there would likely be fifteen hundred fewer such destinations.

Looking on the bright side, the fact that this is merely a lament and not a eulogy is thanks in no small part to the work of the Campaign for Real Ale (CAMRA), an independent organization advocating traditional British ale, community pubs, and consumer rights. When the group launched in 1971, its initial mission focused primarily on that first item, cask-conditioned, hand-pump-served brews that were the foundation of the United Kingdom's drinking culture—the "real" ales for which the organization is campaigning. At the time, the founders rallied against the evolution of the British beer market, which, by that time, had become dominated by mass-produced lagers marketed by growing multinational conglomerates. The organization's biggest concern, aside from pub closings on a colossal scale, has been the escalating encroachment of mass-marketed lagers peddled by a smaller and smaller number of players getting bigger and bigger through accelerating consolidation. Expensive advertising campaigns were wooing a large swath of the population of younger British consumers coming of age during that period, who favored the fizzy, clear, flavor-muted lagers over the cloudy, brownish, inconsistently carbonated ales of their parents' and grandparents' generations.

More than four decades later, stopping that hemorrhaging and introducing new generations to real ale has been the organization's greatest legacy. There's little doubt that without CAMRA, those living, fermented-in-the-cask, naturally carbonated ales would be extinct from Great Britain. (They're only about 10 percent of the beer market as it is.) It's also unlikely that the concept would have much of a following among American craft brewers, a considerable percentage of which dabble in cask conditioning. Its stateside cult following grows every year, and American beer travelers increasingly are making pilgrimages to taste real ale in its natural habitat, even as CAMRA struggles to ensure that Britons continue to appreciate one of the United Kingdom's greatest cultural contributions to worldwide food and drink.

Baltimore's Clipper City Brewing Company, which produces the Heavy Seas brand, has been on the forefront of American cask conditioning. Founder Hugh Sisson has become one of the top authorities on the practice, which really began in earnest throughout the country around 2005. As more drinkers have embraced the method since then, bars in the states have grown far more receptive to carrying it than they were a decade ago. Heavy Seas's home market represents an ideal case study on that evolution.

"In 2005, there were maybe four accounts in the greater Baltimore area that even considered doing anything with cask beer, now there are probably fifteen to twenty,"[19] Sisson observes. "That's still minuscule, but it's a significant increase. One of the big changes we're beginning to see now is a cultural change. By that, I mean consumers understand—not all of them, not many of them, but there's a growing segment that understand what the stuff is."

Ask any seasoned beer geek what a "firkin" is, and at least half of them will be able to tell you that it's the unit of measurement that a typical cask holds ("cask" and "firkin" often are used interchangeably). These days the containers are usually metal, but occasionally, enterprising brewers will use the old-school wooden ones. Casks are characterized by their bulging roundness, versus the taller and more cylindrical standard draught kegs. They also hold less volume; a firkin is equivalent to 10.8 US gallons (nine Imperial/UK gallons, or one quarter of a barrel), versus full-size kegs at 13.2 gallons. The vessels have two openings, a fairly large hole on the side where it's filled and a smaller one on the face for dispensing. There's no forced carbonation; the bartender dispenses either with a previously installed beer engine—also known as a hand pump—or via gravity, straight from the cask into the glass. In the absence of the carbon dioxide that's used to dispense standard draught beer, cask beer is instantly exposed to air. That means bars have to get through the whole firkin pretty quickly. As long as bartenders control the environment—correct temperature and space—they'll get a good two to three days out of it, tops (United Kingdom pubs usually go through a cask in one night).

What ultimately ends up in the pint glass is a bit warmer than what most Americans are used to—the optimal temperature is around fifty-five degrees Fahrenheit ("cellar" temperature), versus the low- to midforties for draught brews. Some detractors have found it to be too flat, but that's really a sign of an establishment that hasn't taken really good care of it or has had it way past its prime.

"It's heavily mitigated by how the product is being served," says Sisson. "If it's a cask that's been sitting on a bar with a gravity faucet in it, you'd better get through that beer in a night."

Though more brewers are following Heavy Seas's lead, cask offerings will never be more than a fraction of any producer's total output.

"It represents probably less than one percent of our business, maybe two," Sisson says. "We're not doing this because we're looking to make a lot of money. We make it because we believe it's the best way that draught beer can be served."

Though many tend to agree with Sisson and cask appreciation continues to grow in the United States, it's gotten harder and harder to make that case in the country that birthed the concept. Aside from the macro-dominance that CAMRA's been battling since day one, there's now a rapidly growing contingent of small British craft brewers that aren't even offering much in the way of cask-conditioned traditional ales.

Once widely lauded as the saviors of British brewing, CAMRA now confronts frequent criticism for being too set in its ways. And, some of the more, shall we say, vocal new brewers have actively railed against cask ales in their marketing messages.

Back in CAMRA's heyday "real ale" versus mass-marketed macro-lager was a far easier distinction to make. Real-ale casks had live yeast that demanded tender loving care from the pub staff to ensure that, pint-after-pint, drinkers enjoyed a top-notch beer experience. The macroproducts, on the other hand, favored efficiency and consistency over flavor. Their draught products filled sterile and sealed kegs free of any surviving yeast. Part of the charm of cask ale is that it is very much a living thing and no two pints taste exactly alike.

It's not always easy in the modern market to argue that cask is better than kegged beer, as there's so much high-quality product coming from artisanal producers. A cask-conditioned porter isn't necessarily superior to a draught porter; it's just a different taste experience with an equal right to exist in a beer lover's vast and growing consumption repertoire. (Though, on a very personal note, drinking a Fuller's London Porter on cask in Chiswick, not half a mile from the brewery, still ranks among my top drinking memories. It's the gold standard by which all porters should be measured, hands down).

In the grand scheme of one's drinking journey, it's best to take the Swiss route on a lot of these matters, especially when it's a question of what makes one thing "real" and others not. But to get a sense of what centuries of British culture and history taste like in a single Imperial pint, ask for the cask.

Week 13
Saké in Spring

More than a century ago, the mayor of Tokyo donated Japanese cherry trees to the District of Columbia as a gesture of good will. The National Cherry Blossom festival has since become Washington, DC's, most significant rite of spring. As beautiful as those blossoms are, they barely hold a candle to the Asian originals. For me, there are few places as stunningly gorgeous as Japan in the weeks surrounding the vernal equinox. And there's nothing more evocative of that natural beauty than the country's native beverages. A good bottle of saké ("sah-kay") with a great meal is always my Japanese spring, no matter what time of year it is or where in the world I may be.

Before we get into exactly what saké is, we need to discuss what it isn't. For starters, it isn't wine. Regardless of the fact that it's popularly referred to as "rice wine," it has about as much in common with wine as, well, rice has with grapes. Its production method is much closer to that of beer. That was hard for me to get my head around when I first discovered Japan's indigenous fermented beverage. It's clear and still, so how much further from beer could it be? But the rice is steeped and brewed, just like most of the ingredients in its heady cousin.

And "fermented" is as far as it goes. It's not distilled; it's not a spirit. Saké far too often is mistaken for one, given its visual resemblance to vodka, gin, or unaged tequila. It doesn't help that it's typically poured into a small glass or ceramic cup roughly twice the size of a thimble (but personally, I wouldn't have it any other way). To the uninitiated, it's a shot with a one-gulp ticket to the belly without a moment to spare to sniff or savor. Not only is shooting it rather gauche, it's also pretty pointless; at its strongest, saké clocks in at 18 or 19 percent ABV (usually closer to 15 percent), so it's actually kind of silly to inhale it like one would a 1.5 ounce glass of rotgut tequila. There's so little burn from the beverage—especially with the finer sakés—that the shooter would get more or less the same effect from a shot of water.

You know what else it is not? A component of an incendiary device. If anyone offers you a "saké bomb," just say no. What's a saké bomb, you ask? Well, you grab a pint of beer and drop a shot glass full of saké into it and watch everything "explode"—everything, including any trace of nuance that may have existed in the nose or flavor of either liquid ingredient.

You might detect a hint of near-militant rigidity in the tone here, but please do not mistake it for pretension. Saké is anything but pretentious. If it's borderline unapproachable to most mainstream Western drinkers, that's mainly because there's so much unintended mystery surrounding it. The importers are probably the most to blame for this, but it's not for any nefarious reasons. It's pretty expensive to import the stuff from the other side of the world, and those who do the importing are going to have to charge a premium to eke out a profit. And what says "Wow, this is really exotic" more than a label dominated by indecipherable (to the average Western consumer) Japanese characters. But that's been a bit of a double-edged katana (see what I did there?) for marketers. There's so little actual branding going on among the hundreds of highly distinct sakés coming into the United States that it's hard for the average drinker to distinguish one from another. It's just a sea of words they, at worst, can't read and, at best, can't pronounce on store shelves and on the menu at the local izakaya (a Japanese-style bar that usually serves small, shareable plates of food).

Some brand owners are starting to recognize this and giving their sakés, simple, easy-to-remember names. For instance, there's one called "Hiro," whose four-letter name is scrawled across the front of the bottle in a giant form of calligraphy (reflecting, as the importers say, "the swift movement of the Samurai warrior in action"). The team behind it wanted something that people could easily pronounce and that didn't have too many syllables. It also jumps out at the shopper perusing the saké aisle (well, saké shelf anyway).

Ichishima may not roll off the tongue as quickly as "Hiro" does, but, visually speaking, it stops traffic just as effectively. A few years back, that brand's US rep, Michael John Simkin, decided it was time to freshen up the offerings from a saké brewery whose history dates back more than two centuries. He replaced the standard Japanese-character-adorned black bottle with a white one and had a designer add a few flourishes of minimalist art to its packaging aesthetic.

To most, the curious icon resembles a puzzle piece, but the true intention was to evoke the flow of water—it's a striking image.

Even if the bottle is readable and/or inviting, what's actually in it is still an enigma to most people. "I think it's got something to do with rice" is the extent of most mainstream knowledge. Learning the basics, however, is far easier than gaining even a rudimentary understanding of wine.

At its most elemental level, saké is the symphonic interaction of four ingredients: rice, water, yeast, and a rice culture—a mold of sorts—called koji. It all starts with a grain of brown rice—in fact, when we eat white rice, it was, once upon a time, brown rice as well, before it was refined. With saké, it's all a matter of polish. Upon harvesting, about 10 percent of the grain is polished (aka "milled," which is used interchangeably) away before it even reaches the saké brewery. There it's milled further. How much further? That depends on the grade the brewer is aiming for to achieve a particular expression. Polishing the grain down another 20 percent brings it to 70 percent, which is more or less where "premium" begins. And that's not necessarily based on quality, but on cost. As more is milled away, the brewer gives up more of the rice's volume, which makes it progressively more expensive to produce.

Generally, sakés at this level are referred to as either junmai or honjozo, but it's a little more complicated than that, and we'll get to that in a moment.

The next polishing level, leaving a maximum of 60 percent of the grain intact, is called ginjo. The trade up from there is daiginjo, where 50 percent or more of the grain is milled away. Some even higher-end expressions go even deeper into daiginjo territory, leaving just 40, 30, or, in rare cases, 20 percent of the rice grain intact (60, 70, or 80 percent of it is polished away). Some elite brewers have gone as low as 9 percent, milling away a staggering 91 percent of the grain, but that's considered by most to be a bit extreme.

The amount of the original grain that remains is referred to as the seimaibuai. So, for instance, a ginjo that has had 45 percent of the grain milled away has a seimaibuai of 55 percent.

So, what's the point of all this polishing? Generally speaking, it's all about desired flavor profile. At the junmai and honjozo level, sakés tend to exhibit rich, dense, nutty characteristics, which make them very food-friendly. The ginjo and daiginjo grades are lighter, with more fruit-like aromas. While those go perfectly well with food, many saké sommeliers say they're better appreciated on their own. "Certainly, [ginjo and daiginjo] have an easy-drinking, elegant quality that junmai doesn't have,"[20] explains Jamie Graves, a respected saké expert and sommelier, who's general manager of the modern izakaya and saké bar, Sakamai, on Manhattan's Lower East Side. "This doesn't make them better, just lighter, more delicate and elusive."

Now, back to the junmai concept. Junmai means "pure," and, in the case of saké, "pure" refers to the fact that no brewers' alcohol has been added.

Its alcohol content is derived entirely from fermenting the rice. You'll often see "junmai ginjo" or "junmai daiginjo" on the label. That simply means is it's either a ginjo grade or daiginjo grade with no added brewer's alcohol. A saké with a seimaibuai between 60 and 70 percent without added alcohol is, simply, junmai. One of a similar seimaibuai with added alcohol is honjozo.

Wait, what? People are actually adding alcohol to, um, alcohol? Again, it's motivated more by flavor than any desire to cheapen the process. "While the no-alcohol-added junmai sounds better in the abstract," Graves says, "adding a touch of refined brewer's alcohol actually makes the texture of the saké smoother and silkier."

There's also going to be a time and place to spend a little more money and savor some sensory complexity with a bottle or two of the more refined stuff. The good news is that it's getting somewhat easier to find sakés of all stripes as American consumers develop a taste for the izakaya experience and more Japanese watering holes (with food!) pop up in major cities throughout the United States. Sushi bars with wine and beer licenses are carrying a greater variety of expressions these days, well beyond US market-share-hogging Gekkeikan. If you're lucky, you might have a few B.Y.O. places and a well-stocked liquor store or Asian grocery near you that carries an impressive selection for you to pair with your nigiri, sashimi, or maki.

We get into a slightly grayer area when we start talking about serving temperature. There's a raging warm-versus-cold debate; there are those who would rather drink formaldehyde than consume heated saké—they consider it a lesser experience. For others, it's more of a right time/right place/right saké scenario.

Both methods are traditional and it's perfectly acceptable to drink saké either way.

Until very recently, I was always of the mind that the types of saké reserved for heating tended not to be the best of the best on their own and they usually lacked complexity. That may be true in many—perhaps even most—cases, but, as I've learned, some über-premium, ultra-rare saké may, indeed, be heated. That also came as a surprise to Graves. "I'd had some great hot sakés before, ones I really enjoyed, but I always thought the best ones, the ones that were going to blow your mind, are the chilled kind of thing,"[21] Graves tells me during a night of saké, shochu, and Japanese small-plate pairing at a Lower East Side izakaya.

That changed when he shared a meal in Niigata, Japan, with the master brewer of major saké producer Hakkaisan (not to be confused with the upscale Chinese eatery, Hakkasan). "The master brewer brought out a daiginjo, saying 'we'll be drinking this today and we don't really sell it outside of this town, blah, blah, blah, it's polished to 35 percent. Would you like it hot or cold? Everything I make is good hot.'"

Graves tried it hot and cold, side-by-side and actually liked the hot better.

"Some are good across a range of temperatures, some have an ideal temperature," Graves adds. "But it's also a matter of opinion."

That's good because I still hold to my opinion that slightly chilled or room temperature is always best, but I have become much less of a inflexible hardliner on the subject. And I definitely will drink it warm if there's something particularly unconventional about the way it's prepared.

On a recent trip to Osaka, I happened upon a hole-in-the-wall restaurant that served its saké piping hot with blowfish fins steeped in it. There was even a bit of ceremony in its delivery: the server would complete its preparation by setting it briefly aflame. Despite my inclination toward mildly chilled saké, there was no way I was leaving that place without ordering a pot of that stuff. Drinking adventurously, indeed.

There actually was a time when the Japanese people only drank it warm. The premium grades are relatively new developments, dating back only to the mid-twentieth century. Before that, flavors weren't very delicate and, therefore, benefited from heating. So, if you were to poll Japanese drinkers to discern the hot/cold divide, don't be surprised if those who favored heating it skewed older.

Whether hot or cold, if you're going to be sharing a full bottle or carafe, be sure to mind one of the essential rules of the road (No one's going to judge you; it's just more fun to enhance your imbibing efforts with a touch of ritual): Don't let any of your dining and drinking companions pour their own. Keep an eye on how empty their cup or glass is getting, and be Johnny- or Janey-on-the-spot with a quick refill. They've got a bit of etiquette of their own to observe. It's always polite for the pouree to lift his or her vessel off the table to assist the pourer.

In some Japanese restaurants where saké can be ordered by the drink, the servers might bring you a small glass inside a wooden or lacquer box called a masu. At first the masu may seem like a high-walled saucer designed to catch any liquid that might accidentally spill over the side of the glass. Then the server keeps pouring for a second or two after it's cascaded past the brim and you realize that this is no accident. That's all part of the tradition, the theater, if you will. There are many tales purporting to be the original story of this practice, and if you average all of them together, you'll conclude that it has something to do with generosity and good luck. That's neither here nor there. It makes for great theater and, hey, more saké!

Saké truly is a liquid worthy of the type of romanticizing that's common on these pages. Therefore, it's quite hard to believe that Japanese consumers steadily have, for decades, been fleeing the category in favor of drinks like beer, whiskey, and, to a certain extent, shochu (more on that next week). Japan's loss, however, is the West's gain, as exporters are seizing on the opportunity abroad, especially in light of the global craft beer boom. Consumers are seeking new flavor experiences and saké fits right in with this quest. In fact, craft saké brewing might be the next phase of the artisanal movement's evolution. It's already happened for beer and spirits, so why not saké? Some entrepreneurial producers have been banking on just that scenario and opening their own saké-making facilities stateside.

Let's not get ahead of ourselves, though. The number of commercial saké producers in the United States is still pretty minuscule; it just cracked the double digits as of this writing. By contrast, there are more than four thousand craft beer brewers in the United States, nearly eighty-five hundred wineries and around eight hundred or so craft distillers (and counting). It's likely that saké will reach only niche status in America, but I would wager it would be a healthy and growing niche.

The best-known US craft saké producer is SakéOne, based in Forest Grove, Oregon, about twenty miles outside of Portland. It opened in 1992, strictly as an importer of brands produced by Japan's Momokawa brewery. Five years later, it started brewing its own, under the Momokawa label, out of respect for its Asian partner. At the time there were a few producers in California, but those were largely satellite breweries owned by their Japanese counterparts.

"[Those breweries] came to the United States and set up shop primarily to brew the entry-level sakés, the ones that you'd get served hot in Japanese restaurants,"[22] SakéOne president Steve Vuylsteke tells me over a couple of glasses of the good stuff at the brewery. "But that's a far cry from the vision that the founders of SakéOne have, to build a brewery to brew high-quality, what we call junmai ginjo-grade saké."

Making it ginjo grade (again, 40-plus percent of the grain polished away) was a conscious choice. But SakéOne couldn't make a non-junmai product even if it wanted to (which it doesn't). The federal TTB licenses saké makers as breweries, not wineries and, therefore, they cannot have outside alcohol added to it.

"So, it's really illegal for any American saké brewer to brew anything but junmai," Vuylsteke continues. "Junmai means pure rice, no alcohol added. The two things put together is what we do and we really think that's the future—[ginjo] and daiginjo are really the future grades that will appeal to a lot of American consumers."

So, what are you waiting for? The future starts here:

- MOMOKAWA ORGANIC JUNMAI GINJO (SAKÉONE):
  The best part of having a brewer like SakéOne in the United States is that it makes premium-level saké much more affordable. Where a 720 mL bottle of a quality imported junmai ginjo might cost around $27.99 at a shop and $45 to $50 at a bar or restaurant, the same size bottle of one of the products in the Momokawa line will be a far thriftier $13.99 at retail and $22 to $25 at a dining or drinking establishment. The organic variety is slightly dry to mildly sweet and pairs well with milder sushi options like salmon or fluke.

- KANBARA BRIDE OF THE FOX (KAETSU BREWERY):
  Kaetsu Shuzo is based in what many consider the Napa Valley of saké brewing, the Niigata Prefecture. That's primarily due to the abundant mountain snow, which melts and feeds the rice paddies with extremely pure water. That same water is used to brew Niigata saké. Medium-dry,

with a slightly sweet finish, Bride of the Fox is a prime example of an accessible (and accessibly priced at about $32.99 per 720 mL in retail shops—affordable by Niigata standards) junmai ginjo from the region. It's equal parts nutty and fruity and its gold-colored label over a deep amber bottle is easy to spot. The saké gets its name from Niigata's annual Fox-Bride festival, which celebrates a local legend about mysterious lights that appeared on Mount Kirin. Locals say the lights were paper lanterns carried in the fox-bride procession.

- DASSAI (ASAHI SHUZO CO., LTD.) It's not hard to figure out which grade of saké you're drinking when you're enjoying a Dassai product. Asahi Shuzo only brews junmai daiginjo. And, it's equally simple to determine how much of the rice has been polished away; the seimeibuai is right there in the name. Dassai 50 is milled to 50 percent of the original grain, Dassai 39 to 39 percent and Dassai 23 to 23 percent. From a culinary standpoint, the 50 is the most versatile; it holds up well against most main dishes. On the other hand, the 23 is incredibly delicate and best enjoyed on its own or with light appetizers. President Obama apparently is a fan of Dassai 23. When the White House hosted a state dinner for Japanese prime minister Shinzo Abe and his wife, Akie, in April 2015, Dassai 23 was the saké of choice for the opening toast.

- ICHISHIMA JUNMAI DAIGINJO (ICHISHIMA BREWERY): Junmai Daiginjo can be quite pricey, but a relatively reasonable one (about $50 to $55 at retail) to try would be from the Ichishima Brewery. Ichishima is even easier to spot on the shelf than Bride of the Fox, primarily due to its modern bottle redesign. The white label over a nearly opaque bottle features Ichishima's "flow of water" icon resembling a jigsaw puzzle piece. All of its saké grades feature this icon, so be sure to look for the green one—that's the daiginjo. It's semidry, very delicate, with subtle aromas of pear. It's perfect with most styles of sushi.

- SEIKYO OMACHI JUNMAI GINJO NAMA (NAKAO BREWERY): You should try at least one nama saké. It's unpasteurized and, therefore, usually has to be kept chilled before serving. Nama typically is released only four times a year, once each season. Because nama sakés don't go through two rounds of pasteurization, they often are zestier and more aromatic from residual koji and yeast. As Graves explains, "I think of it as making the flavor just more direct and forward; you can taste saké as it ages, settling into the middle and then the back of your palate, while the seasonal, unpasteurized stuff just leaps right in." This particular ginjo has a seimeibuai of 55 percent and an alcohol content of 15.4 percent. It's a little sweet and has a deep, nutty quality, balanced by a clean acidity.

***

We're going to stick around in Japan for another week as we sample one of its other incomparable contributions to the drinking world.

Week 14

It's Sho(chu) Time

Just as Western consumers are beginning to get their heads around the concept of saké, there's a whole other form of Japanese beverage alcohol that's trying to find its way into your glass. That would be shochu ("show-chew"), Japan's native spirit and a bit of an enigma in its own right. Younger Japanese drinkers, to a significant extent, turned their backs on saké (after all, it's their parents' and grandparents' drink and it's just not cool to be doing what mom, dad, grandma, and grandpa do or used to do).

In the early- to mid-2000s, shochu experienced its most pronounced modern boom in its home country, spurred by media reports of the potential health benefits of its modern consumption. Most of those reports pointed out its low caloric content relative to other alcohols. That made it especially popular with twenty- and thirtysomethings.

My, how the tables have turned. Not too long ago—just a few decades, really—shochu was considered a low-class drink, not unlike the way the vast majority of US consumers perceived bourbon up until twenty or so years ago. Amazing how food and drink once considered proletarian suddenly becomes fashionable and luxurious in nature. Remember that even lobster was once considered a meal fit for a peasant.

The cynical view is that given its higher ABV, drinkers are embracing it because it offers a much more expedited route to intoxication. While that may, undoubtedly, be true for many who consume, it is far from being the source of shochu's greatest allure. For one thing, even though it's markedly more alcoholically potent than wine, beer, or saké, it's still generally less so than most spirits, save for liqueurs. Whiskeys bottom out at 40 percent, but if you're into the high-end, smaller batch stuff, it could be 45 or 50 percent and, with cask-strength varieties,

55 or 60 percent. Those are quite marvelous in their own right, but a drinker needs a pretty sharp nose and palate to thoroughly appreciate a beverage with such a high ABV, as the alcohol often will upstage other facets of its charred-oak-barrel-aged goodness. By contrast, when a spirit is typically between 20 and 25 percent ABV—as most shochu is, with a few notable exceptions—it tends to be a bit more democratic in terms of dominant flavor notes.

However, it's not just shochu's relative mildness that makes it so accessible. There's so much stylistic diversity and such a something-for-everyone dynamic within the category, that it's almost shocking that shochu doesn't have a more pronounced profile among American legal-drinking-age consumers. A casual drinker would be hard-pressed to tell a bourbon from a Scotch, from an Irish, from a Canadian, from a Tennessee whiskey (until they've read the whiskey chapters in this book, that is). But with shochu, the flavor profiles are as distinct as the array of ingredients from which they're distilled.

Scotch, Irish whiskey, and beer drinkers should be happy to know that one of those base ingredients is barley. And given the fact that it's a very familiar grain to imbibers, barley-based shochu is probably the one variety that tastes remotely similar to a drink they know and love. But not all that similar.

Other common ingredients include black sugar and rice.

Far less common to Western palates is alcohol derived from sweet potatoes, another major fermentable base that's ultimately distilled into shochu. Sweet potato–based shochu is the reigning favorite among Japanese consumers. Those potatoes have found their way into other Japanese drinks, including beer, which we'll hear a bit more about in week forty-seven.

Then there's shochu made from buckwheat (aka soba), which offers a flavor experience completely distinct from all the others. One of my favorites of this ilk is Towari, with its decidedly umami nose and a hint of sour—the closest culinary comparison I could think of is Japanese pickled plum (though nary a plum is to be found in its distillation). There's also the faintest hint of toast. I generally try to be sparing with such note-for-note comparisons, as I find them a bit pretentious and exclusionary. This is an all-inclusive adventure, remember? But with Towari, there's so much complexity going on that simply saying "lots of flavor" would neither do it justice nor paint enough of an enticing picture to get anyone to try it (I hope I've convinced you).

I consulted one of the preeminent shochu experts of the New York City bar scene (and the rest of the country for that matter) to learn how he gets drinkers on board with the spirit and, he says, it's all about progression.

"Rice shochu is the easiest to begin with,"[23] says Takahiro Okada, who runs Sake Bar Shigure in Manhattan's TriBeCa neighborhood. "Rice shochu has kind of a soft taste, it's not a distinctive flavor."

It helps that it's the same core ingredient as saké, which makes it an easy bridge beverage for imbibers already familiar with the undistilled rice-based alcohol.

The barley-based variety is also a relatively easy entry point for the novice, as it's sort of a clearer, lower-alcohol version of Scotch with many of the same barley expressions one would find in Scotland's native spirit. It's also the shochu style that has, perhaps, the widest flavor variation. "Each barley shochu has the taste of the distillery, just like whiskey," notes Okada.

And, like whiskey, some distillers might age it in oak, while others will barely alter it, other than adding water to achieve the desired 25 percent ABV.

The next stage of the shochu initiation process would be for drinkers to try the sweet potato or sugar cane styles. "I prefer those kinds for the person who has some experience with shochu," Okada reveals.

Sugar cane, while not sweet per se, does retain some subtle sweetness that's characteristic of the style. For sweet potato shochu, there's also a pronounced earthy component to it. There's really no other way to describe it, but combined with the sweeter elements, it's understandable why it's so popular now in its home country.

Shochu is by no means limited to the sort made from rice, barley, black sugar, or sweet potatoes. There are more than fifty base ingredients from which shochu may be made, but exponentially more from which it may not. Most fruits, with the exception of dates, are prohibited.[24] Some beyond-the-norm bases that are allowed include those distilled from carrots, milk, aloe, or even coffee beans. A personal white whale of mine is Beniotome, which is the product of sesame distillation. I say white whale because I had it once by happenstance and fell in love with it. I assumed it was ubiquitous (well, as ubiquitous as a shochu can be, anyway). I never saw it listed at another bar after that. Of course, it's easy enough to buy online (in states that permit such a thing), at an Asian specialty store, or one of those liquor superstores with generous selections. Truth be told, I like that it's pretty difficult to find in bars and restaurants. I would have been less likely to experience the full spectrum of shochu styles, as I probably would have made Beniotome my go-to beverage at any izakaya or sushi bar.

And, yes, the unmistakable sesame flavor is very overt.

The spirit's exact origins are sketchy, at best, but the consensus is that it's around five hundred years old. It likely evolved from beverages brought over by Chinese or Korean merchants.

The undisputed center of the shochu-making universe is Kyushu, the southernmost of Japan's home islands. More than 90 percent of the country's shochu output comes from Kyushu[25]. Among the better-known prefectures on the island are Nagasaki, Kagoshima, Miyazaki, Oita, Fukuoka, and Kumamoto.

There are actually three shochu varieties produced on Kyushu that have been granted protected appellation of origin status by the World Trade Organization (WTO):

Satsuma Shochu must be produced and bottled in Kagoshima and use only Kagoshima-grown sweet potatoes. (Satsuma was the name of an old province that now comprises the western half of Kagoshima Prefecture.)

Kuma Shochu is a rice-based spirit that must use water from the Kumagawa River and be produced and bottled in Kumamoto.

Iki Shochu must have a two-to-one barley to rice ratio and be produced and bottled on Iki island in Nagasaki Prefecture.

The island prefecture of Okinawa actually has its own spirit known as Awamori and it, too, has WTO protected appellation status. Awamori typically gets categorized with shochu, but is really a beverage segment unto itself. There are a number of key factors that distinguish it from the more pervasive liquor; the most significant one is that it's distilled completely from long-grain Thai rice. The tradition stems from the days when Okinawa was an independent nation engaged in commerce with the country formerly known as Siam. Awamori usually is aged in a ceramic vessel that mellows the flavor a bit. It also often ends up with higher alcohol content than is common among most shochus; 28 to 32 percent ABV is the norm for Awamori (Okinawa is exempt from a Japanese tax increase on any spirit above 25 percent ABV).

Another regional peculiarity enforced within Japan applies to black sugar shochu. It may only be made in Amami Oshima, a group of islands that are considered part of Kagoshima Prefecture. It historically has been among the highest-ABV shochu styles, often between 30 and 35 percent.

CULINARY ACCOMPANIMENT

Shochu, in general, pairs remarkably well with a broad range of foods, especially since it's on the low side, alcoholically, for a distilled spirit. The spirit boasts a palate-cleansing property that makes it an especially good companion for izakaya fare—Japanese small plates of varying levels of flavor intensity. At Shigure, for instance, a typical meal might include a couple of pieces of delicate, seasonal sashimi; Fried Renkon, a plate of crispy lotus root; Shishito Yaki Bitash, grilled peppers; and Katsuo Tataki, a creation that combines fresh-caught bonito, ponzu sauce, and onion. A sip of shochu between bites enables the diner to fully experience each dish without the invasion of the prior plate's lingering flavor. The cleansing effect is in contrast with saké's primary role at dinner: to amplify the flavor of a chef's innovations.

AS YOU LIKE IT

As with any other spirit from every other corner of the globe, the ultimate question arises: neat, in a cocktail, or on the rocks? There's little difference in the answer: all are correct, at different times and with different shochus. It's best to get acquainted with it neat first, especially to be able to compare and contrast the vastly different flavor expressions among the barley, rice, buckwheat, sugar cane, and sweet potato varieties. Once you've settled on a favorite—very difficult, so no pressure—drop a cube or two in it, if that's how you roll. A couple drops of water also help open up the flavor. It's actually fairly common for Japanese consumers to add even more than that. Sometimes they'll have as much as half of their glass of shochu diluted with water, and sometimes that water is hot! It's also not out of the ordinary to see folks mixing it with green tea.

As for more complex mixed drinks, the higher-end izakayas design their cocktail menus specifically with shochu's delicate sensory nuances in mind, so it's best to stick with the house specialties. Don't be tempted to ask the bartender to put a shot of soda in it or swap out the vodka in a cosmo or martini for shochu. Repeat after me: Shochu is not vodka. Shochu is a journey, so go out and explore it. Don't try to make it come to you.

— STOPS ALONG THE JOURNEY —

It's not hard to get overwhelmed looking at a shochu list. Where does one even begin? A few good places to start are on this list, curated with the help of one of America's top authorities on shochu, Stephen Lyman, founder and editor of Kampai.US:

- IICHIKO SILHOUETTE (SANWA SHURUI COMPANY, LTD.):
  Distinguishable by its short, stout 750 mL bottle, the barley-based Ichiko distilled by Sanwa Shurui Shuzo is the top-selling brand in the United States. It's smooth and easy to drink with light citrus and ginger notes.

- TOWARI (TAKARA SHUZO COMPANY, LTD.):
  Distilled by Takara Shuzo Company, Towari is the shochu that makes me swoon. It's buckwheat (soba) based, and offers a nutty, umami, almost pickled-fruit experience on the nose and palate.

- ENMA (OIMATSU SHUZO):
  The barley-based shochu from the Oita Prefecture is aged for three years in whiskey barrels, so it makes a good crossover beverage for whiskey drinkers new to shochu. Enma takes its name from the Buddhist King of the Underworld.

- KOZURU KURO (KOMASA SHUZO COMPANY LTD.):

A great introduction to sweet potato shochu from Kagoshima Prefecture, where they know a thing or two about sweet potatoes. There's a discernible sweetness to it with a rich mouthfeel.

- KAPPA NO SASOIMIZU (KYOYA SHUZO COMPANY, LTD.): Another great way to acquaint yourself with sweet potato shochu, Kappa no Sasoimizu stands apart as it uses red sweet potatoes—atypical among producers. Produced in the Miyazaki Prefecture, Kappa no Sasoimizu has got a lot of flavor, but not a lot of alcohol—its ABV stands at 20 percent, on the low side for shochu.

- SATSUMA GODAI (YAMAMOTO SHUZO, LTD.): Since sweet potato shochu is the most popular style in Japan, we might as well try one more. Satsuma Godai from Kagoshima Prefecture is a good, no-nonsense spirit that's very true to style—like a reliable comfort food. The label is famous for its sketch of samurai Saigo Takamori, leader of the Satsuma Rebellion.

- KAWABE (SENGETSU SHUZO COMPANY, LTD.): The rice-based spirit from Sengetsu Shuzo Company is what's known as muroka kome shochu—unpasteurized after distillation (technically just the muroka part; kome means rice). The lack of pasteurization and filtration leaves it with a richer flavor accentuated by hints of banana.

- LENTO (AMAMI OSHIMA KAIUN SHUZO COMPANY, LTD.): It would be an unforgiveable omission if I didn't include a black sugar (aka kokuto) shochu from Amami Oshima, the group of islands between Kyushu and Okinawa. It's most famous for a quirk in its production: the distillers play classical music during its three-month aging process to help mellow it.

- BENIOTOME (BENIOTOME COMPANY, LTD.): As I mentioned, this is the white whale/holy grail for me. Immediately apparent on the nose and on the palate is the sesame base from which it's distilled. Grab a glass (or three) of this if it shows up on the menu in front of you.

- ZUISEN HAKURUYU (AWAMORI): I'm hesitant to include this one, not because it isn't deliciously amazing—because it is—but that it's actually Okinawan Awamori, which is its own thing. It's distilled from Thai (Indica) rice.

***

There are few distilled spirits (outside of sweet liqueurs) that are as easy on the palate when consumed neat or on the rocks as shochu. And few foster such aromatic and gustatory harmony when paired with cuisine. It is, therefore, borderline criminal that shochu is not more mainstream in the West. However, it's not exactly a mystery where at least some of the blame is due. Hint: A very similar-sounding spirit from one of Japan's closest mainland Asia neighbors.

Week 15

A Brief Soju Sojourn

Now that you've gotten a primer on just what the hell this shochu stuff is, I'm happy to throw a wrench in it and confuse you further by inviting you to cross the Japan Sea into South Korea to drink the very similar-sounding beverage of choice in Seoul and surrounding regions: soju ("so-joo").

There's no doubt that the two spirits have a fair amount in common, beyond being distilled and clear. Soju's alcohol content can hover around 25 percent (with some as mild as the low teens) much like its Japanese counterpart, but there are a few that could be as strong as 30 or 40-plus percent.

Tastewise, however, the distinctions can be quite pronounced, depending on the brand. That's primarily due to the fact that most sojus are distilled multiple times, similar to the way vodka is produced. The process results in a mostly neutral, yet slightly sweet spirit—the latter due to the addition of sugar and other adjuncts during production. There's definitely a more pronounced hit of ethanol on the nose than in shochu.

That's not to say there aren't shochus similar to vodka. In last week's chapter, we focused fairly exclusively on what's known as otsu-rui. That's the more traditional style wherein the spirit usually is distilled only once and, therefore, retains much of the character of its base ingredient. I didn't get into the less traditional ko-rui variety, which is distilled several times, to the extent that it lacks much taste or odor—essentially the definition of vodka. Shochus that fall under the ko-rui heading are the ones that will be the most similar to soju for that reason.

Now, here's where things start to get really interesting. There are some, not many, bottles labeled as soju that actually contain shochu—as if things weren't confounding and complicated enough! We can thank the laws of certain states—particularly California—for that little maneuver. Some clever lobbying on the part of the Korean restaurant industry in the 1990s secured a special dispensation for soju brands below the 25 percent ABV threshold, enabling those to be sold in eateries licensed to sell only beer and wine. [26] There is no such allowance for shochu, even though a greater majority of the Japanese spirit's brands fall within the designated alcohol limit. Such arbitrariness has had two effects. First, it's made American consumers somewhat more familiar with soju than shochu. Second, it's led some shochu brands to call themselves "soju" to get around the law. So, there's a chance you may have been drinking shochu when you thought you were drinking soju. And even if you were hip to that fact and thought to ask, it's not likely that the establishment is training the waitstaff to let you in on the little secret. (Indeed, the owners may have been duped as well).

Not to alarm you, though. It doesn't happen too often.

One thing soju has that shochu doesn't is bragging rights. The top-selling spirits brand in the world—we're talking all spirits here, including vodka and whiskey—is a soju, according to International Wine and Spirits Research[27], the number cruncher that tracks such things. The brand in question would be Jinro, from Korean drinks conglomerate Hite-Jinro. Remember, this is brands and not categories overall. While soju's definitely up there from a category standpoint, it's still baijiu that retains that top spot. South Koreans have a healthy appetite for soju; the beverage, typically sold in 360 mL green bottles (about the size of your average beer container), accounts for about 97 percent of the country's alcohol sold.

As with many other Asian distilled spirits, the traditional fermentable, distillable base has been rice. However, in 1965, the Korean government put a moratorium on rice-based soju production thanks to a blight that had fallen on the grain at that time[28]. Distillers were forced to get creative with other starchy sources, including, yes, sweet potatoes. And, just as sweet potatoes have surpassed barley as the favorite base among Japanese shochu consumers, they have found quite the following in South Korea as well.

The government finally lifted the rice ban nearly thirty-five years later in 1999, but Korean drinkers had taken a shine to the less-expensive sweet potato soju, so they're quite common today. Rice is still the preferred grain; it just tends to be joined by other fermentable sources.

For instance, Jinro's flagship green-bottle brand uses a combination of rice, barley, and tapioca in its mash.

Brands made from 100 percent rice are reserved for the higher-end of the market—think of it as the single malt of soju. In fact, some distillers have been aging their pure rice sojus in oak, furthering that connection with the top-shelf stuff (Korean consumers also happen to be big whiskey drinkers, so it's an easy leap to make). Many super-premium sojus are single distilled, distinguishing them from the common products that undergo multiple distillation. Distilling once retains more of the grain's character.

Hite-Jinro is cornering that tier of the market as well, with launches like Ilpoom, which sits in oak barrels for a decade before anyone gets to sip it. Where are they getting those barrels? Why, Scotland and Tennessee, of course, two of the most significant whiskey centers in the world.

Soju marketers also have been premiumizing the packaging. Soju's generic-looking green bottle has become a fairly familiar site in Korean restaurants and liquor stores, but expect to see the types of glass containers more likely to be found in the home bars of Cognac connoisseurs.

Whether it's spent ten years mellowing in oak or it's fresh out of the still and into a $4 green bottle, there is, like most Asian drinks, a ritual that must be observed when consuming it. In groups, the eldest member doles out the glasses. The junior participants should accept the glass with both hands.[29] It's a show of respect for one's elders, of course—millennials, take note! Wait for the person who handed you the glass to pour—never pour for yourself. You're also supposed to avoid eye contact with the pourer while you drink it. Shoot the first glass and then sip all subsequent pours, especially if this is the pure-rice stuff. What's the sense of paying extra when you're not even going to get a chance to taste it?

If it's the low-end, mass-marketed green-bottle stuff, there's no shame in shooting every glass. Take a cue from the rest of the table to see what they're doing. But I'd recommend sipping just a little, so you at least get a sense of whatever, if any, flavor there is.

When you finish your glass, hand it to the person who poured your first shot and return the favor.

Soju's close kinship with vodka makes it not only cocktail-ready but remarkably infusion-friendly as well. That's one of the main attractions at Soju Haus in Manhattan's Koreatown. Soju Haus is one of the trendier, lower-lit options in the Midtown enclave, and one of the more striking elements of its décor is the wall full of jars filled to the brim with soju and various infusible botanicals. And it's not completely over-the-top stuff either. Cucumber makes for a particularly delicate, refreshing soju infusion. Servers bring it to the table in a mason-like jar with the center of the lid cut out for easy pouring. It's an attractive addition to the table—usually full of visually as well as gastronomically pleasing dishes like braised pork rib with kimchi and spicy mixed seafood soup. Cucumbers are shredded shoelace thin and collected in a borderline fluorescent green mound within the jar. There's perhaps no better palate reset between such intensely flavored and spicy Korean dishes.

Another popular way to consume the spirit is to mix a bottle of soju with the same quantity of the Korean fermented glutinous rice wine, baekseju—which isn't distilled like the former—for a combination known as Oh-ship Seju or fifty-fifty soju.

Baekseju translates to "one-hundred-years wine," referring to the legend that those who drink it will live to see the century mark. It's infused with supposedly healthful flora, most prominently ginseng, imparting a pleasing herbal element when added to soju. It's quite a hit with younger (legal-drinking-age, of course) Korean consumers.

Beyond flavor and the actual act of drinking it, soju carries vital cross-cultural significance: It's a reminder that the world is actually a much smaller place than people think and that there's more that unites us all than divides us. What is this crazy talk, you ask? Soju loosely translates to "burned liquor" or "burned wine." The Scandinavian spirit brännvin has a similar translation. Geographically and culturally, the two are worlds apart. But when it comes to drinking? We're all the same.

Week 16
PRUNO GETS PAROLE

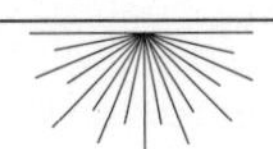

Every culture has its own drink or at least a spin on someone else's traditional libation. Now, every one of those beverages may not be every drinker's cup of tea, but that doesn't discount the value that culture provides to the drinking world at large—even when that culture exists within the four walls of a maximum security correctional facility.

Hardened criminals have a tradition of producing illicit liquids in hidden corners of the Big House, fermenting any sugar-rich bases they're able to smuggle out of the commissary and turn it into the rottenest of rotgut consumable alcohols imaginable. When one's incarcerated, there's a considerable beggars/choosers dynamic happening, so by anything, I mean anything: oranges, fruit cocktail, milk, grapes, ketchup, sugar packets and, as the name suggests, prunes. The cons would use bread to activate the yeast. And those are just the fancy high-end ingredients. If the warden suspects that pruno production is running amok on his watch, he'll halt the delivery of all of that produce and prompt the inmates to get really creative with the fermentables. Sauerkraut, itself having undergone fermentation to get to its present state, often fits the bill. Just imagine how tasty that's going to be.

And if that's not unpleasant enough for you, take a moment to think about where the cons most likely are sourcing the water.

Periodic crackdowns notwithstanding, the guards have been known to look the other way or at least pretend they're completely oblivious to the pruno production plants operating right under their noses. After all, drinking is probably the lesser of a whole lot of evils that could potentially be going on in prison, and the officers know they've got to pick their battles.

On rare occasions, the stuff has been known to get deadly, and not just figuratively speaking from the odor it emits. You'll notice that among the most-used ingredients listed, one of the starchiest, most fermentable vegetables was glaringly absent: potatoes. That's because in the pruno business, as nefarious, unregulated and, well, illegal as it is, the seasoned artisans know to avoid them; it's probably saved their lives.

On two separate occasions in 2012 in the Arizona correctional system, a total of twelve thirsty prisoners ended up in the infirmary, stricken with the often-deadly food poisoning, botulism.[30] Potatoes have been known to provide a safe haven for Clostridium botulinum, the bacteria that causes the dreaded affliction. And, you guessed it, the prison banned potatoes from the cafeteria.

Unless you've got any ex-con friends or are prepping for your own stint in the joint, chances are you'll never get to taste pruno in its purest form.

You, of course, can approximate the experience, sans institutional terroir, by throwing some of these ingredients into a Ziploc with some water and letting nature take its course. I strongly advise against that. If you're really curious, I'd recommend a less stomach-churning option, the legal, commercially available brand, Pruno, which promises to capture the enterprising hardened criminal vibe in a black-and-white-prison-striped bottle. In case the consumer is not quite sure exactly what the beverage is trying to emulate, the company that markets it is called Convict Brands.

Yes, it's a gimmick. Yes, it's essentially a flavored vodka—available in orange and grape, to mimic some of the most popular and widely available fruit bases behind bars.

The admittedly nutty creation was the brainchild of brand developer Brian Pearson, who previously achieved a certain degree of notoriety when he became the first to market a branded Jell-O shot, which went by the name Zippers. Launched in 2000, the brand reached $1 million in sales by 2001. But that's when the trouble began. Various anti-underage-drinking groups joined forces with Hope Taft, wife of Ohio's then-governor Bob Taft, to attack the brand, asserting that it was targeting children. The Zippers office subsequently was raided by the state's liquor control board.

So, in a sense, Pearson shares a kind of kinship with the incarcerated; both have known persecution.

The idea for Pruno was born in a much more innocent place: the Thanksgiving dinner table. When there's a beverage entrepreneur in the family—and a controversial one at that—it's not hard to imagine which direction holiday dinner conversations often go. They frequently begin with, "Hey, you know what you need to bottle?" On this particular Turkey Day, the "what" was pruno.

"You literally saw ten people reaching for their phones to go on Google to figure out what pruno is,"[31] Pearson says. "And, holy shit, there was a whole bunch on Google about pruno. As an entrepreneur, one of the things you look for is not having to explain what it is because Google and history has already done that."

From the get-go, Pearson did not want to go in too serious of a direction with the branding because, well, it's based on the pastimes of convicted felons doing hard time. It didn't take a clairvoyant to predict the first wave of criticism: Why are you romanticizing an involuntary trip up the river?

"I was like, 'Really? If you go to prison, you can't drink my Pruno, so how is it promoting prison?'" Pearson laughs.

The obvious target for the brand is that twenty-one-year old to thirty-five-year-old demographic that spirits marketers fawn over ad nauseam. But Pearson feels he's got a secondary market that no other beverage category can claim: folks around seventy who've been on the inside and are somewhat perversely wistful for the old days.

"I think it's like the case with any consumer product: They can identify with it," Pearson supposes. "They tell their story. It's about the time they spent there."

For the rest of us fortunate enough not to have done any time, it's a conversation piece. And Pearson's okay with that.

But, the way he sees it, it's much more than that. "On my Facebook page I always talk about second chances," Pearson says. "Maybe the only way you can drink Pruno is because you got out, you got a second chance. For me, it was the second-chance drink."

For the rest of us, though, let it be a cautionary tale. We can enjoy a couple of glasses of the curious beverage poured from the bottle that's disguised as a chain-gang escapee and hope that we live the rest of our lives completely ignorant of what toilet-water-steeped inspiration really tastes like.

Week 17
Getting a Grip on Grappa

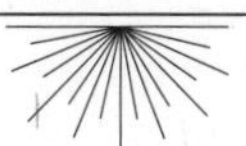

Italy celebrates April 25 as Liberation Day, marking the final expulsion of the fascists and Nazis from the country as World War II drew to a close. So there's no better time to enjoy a rather intense spirit that's a source of great national pride for Italians.

I'm just going to go ahead and say it: When a lot of people hear the word grappa ("grah-pa"), they immediately imagine a spirit whose taste profile is somewhere between furniture polish and lighter fluid. It is not for the faint of heart, that's for sure. It is to alcohol production what offal is to meat butchering. Where snouts, hooves, stomach linings, and ground-up organs are the byproducts of the meat-cutting trade, pomace—the pressed skins and seeds of grapes—are the leftovers of the winemaking process. And, just as organ stews, slow-cooked tripe, and bone marrow originated as the staples of peasants who had to get a lot of mileage out of the animal carcasses on which they feasted, grappa began as a beverage for the Italian underclasses made by distilling the refuse unfit for the wines consumed by the gentry. It is essentially brandy minus the actual good parts of the grape, and its consumption stretches back about seven hundred years.

But, like every other food or beverage with extremely humble beginnings, it's evolved to invite even the most discerning connoisseurs. Over the centuries, it has become a common ritual throughout Italy to consume it after a filling dinner to aid in digestion. A cup or two of espresso commonly accompanies it; often grappa is added to the coffee.

Like many spirits of European origin, grappa now is protected by European Union (EU) guidelines. For one thing, if a distillery on the continent wants to call a beverage grappa and that distillery is based outside of Italy, it is either going to have to call it something else or move to the boot (or at least to the Italian section of Switzerland or the sovereign state of San Marino). Any such beverage that's produced in Europe outside of Italy or Italian-speaking regions may only be called "grape marc" or "grape marc spirit."

The spirit also must be produced from pomace; no cheating by fermenting grape juice. That's really just brandy anyway.

The final rule: The distillation must occur on the pomace, without any added water. In other words, it's distilled in solid form.

The first time I had grappa was in Italy, and it was basically on a dare from a local in our dining party. I felt like Linda Blair when she thought Father Karras was splashing her with holy water in *The Exorcist*. It burns! It burns!

But I'm a sucker for age-old traditions, especially when they involve (barely) potable alcohol, and I wouldn't trade that experience for anything. That's why I'm absolutely giddy that some small US craft distillers have sought to differentiate themselves from those who take the "safe" route—paved with old standbys like vodka, gin, and relatively young whiskey—and embrace a spirit that, for most of the legal-drinking-age population, may never be ready for prime time. And the bonus is they're able to actually market it as "grappa" because they're not based in Europe and not bound by the EU-enforced standards.

The brave ones that are making it have been giving it their own regional spins, applying the unique terroirs of their respective regions. Catskill Distilling Company of Bethel, New York, home of Yasgur's Farm and an intimate little musical gathering that took place there in the summer of 1969, has been using three kinds of grapes—Muscat, Riesling, and Traminette from the Napa Valley of Upstate New York, the Finger Lakes, to fashion three distinct grappa flavor profiles.

For Catskill founder Monte Sachs, the brand was thirty years in the making. Sachs, a veterinarian, attended vet school in Tuscany in the late 1970s. He had some friends at a vineyard and decided to learn how to make wine on the side, the task, as he puts it, "was way too much goddamned work." However, while there, he befriended a group of older Italian gentlemen who taught him how to make grappa out of the same grapes with which he was trying to make wine.

"These old Italian guys were pretty amused that this American kid wanted to learn how to do this,"[32] Sachs tells me.

What attracted him the most to the grappa-making practice was the notion of "making something out of nothing," particularly creating a product from the bits and pieces of grapes that otherwise would have been composted or completely discarded.

He points to those days at the end of the grape harvest season circa 1979 as the inspiration for opening his own distillery some three decades later.

And the spirit certainly has come a long way from the time when Sachs was just learning how to make it.

"The thing is, grappa, not unlike tequila, has gone through an evolution," he explains. "Tequila in the early days was pretty rotgut, but the distillation technique and equipment have gotten so much better."

The same holds true for grappa. "It needed to be a more sophisticated type of distillate."

Sachs believes that he has done his part, in some small way, to elevate the public's perception of the spirit with his Bosco Monte Vecchio brand. At the very least, he's made the uninitiated curious enough to try it and decide for themselves. Generally they'd be pleasantly surprised. For a grappa, it's fairly smooth, faintly reminiscent of a white dog (off-the-still, unaged whiskey).

The secret has been to let the grapes speak for themselves. Each of the varietals he's used brings a floral element to grappa, a characteristic that drinkers tend to find appealing in other beverages, be they beers, wines, or spirits.

The best way to appreciate those notes is to nose a one-ounce pour in a small-stemmed tulip glass; the small-rim design concentrates the aromas.

All of Catskill Distilling Company's efforts seem to be paying off: Bosco Monte Vecchio actually managed to score an impressive ninety-one-point rating at the 2013 Ultimate Spirits Challenge, one of the distilling world's most respected competitions.

Will grappa soon conquer the palates of American spirits drinkers from coast to coast? It'd be a bit of a reach to make that prediction for such a polarizing tipple. But when taken in the right context—with a double shot of espresso after some antipasto and Osso Bucco—it makes for a nice ritual as the final sip to wind down the day.

The quality of the grappa enhances that ritual. Here are a few to try:

ITALIAN GRAPPA

Grappa Cru Monovitigno Picolit (Nonino Distillery):
The Nonino family's distilling heritage dates back to the late nineteenth century, but it was in 1973 that they first distilled this grappa with the Picolit grape, native to Nonino's home region of Friuli. The grappa is famous for its crystal decanter with spherical neck, long base, and its notes of honey.

Le Diciotto Lune Grappa Stravecchia (Distillery Marzadro):
Barrel aging mellows the spirit and imparts the expected woody flavors and amber hue. The youngest grappa in the blend is eighteen months old, hence Diciotto Lune, which translates to "Eighteen Moons."

AMERICAN GRAPPA

Bosco Monte Vecchio (Catskill Distilling Company):
Sachs crafted this grappa to make it accessible to American drinkers either unfamiliar with grappa or those whose prior experiences haven't been positive. Floral aromas and notes of pear characterize this one.

Hudson Valley Grappa (Harvest Spirits Farm Distillery):
There really must be something about the Upstate New York terroir, as Harvest Spirits also calls the Empire State home. Distiller Derek

Grout sought to replicate his European travel experiences, when he'd drink grappa after fondue or any other heavy meal. His main objectives were smoothness and drinkability—words not often associated with the spirit—and he's delivered with a grappa made from leftover grape pressings from the local Hudson Chatham Winery.

Grappa Moscato (Clear Creek Distillery):
Portland, Oregon's, Clear Creek dubs the moscato-grape-based creation as "perfect for someone who has never had grappa before" (think of it as a gateway grappa). It's floral, smooth, and has a clean finish. The distillery makes four other grappas for those ready to advance their palates to the next level.

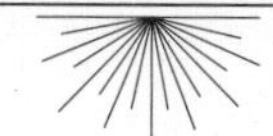

Week 18

BEYOND CINCO DE MAYO

SAVORING TEQUILA AND MEZCAL

Cinco de Mayo, as it is celebrated in the United States, is riddled with inauthenticity. It is often mistaken for Mexican Independence Day, which actually is September 16 (we'll get into that in due time). The May holiday commemorates an epic Mexican victory over the French in 1836, but Americans, especially those in beverage marketing, have co-opted the Mexican observance as yet another excuse to get monumentally inebriated. Let's bring a little authenticity back to Cinco de Mayo with a look at Mexico's proud distilling heritage.

Up until the beginning of the twenty-first century, Mexican spirits had suffered (and some would argue still do suffer) from an image problem. When most Americans thought of tequila—beyond its role as the requisite alcohol in a margarita—it was as a cheap liquor consumed in quick succession of shots to get one as drunk as possible—a reputation it gained in the immediate post–World War II period when returning GIs' demand for inexpensive spirits prompted importers to bring some rather subpar liquor across the border. The frat boy demographic hasn't done much to remediate that image.

The first and last time I indulged in the traditional college spring break ritual of sand, sun, and slosh, it was 1993 in Cancun where tequila flowed like water—which wasn't necessarily a bad thing because we were advised not to drink the water. My most vivid memory of all the debauchery is being at one of those meat-market dance parties—at Señor Frog's or Fat Tuesday's or some such ridiculousness—where the emcee stood on a table with a bottle of the stuff and poured shots directly in the mouths of revelers swarming around him. Now that's class.

So, there were some serious headwinds for tequila to overcome to achieve a certain level of respectability.

Luckily, the spirit was able to ride the premiumization wave that pretty much defined the global distilling market since the turn of the millennium. Much, but not all, of the credit goes to a certain brand called Patrón for convincing modern-day consumers that tequila could indeed be fancy. Actually, it wasn't even the creation of the brand, it was its sort of reinvention after 2000 when a man named Ed Brown took over as CEO and took a cue from what was happening in the vodka world with brands like Grey Goose and Ketel One.

Most drinkers by now know that tequila comes from the blue agave plant, which, despite its visual and tactile similarities, is neither a cactus nor a close cousin of aloe. The government of Mexico dictates that the spirit must be produced in the state of Jalisco (home to the town of Tequila, where the especially sweet nectar of the blue agave is in abundance), as well as a few specially designated towns in the states of Guanajuato, Michoacán, Nayarit, and Tamaulipas. The United States generally complies; it's produced in Mexico, but a lot of times it's actually bottled in the United States. Mexico tried, unsuccessfully, a decade ago to restrict bottling to inside its borders.

Now, you've got to make sure you read the label very carefully. Most of the labels are going to read "agave tequila." But they're not all going to specify "100 percent agave tequila." There's a very clear distinction there. The finest tequilas are of the latter variety. Similar to the way bourbon can't be called bourbon unless at least 51 percent of it comes from corn, tequila can't be labeled tequila unless a minimum of the same percentage is distilled from an agave base. The difference is that many fine—very frequently finer—whiskies are made from other grains. You won't find corn in a single-malt Scotch, after all. But with tequila, agave nectar is what gives the spirit its complexity. Why would you want that diluted with other sugars?

The other 49 percent is open to all sorts of cost-cutting shenanigans. If you're sitting at a bar and not quite sure about the top-shelf-looking brands on display, politely ask the bartender to show you the bottle.

Don't worry, it doesn't have to be expensive. There are different grades and different levels of aging that usually determine how pricey something's going to be.

Silver, sometimes known as blanco (white), is the clear, right-out-of-the-still variety with no or extremely minimal aging (sixty days in a stainless steel tank is the absolute max). Another term you're likely to encounter is reposado, which translates to "rested" or "restful." That's exactly what the liquid does, enjoys a modest repose, anywhere from that two-month threshold to nine months in wooden aging vessels. Then there's añejo, meaning "aged"—at least a year, but the better-quality añejos will spend two to four years in wooden barrels. As it does with whiskey, the wood will impart a brownish tint to the spirit. Don't get confused, however, with "Gold" tequilas. They may look considerably darker than their blanco counterparts, but the hue comes from added caramel coloring; Golds are very young and usually of the "mixto" (blended, not 100 percent agave) varieties.

A common question I hear is, "What's the difference between tequila and mezcal?" They're both Mexican, they're both distilled from varieties of agave, with the better ones derived exclusively from the plant. But that's essentially where the similarities end. For one thing, mezcal production isn't as regionally restrictive as it is for tequila. Having said that, most of it is produced in Oaxaca—around 90 percent—but it's commonly made in at least seven other states as well. It also must be bottled in Mexico. It may not, like tequila, be shipped in bulk to the states and bottled there.

Let's get something out of the way right now: the worm. Yes, some brands have a worm at the bottom, but it's actually only a few of them that put the gusano rojo ("red worm") or weevil larva in the bottle—certainly the exceptions, not the rule. Brands that popularized the practice were Monte Alban and the appropriately named Gusano Rojo. It's a relatively recent development; it's not common in more traditional mezcals. Throughout Oaxaca, worms and other insects had been typical delicacies available as street food. They're known to have a sort of baconish flavor, giving those mezcals a little extra something.

And that "something" is a kick the spirit doesn't really need. Mezcal tends to have a fairly pronounced smoky character, an element that immediately distinguishes it from tequila, even with untrained palates. That results from a process unique to the spirit. The distillers bake the heart of the agave plant, known as the piña, in underground charcoal-heated ovens, versus steam ovens for tequila, which converts the starch to fermentable sugars.

The charcoal from those ovens is what imparts the smoke, which is more apparent in some brands than others.

Those ovens are so deeply ingrained with the culture in the region that there is archaeological evidence suggesting the ancient indigenous peoples were using them as far back as nine thousand years ago to cook agave as a sugar source.

The birth of modern-day mezcal making occurred during the sixteenth century, which saw the arrival of the Spanish Conquistadors in Mexico.[33] When the Spanish ran out of the brandy that they had brought with them, they had to find something to distill and ultimately turned to agave. Today's producers still use the same type of rustic copper stills the Spaniards first imported.

The decidedly smoky character for which mezcal is known is not entirely unlike a moderate to intensely peated whisky from the Islay region of Scotland (without the grain expression, of course). I usually recommend that Scotch drinkers, especially those who gravitate to the peaty offerings, try mezcal when they swear they're not into Mexican spirits (mostly the tequilas of their drunken college years).

Mexican guidelines state that tequila producers must use only one variety of agave, while mezcal distillers are allowed to use just about any of them. Getting to know each one is like discovering the nuances of different wine styles. "Every different variety of grape has a different flavored wine and every different variety of agave has a different flavored mezcal,"[34] explains Douglas French, the master distiller of Oaxaca's Scorpion Mezcal (a brand that actually one-ups the worm concept by putting an actual dried scorpion at the bottom of the bottle).

There are nearly thirty different varieties that mezcal makers currently are using.[35]

Mezcal hasn't always had the best reputation, thanks to so much rampant adulteration among some producers.

Exporters often would buy quality mezcals from some of the five hundred-plus small-village mom-and-pop distilleries, blend them, and mix in cheap additives for large-scale volumes. But things have changed a bit. In 1995, mezcal received its Denomination of Origin designation, internationally recognizing it as a product native to its specific region. Then in February 2005, the law standardizing mezcal production went into effect.

"That's when the hammer came down," French says.

The regulatory body, Consejo Regulador del Mezcal (CRM), has certified about one-third of the mezcals being produced. The distillers of many of those had a prior history of adulterating their spirits, but have been forced by the standards to clean up their acts. Those that want to maintain their certification have to keep detailed records for the CRM to audit.

The standards clearly define two mezcal categories, which are similar to those within tequila: 100 percent agave and those that combine the main ingredient with other similar ingredients. The difference, however, dictates that mixes must contain at least 80 percent agave—stricter than the 51 percent mandate for mixto tequila.

Not only has that improved mezcal's reputation, it brought more attention to products on the premium side of the category, creating greater opportunities to educate drinkers about more upscale offerings—similar to the perceptual shift in tequila. That's a welcome development for someone like French, who's been crafting fine mezcals for two decades.

"Thank God, after all these years, it's finally being invited in by a small segment of the connoisseur market," French says. "The general population still has no idea that mezcal exists, but the upper echelon of the industry is aware of it. Basically they regard it as a high-end artisanal product."

Scorpion, Fidencio, and Mezcal El Silencio are among the brands that have been appearing on high-end bars and Mexican restaurants' radar.

Some of those get fairly bold with their ultra-premium expressions. Scorpion, for instance, offers a triple-distilled Gran Reserve Añejo that spends a staggering seven years in the barrel. It also comes in a pretty classy French decanter-like bottle that would look more at home containing some of the most connoisseur-friendly Cognacs than the smoky Mexican liquor. They're best enjoyed in a similar fashion to that European spirit.

"I make a lot of añejos, and I sip them like a fine single-malt Scotch—even the silvers I like to sip in either a tulip glass or a brandy snifter," French offers. "With thirty different distillate flavors coming out, we really try to focus on appreciating the flavors of each specific variety."

For both tequila and mezcal, the tide is finally shifting, and that's a breath of fresh air for inquisitive imbibers. It's also a welcome development for the artisans whose life's work and passion is distilling. They're having their moment and they're employing entire villages in the process.

So, ditch the frat party, pour out that margarita, and go enjoy the distinctive spirits of Mexico as half a millennium of tradition has intended.

Get acquainted with mezcal:

EL SILENCIO JOVEN (EL SILENCIO HOLDINGS, INC.)

Joven, meaning "young," blends three types of agave: Espadin, Mexicano, and Tobaciche. It's considered one of the more accessible mezcals for those new to the spirit or looking for something a little different than tequila. Interesting bit of trivia: the name El Silencio is a reference to the mysterious nightclub in David Lynch's *Mulholland Drive*.

SCORPION AÑEJO (SCORPION MEZCAL)

Aged in oak for a year, the 100 percent agave, amber-colored spirit balances the smoke with a hint of mellow. And, like Scorpion's other offering, there's a real scorpion at the bottom of the bottle.

FIDENCIO CLÁSICO (FABRICA DE AMIGO DEL MEZCAL)

Fidencio uses 100 percent estate-grown Espadin agave for its Clásico product. It's unaged and is produced through organic means, though its organic certification is pending.

DURANGO (MEZCALES DE LEYENDA)

Mezcales de Leyenda likes to showcase the unique terroir of individual states in its silver mezcals. This one in particular spotlights

Durango (the company also has one for Guerrero and, of course, Oaxaca), particularly its Agave Duranguensis. The central valleys of Durango are known for their rich volcanic fields—the agave is cooked underground in a lava rock–lined pit.

Week 19

Before There Was Beer, There Was Pulque

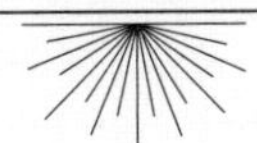

We're going to stick with the agave theme for another week, backtracking a bit to a fermented form of the plant's nectar that does not go through the distillation process. Pulque is the mildly sweet, considerably viscous beverage with a milky-watery appearance that results from fermenting agave sap directly from the plant. It wouldn't technically be accurate to call it a mezcal precursor, as it is tapped directly from the plant.[36] Mezcal is made from crushed agave hearts or piñas.

Pulque's origins date back to sometime during the Aztec empire. Exactly when that was is anybody's guess. There's a creation legend associated with it that's more entertaining than it is historically accurate (which is to say, not at all). During that ancient era, a woman was doing her daily gathering when she encountered four hundred rabbits (Rabbits are a particularly significant part of Aztec culture). When she approached, they all scattered—all but one, that is. This curious little critter just kept running in circles like a lopsided drunkard. The woman decided to follow the rabbit, which eventually led her to an agave plant leaking nectar. It had spontaneously fermented and intoxicated the animal. Intrigued, the woman brought it back to her village. The villagers believed it was a sign from the gods and dubbed the woman Mayahuel, goddess of the maguey plant.[37]

Pulque was fairly pervasive throughout Mexico from that period until about a century ago, but slowly faded from the country's general consciousness as generation replaced generation in the modern era. The typical serving establishments, known as pulquerias, had descended into divey disrepute as cerveza became the fermentable of choice,[38] and they all but vanished in major Mexican metro areas during the twentieth century. That is, until recently of course (and who doesn't love a good comeback story?).

If another kind of myth is to be believed, its near-extinction was by nefarious design, not changes in consumer tastes. The emphasis is on myth, so take this tale with a very fine grain of salt. The general conspiracy some mom-and-pop pulque purveyors have kicked around posits that seventy or so years ago, the beer distributors teamed up for an anti-pulque smear campaign. The supposed rationale was that the beer wholesalers feared the cost of pulque would undercut that of their products, so these mustache-twirling, black-hat-sporting distribution villains circulated stories about pulque's "unsanitary" production methods. Whether there's any truth to that story is anyone's guess. Usually the truth lies somewhere between verified historical fact and complete fabrication.

If it is true, it's hardly fair to call a beverage whose inception is rooted in pre-Columbian indigenous cultures "unsanitary" when it was keeping people alive for well over a millennium.

Regardless of such a claim's veracity, it does inject a little irony into the setting of my own inaugural encounter with the Mexican staple: a trade show for beer distributors. It was the early 2000s and a group of entrepreneurs had put their own recipe in a bottle, slapped a label on it, and began their quest to woo both the Mexican-American population and curious non-Latin legal-drinking-age adults tired of ordering Coronas and strawberry margaritas at their local cantinas.

It was indicative of a small pulque renaissance that was taking place as newer generations were attempting to connect with their roots, their inherent Mexican-ness. Pulquerias remain rough-and-tumble dives, but dive bars are cool again. (Thanks, hipsters!) "They're definitely more divey, on the side of the road, locals-only kind of places,"[39] says Mishi Torgove, bar manager of a Mexican-themed underground speakeasy called, simply, Pulqueria—incongruously tucked away in New York City's Chinatown. The dimly lit, literally underground establishment boasts all of the requisite South-of-the-Border décor, but it's considerably more upscale than the joints that inspired it.

Pulqueria is one of the very few places in New York (or most of the East Coast, for that matter), where a drinker actually can taste the real deal. A producer in Mexico cans and ships pulque to the bar, and it's a pretty close approximation to what those brave enough would happen upon in one of those "locals-only" holes-in-the-wall. The only difference is Pulqueria's is pasteurized—otherwise it would never survive the trip. The house-made stuff in Jalisco is consumed pretty quickly, so there's no need for pasteurization. Pasteurizing makes it slightly less viscous; in Mexico, it has a more sap-like consistency. Beyond that, the flavor's more or less the same. "Ours is more similar to saké in terms of its color and texture," Torgove notes. "If you're in Mexico and you go into a pulqueria, chances are they'll have a big vat of it and you'll just dip your mug into it. And when you lift your mug up, it'll be very slimy and drip down the side of your mug, whereas ours is more of a liquid."

Flavorwise, it's best described as "earthy" with some citrus elements. Its notes aren't terribly unlike those of coconut water. Its alcohol content lingers on the low side, in the beer zone of 4 to 6 percent ABV.

Pulqueria offers its version of the drink on its own, which it dubs "Pulque Classico," served with a slice of lime. Those who want more of a kick can order it in a cocktail. The bar offers everything imaginable on the sweet-savory spectrum, from El Tigre (pulque, blanco tequila, house-made strawberry syrup, mint, and lemon) to Tijuana Flashback (pulque, mezcal, tomatillo, cilantro, habanero-infused bitters, and lime).

Most American clientele entering such an establishment for the first time probably have had no exposure to pulque before, nor have they likely even heard the word before. Torgove usually encourages bar-goers to try the Pulque Classico to get a sense of the flavor before they order it in a cocktail. He also recommends they sample it first without the lime to get an idea of what it's all about. After that, they're more likely to squeeze the citrus fruit's juice into it because it cuts much of the earthiness that may be too intense for some people.

Right now, pulque's virtual lack of availability in the states has proved to be one of its greatest assets. "People are drawn to the fact that it's not readily accessible in the United States," Torgove supposes.

In the age of social media, there's no underestimating the power of a cult following—especially when it's based on a perceived scarcity.

Week 20

Why So Bitter?

Artisinal Bitters

Normally I would advocate drinking well-crafted spirits neat, but with this week's adventure, I can't really recommend it. But that, in no way, is a condemnation. Quite the contrary, it's a hearty endorsement for what's perhaps the most misunderstood and taken-for-granted component of the world's greatest classic cocktails. May 13 has been designated National Cocktail Day, so the twentieth week of the year is the perfect time to shine the spotlight on bitters.

If whiskey and rum are the stars of said cocktails, then those small bottles of bitters are the stalwart character actors, the supporting players whom you'll never see in a lead but without whom you could never imagine your favorite films actually working as well as they did. And they continue to get cast in high-profile roles well into their sunset years, long after the once-A-list superstars are well past their prime and making a living on reality TV and infomercials.

Now, somewhat ironically for a book about potable adventures, the class of bitters I'm talking about here is typically referred to as "non-potable." "Potable" bitters include the likes of Campari and Fernet, the latter of which we explore next week. Nonpotables, by contrast, tend not to be drunk on their own, though it's perfectly safe to do so if one were so inclined.

Bitters' humble beginnings were, like many alcohol and nonalcohol beverages (Coke and Pepsi included), rooted in supposed medicinal benefits. Across Europe, most countries had some version of a potable liquid made from a combination of bittering agents, bark, fruit, and spices that promised some sort of positive physiological effect. Such concoctions often were prescribed as hangover cures—hair of the dog long before Bloody Marys and Mimosas came into fashion.

And then the global cocktail movement started sometime around the turn of the nineteenth century and bitters became an essential component of the very early days of what would, two centuries later, become known as "mixology." In fact, the word, "bitters" appears in the first recorded definition of cocktail in the May 13, 1806, (hence, the holiday) edition of the publication, The Balance and Columbian Repository, which describes it as "stimulating liquor, composed of spirits of any kind, sugar, water, and bitters."[40] (Of course, there's still a rabid debate over why it's called a "cocktail." But we won't get involved.)

The best-known brand that's still on virtually every bar today is Angostura, produced by House of Angostura in Trinidad and Tobago. As the story goes, at least according to the modern standard-bearers for the brand, Dr. Johann Gottlieb Benjamin Siegert developed Angostura Bitters in 1824[41] when he was serving as surgeon general to Simon Bolivar during the South American wars of liberation. Bolivar stationed Siegert in the town of Angostura (since renamed Ciudad Bolivar) in Venezuela, where he harvested the native flora as curative ingredients. Siegert's sons relocated the business to Trinidad about a half-century later.

The other game in town has been Peychaud's Bitters, created in New Orleans fourteen years after Angostura by pharmacist Antoine Amedie Peychaud.[42] Peychaud's Bitters was among the alcoholic inventions the namesake apothecary's customers enjoyed. Soon one of Peychaud's creations evolved into the Sazerac cocktail, of which Peychaud's Bitters is still a signature component to this day. What is now known as Sazerac Company, Inc., still owns the brand (not to mention the eponymous rye, which, interestingly, finds its way into the vast minority of the cocktail's iterations).

The premiumization movement and the ensuing classic cocktail renaissance—best illustrated by the popularity of Prohibition Era–themed neo-speakeasies in the first and second decades of the twenty-first century—has been a welcome development for the bitters business, albeit on a considerably smaller scale than it has been for whiskey and rum. The retro-chic Clover Club in Brooklyn, NY's, trendy Carroll Gardens neighborhood offers a veritable shrine to bitterness, proudly displaying its impressive selection front and center on the bar.

"When some people see them and know what they are, they say, 'This is a serious cocktail place because they have bitters,'"[43] half-jokingly observes Clover Club head bartender Tom Macy. It also adds to the theater that is modern mixology.

"Seeing the bitters on the bar and reading the bottles, it's like having a little apothecary," Macy adds. The bottle's turn-of-the-twentieth-century-text-adorned paper wrapping gets wrinkly and slightly stained quite easily, adding to the visual feast. "It looks like you use them a lot," Macy explains. "Especially here, it fits right in with the aesthetics and the décor."

And Brooklyn, being the incubator of hipsterdom that it is, also happens to be the creative capital for the burgeoning artisanal bitters movement. Bittermens, founded by Avery and Janet Glasser, began experimenting during their time in the San Francisco cocktail scene. They started producing in 2010 in Massachusetts, before relocating the operation to Brooklyn a year later (they've since moved to the birthplace of Peychaud's itself, New Orleans).

The Clover Club stocks some of Bittermens's more exotic flavorings, starkly labeled and packaged in blue glass dropper-top bottles, harkening back to bitters' medicinal origins. Among those is Elemakule Tiki bitters, ideal for those Polynesian rum-based drinks, and Hellfire, a habanero-infused variety for a little added heat.

Another Brooklyn-born bitters-making startup is Hella Bitter, whose existence, like some of the most successful beverage companies, is rooted in a hobby gone unexpectedly commercial.

Even when the founders decided in the spring of 2011 to turn to Kickstarter for some supplemental funding, their goal was to just be able to make some more to sell to family and friends. But the Kickstarter campaign proved far more successful than they had anticipated, providing them with the seed money to expand beyond their immediate social and familial circles.

The Hella Bitter team, consisting of Tobin Ludwig, Eduardo Simeon, and Jomaree Pinkard, recently moved their operation to a small facility in a shared industrial space designed to nurture entrepreneurial endeavors in the Long Island City section of Queens. The bursting-at-the-seams space serves as corporate HQ, production plant, and R&D lab as the managing trio prepare for their next phase of growth.

"Prohibition ended and people started drinking again, but I think it took a while for the cocktail to come back and resurge,"[44] Ludwig points out. "We have amazing cocktail books from the first half of the twentieth century—there were people out there who were doing this, but widespread it wasn't. [Cocktails] culturally weren't a phenomenon like they had been."

That would start to change in the late 1980s and 1990s when noted cocktail experts like Dale DeGroff and Gary Regan were in their heydays. Then, for the first few years of the twenty-first century, anyone who fancied him- or herself a cultural pundit of one sort or another joined the Carrie Bradshaw chorus, asserting that the popularity of *Sex and the City* was, if not single-handedly responsible for, one of the primary forces behind modern cocktail culture.

Regardless of what's driving the classic spirit and cocktail resurgence, it's pretty damned cool that it's happening. The Manhattan, Old-Fashioned, Sazerac, and Negroni are among the mixed tipples that have come back in a major way, and all would be a hollow shell of their former selves without their respective bitters contents.

"We saw the opportunity to offer people small-batch premium alternatives to the mass-produced stuff that was out there," recalls Ludwig. "We were going for versatility and usability."

Initially, the company produced two flavors: Aromatic and Citrus, which many, including the Hella team, consider the salt and pepper of the bar.

Aromatic bitters tend to be more assertive and redolent with notes of baking spice and pair well with aged spirits—bourbons, brandies, and aged rums, for instance.

However, that's more of a guideline than a rule.

The citrus variety offers considerable versatility. "An orange or citrus bitters could be a complement to pretty much any cocktail that calls for bitters," Ludwig points out. "It's light and bright enough that it won't overwhelm a gin or a vodka or an unaged tequila or rum. But it also has enough depth and structure that it actually does quite beautifully with aged spirits as well."

The small company recently expanded its product line to include Ginger Lemon, Smoke Chili, and Orange bitters—the latter was based on drinkers' demand for a pure orange bitters, in addition to Hella's existing mixed citrus version.

The bubbling cauldron (okay, tank) of Hella's citrus-bitters-in-progress is quite the sight to behold. Tens of thousands of orange, lemon, and other tropical peels blanket the surface of the neutral grain spirit as a cheesecloth bag full of dry botanical ingredients—on the particular day that I visited it was allspice berries—steeps below the surface. Bundling those components allows for precise control over how much each of the ingredients infuses the liquid. "Because we use fresh, natural dried spices," Ludwig concedes, "there is a certain level of inconsistency, batch to batch. Sometimes the spices are incredibly volatile and sometimes, for whatever reason, the oils are a little less pronounced and that obviously will affect the bitters."

That all sounds lovely, but it's time to drink! Bet you're intrigued enough to take a bottle—let's stick to the classics and say Angostura—and just sip it straight. Feel free, it won't kill you. Typical bitters brands tend to range between 45 and 55 percent alcohol by volume and are traditionally packaged in bottles no bigger than standard hot sauce containers, so they're not likely to do that much harm from an intoxication standpoint should you decide to take a few swigs (of one bottle, mind you). "The average person should probably stay away from doing that, but there are some very bitters-forward cocktails out there," advises the Clover Club's Macy.

For instance, Macy mixes a mean Old-Fashioned at the Clover Club with not one, not two, but three different types of bitters (the recipe's in the back).

Macy and most other mixologists would agree that bitters are like snowflakes. No two are exactly alike; each one brings its own complexity with a drink.

You can't go wrong with Peychaud's and Angostura and virtually every bar will stock those. But keep an eye out for some of the smaller, artisanal products finding their way into cocktails:

- SMOKED CHILI (HELLA BITTER): The Hella team sources its smoked chili from Mexico with tequila in mind. It doesn't just add a bit of heat, it adds smoky, rich aromatics.
- BURLESQUE BITTERS (BITTERMENS, INC.): Hibiscus, acai berry, and long pepper are the stars of this racy little show, marrying floral, sour, and peppery spice notes.
- BITTERCUBE TRINITY (BITTERCUBE, LLC): Bittercube combines three of its signature bitters recipes into a single proprietary blend: Cherry Bark Vanilla, Orange, and Bolivar—the third of those is an homage to a recipe from a nineteenth-century cocktail book, revealing notes of chamomile, jasmine, cinnamon, and dried fruits.
- CHESAPEAKE BAY BITTERS (THE BITTER END): Although The Bitter End calls Santa Fe, New Mexico, home, it doesn't mean the small producer doesn't know how to evoke seaside summers on the East Coast. Bay leaf, black pepper, and cayenne do most of the heavy lifting in that regard.

***

Now that you've acquired a taste for botanical bitterness, next week it's time to move into the big leagues with Fernet.

Week 21
The Force of Fernet

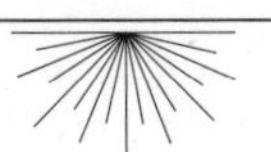

Fernet ("Fur-net") is one of those liquids that's just an inexplicable mystery to me. I first discovered the herbal tipple, which falls under the broader heading of amaro, on a trip to Buenos Aires. The stuff is something of an adopted native spirit there. Its origins are in Italy, but Argentina historically has been a hotbed of Italian immigration and the newcomers brought the homegrown digestif with them on their voyage to the birthplace of tango.

The origins of the best-known brand, Fernet-Branca, date back about 170 years. In 1845, Bernandino Branca created the bitter[45] and what ultimately became the Fratelli Branca Distillery.

The Argentines who still drink it commonly do so either straight or mixed with Coca-Cola. I was at an empanada and pizza restaurant when I first drank it, and I decided to sample it as part of the Coke concoction. Little did I know that the waitress was going to bring it to me in deconstructed form—a bottle of Coke and a small glass of Fernet-Branca. On the one hand, this was completely terrifying because I had no idea what the right proportions were to make this combination palatable. On the other, I was glad that I could get the best of both worlds and sample the spirit both in its most naked state and as part of a rather rudimentary cocktail.

Let's talk about appearance first. It's dark. Really dark—opaque even. It's also quite viscous.

As for the flavor . . . well, to call it an "acquired taste" is a bit of an understatement. Imagine stuffing a handful of Good 'n' Plenty candies in your mouth. And then chase those with a spoonful of Robitussin and a shot of Scope. That's about as close a description as one could muster. The Coca-Cola, of course, adds a whole other level of complexity to it that neither improves on nor detracts from the au naturel iteration.

Back in the Northern Hemisphere, Fernet is enjoying a cult-like renaissance, driven largely by folks in the bar and food-service industries—especially in San Francisco. When Fog City cooks and bartenders would finish their shifts, they'd meet up at their favorite local dives and decompress over a Fernet-Branca—sometimes chased with a sip of ginger ale.

San Francisco–based celebrity chef Chris Cosentino, of the famed, recently closed Incanto and now a partner at the newly opened celebration of the city's diverse culinary tradition, Cockscomb, has had his fair share of the bitter amaro throughout his career and has watched it evolve into a full-on phenomenon.

"Everyone wants to find the cool, new, hip thing,"[46] Cosentino observes. "It's become this cook-driven, industry-driven after-work beverage."

Its role as a digestive definitely fuels that late-night craving.

"It's kind of, 'Okay, we've been drinking all night, we're going to have a shot of Fernet before we go home,'" Cosentino explains. "And it's become huge."

The Bay Area provided particularly fertile ground for the Fernet-aissance because the region boasts such an intense connection with Italian food, especially dishes that had been hard to get outside of the old country. Having access to this once relatively obscure imported Italian spirit just enhanced that allure.

Cosentino actually had his first sip of the drink nearly six thousand miles from the Bay Area.

Known for his penchant for offal, Cosentino was enjoying a night out with kindred spirit Fergus Henderson—the London-based chef, offal expert, and partner in the United Kingdom's St. John group of restaurants.

"If Fergus wants me to try something, I'll try it," he recalls of his inaugural Fernet experience. "I'd had plenty of amaros in the past, but this one was just such a punch in the mouth, kind of bracing, in your face. Especially after having a heavy meal, it actually made sense."

At any given time, Cockscomb carries five Fernet brands on its menu of digestivos.

My cousin, Tom Cioletti, who worked as a pastry chef in San Francisco before relocating to Los Angeles, talks about the stuff like it's sacramental wine. His first encounter with Fernet was when he was flying solo one night after just starting culinary school. A bartender gave him a shot of it and told him, "Get used to this, you'll be drinking it a lot if you're going to be working in the industry." (He was so inspired that he ultimately created a Baked Alaska–style dessert with Fernet-Branca ice cream and an anise meringue.)

Three thousand miles away, Tom Macy, head bartender at Brooklyn's The Clover Club, doesn't have a fond recollection of his first encounter with the Italian tipple.

"I really hated it the first time I tried it,"[47] he reveals. "But I really like it now. I think that's from working in the industry."

He concedes that there's an "adapt or die" mentality when it comes to Fernet.

In the greater Washington, DC, area—Alexandria, Virginia, to be precise—the cocktail bar Jackson 20 serves a rather earthy, spicy, bitter creation it calls, with a nod to the Confederate general, Lee's Temptation: Fernet-Branca is joined by Bulleit rye, sweet vermouth, and flamed orange peel. The bartender pours it into one of those pretty, stemmed martini glasses, making it appear to be in the cosmo family. That's very deceptive—for this, my friends, is no cosmo. You have received fair warning. In the colder months, the bar mixes the Fernet Me Not: Fernet, Meyers rum, house-made hot chocolate, and campfire-toasted marshmallows.

The Fernet-Branca brand has been attempting to push into the mainstream in recent years with strategically placed marketing in the most trendsetting of US cities. San Francisco was a natural fit for the ubiquitous outdoor ads posted everywhere from transit stations to parking garages. I'd be the first to admit that the spirit was barely on my radar until I had tried it in that Latin American eatery in the Southern Hemisphere. After that, it seemed like it was following me.

On TV and in movie franchises, there's this notion of retconning—retroactive continuity, for the uninitiated—a sort of creative time travel mixed with *Inception* where new ideas are shoehorned into earlier storylines to become canon. It's as though writers are traveling to past episodes and implanting new memories into the characters' heads so they jive with new story developments. That's how I felt with Fernet advertisements. It's as though they didn't even exist for me until after I discovered the liquid and then suddenly they were everywhere and always had been. And it wasn't just in San Francisco. The posters were showing up in my everyday stomping ground in New York City.

"I do see it quite a bit in New York, Portland—it's definitely expanding," Cosentino observes. "It's definitely a global beverage."

Fernet also started transcending the spirits category and spilling over into my first love: beer. Colorado's Odell Brewing Company, based in what has been fondly dubbed the "Beermuda Triangle"—the city of Fort Collins—for its extraordinarily high density of craft breweries, has produced a porter aged in empty Fernet barrels. The used cooperage comes courtesy of nearby microdistillery Leopold Brothers. Yes, even small US craft spirits producers are trying their hands at this venerable bitter. Leopold Brothers's version includes a subtle mix of botanicals including lavender, honeysuckle, ginger root, bitter aloe, dandelion root, rose petals, chamomile, and pepper. When the residual spirit on the barrels' wood is combined with the roasty, chocolate notes of the porter, the result is something not unlike an alcoholic version of Andes Candies or any variation of those one might find on one's pillow following nightly turndown service.

Fernet's reemergence has not been lost on its creators—well, the modern stewards of the century-and-three-quarters tradition anyway. A few years back at its production facility near Milan, Fratelli Branca Distillery cut the ribbon on an eleven-thousand-square-foot museum/visitors center for anyone with even a mild curiosity about this enigmatic and storied spirit.

If you don't feel like going all the way to Italy—though I couldn't understand why anyone wouldn't—you probably don't have to travel much farther than your corner dive bar to get a bit of living Fernet history. Just order a glass and you're likely to get an earful from the regulars about their amaro-soaked adventures back in the day.

Week 22

Respect Your Elders

Elderflower Liqueur

If I had a nickel for every time a beverage public relations or marketing specialist told me that a particular flavor or ingredient was "trending" . . . well, I'd have a whole lot of nickels.

But sometimes they're able to pierce the armor of my knee-jerk cynicism and convince me that, "Yes, this is indeed a thing."

That's elderflower in a nutshell. And, since late May ushers in elderflower season in Europe, let's talk about that floral curiosity a bit. It was definitely odd that brand owners had started putting flowers in a drink and even odder that people were actually drinking the stuff. Brewers started putting it in beer—as if many hop varietals weren't floral enough for beer geeks. Okay, it's a different kind of floral, more sweet and perfumey than earthy, and it really brings flavor and aroma elements to beer that weren't traditionally there before. Back in 2012, in honor of the impending end times heralded by the Mayan calendar, Seattle's Elysian Brewing Company each month released one of its Twelve Beers of the Apocalypse. Number six was Wasteland Elderflower Saison, a riff on the classic Belgian farmhouse style that balances the typically dry ale with a touch of sweetness.

Elderflower has found its way into cider as well, as none other than the Boston Beer–owned Angry Orchard—now the number one cider brand in the United States—launched a version with that floral component, complementing the crisp apple flavor of its flagship beverage.

Europeans were early adopters of consumable elderflower, and it's really by way of the continent across the pond that Americans started to discover it. It has been particularly successful as a liqueur, most famously the French-made St-Germain, which exploded onto the nightlife scene in 2007 and has been a favorite arrow in the quiver of mixologists across America ever since. Even the *New York Times*'s Dining & Wine section has sung its praises for its role as a game changer among bartenders in the past decade, noting, in 2009, that every liqueur "wanted to be as big as St-Germain when it grew up." Not bad for a brand that, at that time, had been on the market for just two years.

The bottle alone is enough justification for bars to stock up on it. It combines the best elements of the Art Deco and Belle Epoque periods, resulting in what seems more like a fancy lamp or vase than a beverage container.

There's also a fair degree of romance surrounding its production—and why wouldn't there be; romance and flowers go hand in hand. As St-Germain's founders tell the story in their marketing materials, it's made in the "artisanal French manner" from 100 percent fresh, hand-selected blossoms, harvested during a four-to-six-week period in late spring. The flowers are then delivered to small collection stations where harvesters reportedly are paid by the kilo for their flowers, "often using specially rigged bicycles to carry them." Each harvester works independently, so there's a sort of Fair Trade element to the process. The blossoms then are macerated.

Of course, a recent ownership change could augment that process a bit and bring a bit of that logistical, cost-cutting efficiency that larger companies like to brag about in their corporate communiqués.

Originally marketed by New York–based Cooper Spirits International, owned by St-Germain creator Robert Cooper, it wasn't long before the big guys started taking an "if we can't beat 'em, join 'em," path with the liqueur. Bacardi Limited in early 2013 acquired St-Germain from Cooper,[48] who, for a brief time afterward, remained on board as, in Bacardi's words, the liqueur's "brand guardian" and essentially its spokesman. But he guards the brand no more.

The acquisition did not come as much of a surprise. Bermuda-based Bacardi, known, of course, for the most iconic rum brand in the world, has done quite well with another French-sourced spirit. In 2004 it bought Grey Goose—which almost singlehandedly led the superpremium vodka revolution—from original owner Sidney Frank Importing Company for a cool $2 billion.[49]

Bacardi's purchase of St-Germain, however, has ruffled its share of feathers in the bar and nightclub world.

More than a few bartenders have been vocal about their fear that St-Germain has become a victim of its own success. Those in the "craft cocktail" set like to think of themselves as tastemakers, influencers, or whatever word marketers are liberally throwing around these days to mean "ahead of the curve." There's a hipster element to it; the moment a certain band reaches a critical mass and gets "discovered" by more mainstream audiences, the skinny jeans, ironic T-shirt, and mutton-chop-sporting crowd start to lose interest (like a hipster-ribbing shirt I once owned that read, "I'm into bands that don't even exist yet"). St-Germain may have lost its "specialness."

While there's some validity to that assessment, it's not the entire story, nor is it completely fair. Mixologists actually love using elder-flower. They also love the fact that St-Germain helped put the botanical on the map for so many people who had no prior exposure to it. What they're not particularly enamored of is its sometimes-overpowering sugar content.

"Anything that you put it into, guess what it's going to taste like—St-Germain!"[50] complains New York City mixologist Ben Paré, aka "The Cocktail Snob." "Sweetness is the crutch. It's so sweet that anything you add it to is going to fall by the wayside."

Paré, who operates out of SoHo's Sanctuary T and frequently teaches cocktail classes, says fresh elderflower is easy enough to procure, even grow. It's also simple enough for bartenders to make their own elder-flower liqueurs or infusions without sticky high-fructose corn syrup. The flower could even be infused in a gin as the dominant botanical. As cocktails that emphasize fresh ingredients are enjoying a resurgence, elderflower should find a fairly permanent place on the bar. Paré is an evangelist for such drinks, especially those that have a vegetal component. He's been known to mix drinks with everything from kale to arugula, and elderflower is a natural partner for those.

"I can make something like St-Germain that has the same sweetness, but with a different complexity because of that fresh element," Paré points out. "For an arugula drink, you can add some elderflower to it—it has a nice, delicate flavor to it without it being overbearingly sweet.

Some, like Paré, may feel that St-Germain is played out, but most would concede that there's a reason it's become as popular as it has. Something about the flavor has really connected with drinkers. A key component of Paré's repertoire is his bespoke cocktail offerings—patrons tell him what spirits they like and he customizes drinks based on those flavor profiles. St-Germain makes a frequent appearance.

"People do look for it," Paré admits, as he motions to his own bottle on Sanctuary T's shelf. "That's the only reason it's on that bar there. People order it by name."

It's also likely to be the only way most pub-goers are going to be able to get even the remotest sense of what the flower tastes like, since only the most ambitious barkeeps of Paré's ilk are going to have fresh blossoms and infusions at the ready.

As far as this author is concerned—not to mention the vast majority of the legal-drinking-age population—there's still an adventurous element to a relatively exotic liqueur made from a piece of plant life previously more at home in a wedding table centerpiece than a bottle of booze. And, from a brand standpoint, St-Germain may have most of the market share, but it's far from being the only game in town. There are plenty of smaller brands to try—before it's not cool anymore:

- PÜR LIKÖR BLOSSOM (PÜR SPIRITS): Pür Spirits accesses centuries of its native German distilling heritage to craft its elderflower liqueur. The company claims to handpick the flowers from forest clearings specifically to craft this fruity, amber-hued spirit.
- THE BITTER TRUTH ELDERFLOWER LIQUEUR (THE BITTER TRUTH GMBH): Known for its bitters, The Bitter Truth also has a pretty extensive liqueur portfolio. Its elderflower product pours more of a pale golden than an amber and tickles the tongue with a couple of faintly spicy notes.
- ST. ELDER (ST. ELDER, LLC): There seem to be plenty of "saints" and not enough sinners among the elderflower liqueurs available. St. Elder is produced in Massachusetts, using an American species of elderflower known as Sambucus Canadensis. Floral and sweet notes are tempered by a slightly tart, citrusy kick.

Week 23
The 'Shining
Moonshine Goes Legit

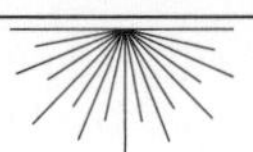

It's funny how we drinkers love to romanticize past illegalities.

The Prohibition-chic movement has been one of the livelier modern trends in nightlife and the most visible manifestation of that has been the speakeasy-style bar.

I love kicking back for an evening in one of those tucked-away, often exclusive Roaring 1920s–themed bars with classic cocktails and era-specific jazz music (live or otherwise).

But legally embracing alcohol's illicit history takes many forms, and one that always manages to make me chuckle with delight and scratch my head in equal measure has been the emergence of legal moonshine. Sounds like a bit of an oxymoron and, to many, it is, but it has become a bona fide spirits category. As that has happened, drinks enthusiasts, bartenders, and brand marketers all have been putting a note next to June 5 on their calendars: It's National Moonshine Day.

My first encounter with a marketable form of the product was at a spirits' expo in New York around 2010, just as the concept was starting to catch on. The brand ambassador pulled out a mason jar filled with a clear liquid and proceeded to pour it into my tasting glass, explaining that it was from an old family recipe dating back generations. The only difference is that the family doesn't have to hide it from the authorities anymore. Well, that and the fact that it was incredibly smooth—astonishingly so. It was a far cry from the near-toxic burn one thinks of when one hears the word moonshine.

Prohibition was really the heyday for moonshiners, as that was when they saw the greatest spike in demand for their products.

Their families had been producing the stuff for at least a century prior to that, mostly for family and local consumption. But when the rest of the country went dry, they seized the opportunity to give the public what it wanted. Of course, to keep up with demand, product quality took a bit of a back seat to quantity and some batches wound up being downright poisonous (some cut corners with ingredients like antifreeze and paint thinner). Ever hear the term "blind drunk"? Well, you can thank the not-so-conscientious quality control going on in the era for the literal loss of vision that was known to happen on occasion.

Appalachia remains an epicenter of moonshine activity, just as it had been during more illicit times. The funny thing is, distilling only became legal in a large swath of that area barely half a decade ago. Prior to 2009, the state of Tennessee only permitted distilling in three counties, most notably Moore County, the home of Jack Daniel's. In an effort to create jobs and boost the economy, the state legalized spirits production in more than forty additional counties across the state.[51] That included eastern Tennessee, where moonshining had been the most robust for about two hundred years. Among the 'shiners to find success in that region after the change in law is Ole Smoky, based in Gatlinburg.

"We saw an opportunity to go into the market with a moonshine recipe that our family had been messing around with for many years,"[52] says Ole Smoky's cofounder, Joe Baker.

Its Original Moonshine is an unaged whiskey whose grain bill is 80 percent corn. The other 20 percent the distillery won't divulge because it's an old family secret that the producers say makes it distinct from its peers. "Originally our families were just making corn whiskey because that was the ingredient that they could get their hands on easily and distill it," Baker offers.

Ole Smoky's portfolio also includes White Lightnin', a term that may be at least vaguely familiar to most. It was the name of the 1973 Burt Reynolds action caper with moonshine at its center (okay, White Lightning wasn't missing its 'g', but you get the idea). The movie was so successful it spawned the sequel, Gator, bringing back Reynolds' ex-con character, Gator McKlusky.

Ole Smoky's White Lightnin' is much closer to a vodka than it is a whiskey. It's a grain-neutral spirit distilled six times to a remarkably smooth flavor. The distillery recommends that drinkers use it in place of vodka, gin, or tequila in their respective cocktails. Both of those are one hundred proof. The distillery actually crossed over into more conventional whiskey territory recently when it partnered with Harley-Davidson. Yes, that Harley-Davidson. The licensing partnership resulted in the creation of Harley-Davidson Road House Customs Charred Moonshine, which is aged in barrels, just like any fine bourbon or Tennessee whiskey.

Ole Smoky also has brought moonshine into the liqueur realm with an entire range of fruit creations. One of those is Apple Pie, which the distillery created to evoke the smell of an Appalachian grandmother's apple pie cooling on the windowsill. It combines the flagship white whiskey with apple juice, ground cinnamon, and other warm spices. It's another tradition rooted in the region's extralegal activities. "As far as I can remember, apple pie was always the number one—everyone was always interested in it," Baker remembers. "If you were at a party and had a jar passing around, you were just as likely seeing an apple pie as you were a clear."

Drinkers are generally surprised when they taste the products because they're expecting it to be, well, awful.

"The idea of moonshine for most folks is something that's going to be a harsh, strong taste and high proof," says Baker. "But when they taste it, you get a lot of 'wows'—that's exactly what they'll say. Just because it's moonshine doesn't mean it has to take the varnish off the furniture. It can be sipped and enjoyed. We make an enjoyable spirit in a variety of proofs."

Ole Smoky may have family heritage to draw upon, but North Carolina's Piedmont Distillers went right to the source for its 'shine line: NASCAR legend Robert "Junior" Johnson. Prior to his years on the stock car circuit in the 1950s and 1960s, Junior worked in the Johnson family bootlegging business. (The very origins of the sport stem from Prohibition-era 'shine running. Bootleggers would strip the cars of any unnecessary components that would weigh them down and hinder their ability to outrun the cops.) In 2007, Johnson joined forces with Piedmont, whose Midnight Moon range includes everything from forty- and fifty-proof versions of its signature corn-based moonshine to its own apple pie-, berry-, and cherry-based concoctions.

One of the more recent startups to throw its jar into the ring, Nashville-based American Born, has sought to bring the concept closer to its roots. Founded in 2012 by the alpha duo of former Notre Dame quarterback Patrick Dillingham and US Marine Corps. Captain and

Iraq War vet Sean Koffel, the company launched its first products in the fall of 2013.

"The US Marine Corps is fueled by the South with strongholds in Parris Island and Camp Lejeune, and there are a lot of Southern boys who make up the locker room at Notre Dame,"[53] Koffel says.

Like its Appalachian predecessors, American Born markets an Original corn whiskey and the requisite Apple Pie creation.

Its bag of tricks features a third variety, Dixie, which it touts as the first sweet-tea-flavored moonshine (a huge dose of Southern culture).

In true Semper Fi–form, Koffel is never timid about calling out the inauthenticity of some of its competitors.

"We were at a wedding and a lot of our friends were really offended by the way moonshine was being portrayed in the legal market," he reveals. "Basically a lot of people were putting cheap neon-orange spirits in a foreign-made mason jar at forty proof and calling it moonshine—making fun of Southern mountain culture and making a caricature of it with the branding. We just thought there was an opportunity to make moonshine the authentic way, just corn, sugar, and water."

The moonshine phenomenon has expanded beyond the South and has caught on nationwide, especially since it enables distillers to market a new-make whiskey without having to age it. A bottle (or jar) labeled moonshine is just as likely to come from California or New York as it is from Appalachia.

Now, I'm going to guess there's a nagging little voice in the back of your brain asking, "Is it truly moonshine if it's legal?"

There actually is a great deal of debate in the spirits community over the use of the term, given the fact that the word refers to the unlawful, under-cover-of-night shenanigans involved with its production and distribution. Some prefer to call it "white whiskey," "white dog," or "unaged corn whiskey," or some variation of those (sometimes, when its base ingredient is something like cane sugar, it's not even technically whiskey and is just, simply, "neutral spirit"). But there's a lot more fun embedded in the term "moonshine" and it's pretty damned evocative, so I'm going to stick to calling it that. Having said that, I acknowledge wholeheartedly that there's more than a generous helping of overly romanticized marketing associated with it in an industry already drowning in marketing bullshit. Whatever you choose to call it, at the very least it's a tiny bit of culture and a light touch of a history lesson packaged in an industrial glass jar that otherwise wouldn't find its way into your local bar or liquor store. For a sip of that history, you might consider a flight of the following.

Junior's Midnight Moon 100 Proof (Piedmont Distillers): The one-hundred-proof version should satisfy those looking for a bit more of a kick than Midnight Moon's original eighty proofer offers. Despite its added strength, the corn-based spirit is still pretty smooth.

Kings County Moonshine (Kings County Distillery): You might overlook the Brooklyn-based distillery's white whiskey if you're looking for a mason jar; it's actually bottled in 200 mL glass flasks. Kings County combines 80 percent New York State organic corn and 20 percent Scottish malted barley for a remarkably smooth, eighty-proof spirit.

Dutch's Sugar Wash Moonshine (Dutch's Spirits): Dutch's is another New York producer that foregoes the mason jar—the distiller favors a classic 750 mL jug-like bottle with a handle. It also foregoes corn altogether and crafts its 'shine from 100 percent cane sugar. The "Dutch" in question is notorious Prohibition-era mobster Dutch Schultz. The distillery was built on the footprint of what was believed to be Schultz's clandestine bootlegging operation.

American Born Apple Pie (Windy Hill Spirits, Inc.): It's quite common for moonshiners to produce an apple pie-flavored product. A key distinguishing factor for the American Born offering is that it steers clear of lower-ABV liqueur territory, bottling its apple offering at eighty-three proof (41.5 percent ABV). It's great chilled or in a cocktail.

Moonshine Cherries (Ole Smoky Moonshine):
Another Appalachian tradition that found its way into an Ole Smoky mason jar is Moonshine Cherries. It's just what it sounds like: a healthy helping of maraschino cherries soaked in one hundred proof moonshine. In the region, it wouldn't be a party until someone remembered to bring the cherries.

GIN UP (AND TOSS THE TONIC)

Moonshine may be one of those spirits popular enough to get a "National" day, but the much more universally consumed gin one-ups it with a global one. World Gin Day has caught fire internationally since Neil Houston, founder of the blog YetAnotherGin.com, launched it in 2009. It's typically observed on the second full weekend in June.

My own experience with gin has been one of the great paradoxes of my legal-drinking-age existence. I've never been a gin person and, for a good chunk of the late 1990s, I was almost exclusively a gin person by default. Back in those days (as in 'my midtwenties') a person didn't have much time to decide what to drink, especially in the loungey starter bars of Manhattan's East Village. For the microsecond that the aloof bartender made eye contact with you, you'd have better made up your mind about what you plan to consume lest the tiny well-drink-delivery window slam shut indefinitely. Keen to mask my indecision, I'd usually just shout the first thing that popped into my head: "gin and tonic." It felt "adult." No more was I ordering the cheapest watered-down lager on tap or in bottles. This was the cocktail that was going to take me into my grownup-ness.

Except that it wasn't. I didn't realize it, but I actually loathed most of the gins that bartenders were putting in well drinks (again, I was a broke twentysomething), which was a testament to just how watered-down these drinks actually were, between the overabundance of ice and the hypergenerous tonic pours. When I actually had occasion to drink one of those gins straight, it was worse (I'd imagine) than drinking lighter fluid.

Fast-forward a decade and a half or so, and I found myself drinking gin again—for the first time.

It wasn't the case of my palate finally catching up with gin, but with gin finally catching up with my palate. Gin, like vodka, had more or less become commoditized. Marketers of industrially produced brands—those designed for well G&Ts—likely figured that imbibers were diluting the spirit so much that the complex interplay of botanicals was of little interest to them. No judgment there. The market wants what the market wants.

And back then I couldn't even tell you what the difference between gin and vodka was. Luckily, I've had plenty of time to bone up since then.

Gin more or less evolved from the Dutch beverage, genever, whose exact origins have been the source of great debate. Many have credited a sixteenth-century Dutch chemist with its creation, but others have traced its origins even earlier to the late Middle Ages, in what is now modern Belgium.[54] The word itself derives from the Dutch word for juniper, which is the primary component that defines what is and isn't gin. It's usually combined with any number of other botanicals, either exhibiting a juniper-forward expression or letting those berries hang in the background and allowing the other parts of earth's bounty to enjoy the spotlight.

Of course, like all good things, the English co-opted it and made it their own, ultimately giving it the simple three-letter, one-syllable moniker with which we've all become familiar.

Naturally, like many other spirits that you'll find in this book, gin's early applications were primarily medicinal, hence the reliance on the complex combo of herbal ingredients. I'm going to go out on a limb and say not too many modern physicians have been prescribing the stuff (save for during Prohibition when patients sought it to heal all manner of "ailments"—anyone who has ever visited a present-day medical marijuana dispensary might identify with many of those horrific maladies).

Fascinatingly enough, the good old G&T itself was a mixture responsible for saving countless lives during the days of British colonialism (either a good or a bad thing, depending on whether you were a colonist or the colonized). The Brits discovered that quinine, which they would add to water to create tonic, was an effective antimalarial agent.

And the gin? That masked the rather intensely unpleasant flavor of the quinine.[55] Today's tonics contain a fraction of the compound used in their nineteenth-century forebears.

Gin and its earliest cocktails may no longer be treated as curatives, but there still are some serious standards governing the spirit's production and labeling, especially in the European Union where the stuff was born. The EU updated the definition as recently as 2008. The new(ish) definition, in a nutshell, states that all gins are made from ethyl alcohol flavored with juniper berries and other flavorings. The ethyl alcohol must be distilled to the minimum standards set by the EU, in this case 37.5 percent alcohol by volume.[56] EU Spirit Drink Regulations define three styles of gin: gin, distilled gin, and London gin. Here's the technical definition,[57] in its most naked form:

- A. Made from suitable ethyl alcohol and flavorings
- B. Ethyl alcohol does not have to be redistilled
- C. Flavoring can be either approved natural or artificial flavorings
- D. Flavorings can be simply mixed together with the ethyl alcohol to form the gin
- E. There is no restriction on the addition of other approved additives, such as sweeteners
- F. Water is added to reduce the gin's strength to the desired retail level, but not below 37.5 percent
- G. No restriction on coloring gin with an approved coloring

DISTILLED GIN

- A. Made in a traditional still by redistilling neutral alcohol in the presence of natural flavorings
- B. No minimum strength for the resultant distillate
- C. After distillation, further ethyl alcohol of the same composition may be added
- D. Additional flavorings may be added after distillation and these can be either natural or artificial flavorings
- E. The distillate can be further changed by the addition of other approved additives

- F. Water may be added to reduce the strength to the desired level.
- G. No restriction on the coloring of distilled gin with approved colorings

London Gin

- A. Made in a traditional still by redistilling ethyl alcohol in the presence of all natural flavorings used
- B. Ethyl alcohol used to distill it must be of a higher quality than the minimum standard expressed for ethyl alcohol. The methanol level in the ethyl alcohol must not exceed five grams per hectoliter of 100 percent alcohol by volume
- C. Flavorings used must all be approved natural flavorings and must impart the flavor during the distillation process
- D. The use of artificial flavorings is not permitted
- E. The resultant distillate must have a minimum strength of 70 percent alcohol by volume
- F. Further ethyl alcohol may be added after distillation, provided that it is of the same standard
- G. A small amount of sweetening may be added after distillation provided that the sugars do not exceed 0.1 grams per liter of finished product
- H. The only other substance that may be added is water
- I. No coloring is permitted

The distinctions might appear esoteric and indiscernible to the average drinker—they apply largely to production methods that are lost on most of us. But, for all intents and purposes, London gin often is regarded as the premium style. It was not until the 2008 guidelines that London gin received the special designation, protecting its process and cultural heritage. Unlike a product such as Scotch, however, production of London gin is not specific to its point of origin. In fact, very few gins are even produced in London these days.

Within London gin, there's a further distinction, London Dry versus Old Tom Gin, the latter being the sweeter of the two. London Dry typically is considered the gold standard on the style quality spectrum but, like just about anything else, that depends on whom you ask. Dry more or less usurped Old Tom as the gin of choice after the nineteenth century. [58]

TERROIR, BOTANIVORE, AND DRY RYE (ST. GEORGE SPIRITS):

The craft distilling movement in the United States has precipitated further stylistic revolutions, challenging perceptions of what drinkers typically think of as gin.

An early pioneer on the scene was Alameda, California's, St. George Spirits, which now offers three very distinct expressions: Terroir, Botanivore and Dry Rye.

Whenever and wherever possible, I'd recommend tasting these three side by side to get a true sense of the distinct variations among them. And if you ever visit (or live in) the greater San Francisco area, you must make time to taste it at the source. St. George occupies a very spacious former Navy aircraft hangar right on the Bay, with a stunning view of the city. Don't let the enormous movie prop shark guarding the barrels scare you off!

Terroir proves that the wine industry that has defined St. George's immediate region doesn't own the term. This particular gin celebrates the same flora and climatological character that have made Northern California famous.

I'll admit, upon pouring my first glass and nosing it, the scent of an entire forest of Douglas firs wafted to my olfactory nerve. In fact, if you ever find that you need a little Christmas, just crack open one of these babies and let the piney scent engulf your home. I'm kidding of course, but you get the idea. The actual sipping reveals hints of the other botanicals: fennel, bay laurel, sage, and, of course, juniper berries.

Botanivore boasts a whopping nineteen botanicals, ranging from cardamom and cilantro to citra hops(!) and star anise. After experiencing the earthiness of Terroir, this one is markedly sweeter and fruitier.

As for Dry Rye . . . well, even the uninitiated would figure out that this is the gin for whiskey lovers without even knowing that St. George markets it as such. Indeed, on the inaugural nosing, you'd swear it was an unaged white whiskey—the grain punch is that pronounced. And it should be because the base is 100 percent pot-distilled rye. All of the spicy complexity one would expect from a rye whiskey dominates each sip, but there's a nice, subtle interplay with the juniper berries, caraway, and black pepper that reminds drinkers it's actually a gin they're drinking.

"The biggest thing is to let [tasters] know that because they have certain expectations of what a gin is supposed to be, they need to put those aside,"[59] says Lance Winters, master distiller at St. George Spirits. "This is not your dad's or your grandfather's gin; this is a completely unique experience. Your dad and your grandfather really didn't have a chance to have this gin experience. You do."

BLUECOAT AMERICAN DRY GIN (PHILADELPHIA DISTILLING COMPANY):

Bluecoat American Dry Gin, the flagship brand of Philadelphia Distilling Company, has, since 2005, become a rather prominent example of this new style. The name Bluecoat, naturally, is the colonial answer to the Redcoats' centuries-long gin dominance. The brand's key botanicals include natural coriander seed, American citrus peel, natural angelica root, and, of course, juniper berry (organic berries, to boot). A major distinction for the product produced in the City of Brotherly Love is that it's not quite as juniper-forward as its British brethren. Bluecoat's blend creates more of a citrus experience on the palate.

AVIATION GIN (HOUSE SPIRITS DISTILLERY):

The Pacific time zone's answer to the cobalt-bottled mid-Atlantic creation is Aviation American Gin, one of the better-known brands to emerge from Portland, Oregon's, rapidly expanding distiller's row. The distillery in question is House Spirits, which touts Aviation as the result of the rare partnership between distiller and bartender. The story that House Spirits likes to tell begins at a summer 2005 tiki party in Oregon's neighbor to the north, Washington State—West Seattle to be precise. A Portland-based friend hands mixologist Ryan Magarian a botanical infusion unlike anything he's ever tasted. That prompts him to head south to old Stumptown and seek out the creators. They soon collaborated on thirty or so iterations of that original blend until the new partners got it quite right and Aviation took flight. "That was really, for us, a very intentional attempt to create a style of gin that was not London gin,"[60] explains House Spirits founder and head distiller Christian Krogstad. "I love London dry gins, but the world didn't need another London dry gin."

So, Krogstad and his team backed off the juniper a bit, let the other botanicals shine, and introduced Aviation as a distinctly American dry gin.

REHORST GIN (GREAT LAKES DISTILLERY):

World-class craft gins aren't limited to the coasts; the Midwest has its fair share as well. One of those is Rehorst, whose namesake, Guy Rehorst, founded Milwaukee's Great Lakes Distillery. Most Americans exhibit some form of pride for their home state, but some of the most rabidly proud I've encountered hail from Wisconsin. And for good reason; the state has a great deal to offer from those delightfully addictive (and squeaky) cheese curds to the Wisconsin Old-Fashioned cocktail to some of the most iconic beer brands (and, lest I get pummeled for not mentioning them, the Green Bay Packers.) Of course, any spirit brand distilled in the state would have to have some distinctly Wisconsinite attributes. That's why Wisconsin ginseng—considered among herbalists as the best of its kind—is included among Rehorst Gin's nine botanicals. Rehorst also includes sweet basil, another rarity in gin.

BOOTLEGGER 21 GIN (PROHIBITION DISTILLERY):

"I love old-school gins, I love Beefeater—I love the classics,"[61] declares Brian Facquet, the cofounder and principal distiller of the ironically named Prohibition Distillery, which operates out of a converted 1920s firehouse in Roscoe, NY, about 120 miles outside of New York City. "So what I wanted to do was make a modern twist on a classic." The result was Bootlegger 21 Gin, which achieves its distinct flavor with just five botanicals: coriander, lemon verbena, orris root, bitter orange, and, of course, juniper. The ninety-four proof (47 percent ABV) gin is unabashedly juniper-forward.

»→ To Tonic or Not to Tonic

There truly is something for everyone in the gin world, which likely comes as a surprise to many. With so many choices of what to drink, the real question is how to drink it. The answer is, there is no wrong answer. But before you douse it with carbonated quinine water and lime, try it neat, at room temperature. If you're an ice person, your next glass can be on the rocks.

"As gins are becoming more approachable in their flavor profiles, I am definitely seeing more and more people drinking it on the rocks or just as a nice gin martini with very little embellishment," observes St. George's Winters. "You've got people making gins that are designed to be sipped."

Once you've had the full flavor experience in its most naked form and are still looking for something refreshing, go ahead and have the bartender mix that G&T.

»→ FERMENTED and FORTIFIED

Ever go to a fancyish restaurant, have the waitperson present you with a list of fortified dessert wines, and then realize you never figured out the difference between a port, a Madeira, and a sherry (I can't be the only one)? Over the next three weeks, we'll be looking to the Old World empires of Iberia to help get to the bottom of the mystery.

Week 25

OH, SHERRY

Our fortification journey begins in Spain. It's impossible to have a conversation about sherry without mentioning the town with which it is most closely associated, Jerez de la Frontera, in the southern region of Andalusia.

One of the primary differences between sherry and its Portuguese sister, port (which we'll get into next week), beyond geography and terroir, is that most sherries are produced with white grapes, while ports are usually derived from red ones. There are always exceptions, as in the case of white port.

A substantial majority of sherries—in the neighborhood of 95-plus percent—derive from Palomino grapes.[62] The remaining ones begin as muscatel or Pedro Ximénez varietals, but those are reserved for the sweeter offerings.

Another significant distinguishing factor and one that sherry aficionados believe should distance their beloved wine considerably from others of the fortified school is that the finer ones are bone dry. Residual sugar barely plays a part in its flavor profile, as it so often does in many ports and Madeiras. "We have this popular image of sherry being a sweet drink and, to be fair, historically a lot of it was,"[63] says Peter Liem, noted wine critic, author, and cofounder of New York City's Sherryfest. "But in today's world of sherry and especially the fine sherry we're talking about, most of the best examples are dry."

In that regard, the beverage is more of a kindred soul with white table wine—Chardonnay, for instance—than the other fortified wines, despite the bonus alcohol content.

Sherry producers are fiercely protective of their heritage. Many believe the ultimate flavor nuances that their beverage exhibits today are the result of three millennia of successive cultural influence in the Mediterranean region. First it was the Phoenicians for three thousand-odd years, followed by the Romans about one thousand years later, and then the Moors another one thousand years after that. As sherry makers tell it, all had some influence on the grapes that ultimately ended up in a bottle of twenty-first-century sherry.[64]

Sadly, that hasn't stopped other countries from claiming the word for their own products. A century and a half ago, sherry was among the most popular beverages in the world, so it's no surprise that any number of grape-growing regions outside of Spain try to claim the concept for themselves. The price one pays for fame, I guess.

Most American imbibers have, at some point, encountered a "California sherry" and those in Cape Town are no doubt quite well acquainted with a "South African sherry." Despite the fact that the European Union has made it a protected appellation, not every country wants to play ball. It's beyond disappointing to report that the United States has been incredibly stubborn in its disregard for such rules (after all, this is the same country whose Korbel brand calls itself "California Champagne"). Canada, on the other hand, has been far more amenable. The Canadian product's reputation was that of a fairly cheap, cloyingly sweet, highly alcoholic interpretation of the Spanish classic. But in 2013, the country agreed that it no longer would label the beverage as "Canadian sherry."[65]

Stylistically, the diversity within the extremely vast realm of dry sherry is staggering, but all such classifications generally fall close to one of two camps: Fino and Oloroso.

Fino

Fino sherries are those aged in a barrel under a film of yeast called flor, which acts as a barrier between the liquid and the air. The flor helps Fino achieve its signature character—typically light in body, with a pronounced minerality often found in soil-driven wines like white Burgundy.

Oloroso

An Oloroso sherry, by contrast, has not been aged under flor and tends to be richer, more textural, and far fuller in body than a Fino. In the sherry-producing region, it's fairly common for the locals to consume it like they would a red wine, pairing it with meats, stews, and wild game.

Sherry is pretty flexible from a food-pairing standpoint. It works well with all sorts of main courses, an attribute that is frequently forgotten at many restaurants.

"Inexperienced sommeliers will take a Fino and put it on a dessert wine list and that's a disaster," Liem contends. "Here you have bone dry wine; it should be put on the white wine list. My point is you can find a style of sherry to pair with just about any food you put on the table."

Finos are known to be the most flexible when it comes to finding dinner partners.

"It's almost like a joke with sommeliers," Liem says. "If you get some impossible pairing and you don't know what to say, just say 'Fino.' It'll work."

That even includes such notorious viticulture Kryptonite as asparagus, artichokes, eggs, and anchovies, or anything that's considered too assertive or too vegetal for most conventional matches.

Beyond Oloroso and Fino, there are a few other terms you're likely to encounter on a restaurant's list.

MANZANILLA

Best described as a sister wine to Fino, Manzanilla bears a different name than its sibling essentially due to extreme local pride. It's unique to the town of Sanlucar, whose resident winemakers wanted no association with Fino—otherwise there's very little discernible difference from a Fino. Manzanilla is produced in a similar aged-under-flor fashion and shares the same lightness of body as a Fino.

AMONTILLADO

Kind of the best of both worlds, an Amontillado begins its life under flor like a Fino, but finishes as an Oloroso after it's exposed to oxygen. As one would expect, it exhibits characteristics of both styles. It's typically darker in appearance than Fino, but noticeably lighter than Oloroso. (If the name sounds vaguely familiar, you're probably thinking of the Edgar Allen Poe short story, "The Cask of Amontillado.")

Palo Cortado

Like Amontillado, Palo Cortado sports hints of Fino and Oloroso. It starts out with every intention of becoming a Fino, but at some point the flor film disappears and oxidation sets in, pulling it into Oloroso territory. Traditionally, this occurrence is supposed to be complete happenstance, though some producers have sought to simulate its key flavor, appearance, and body elements through blending. Palo Cortado literally translates to "cut stick," signifying the mark drawn on casks of the style. When it originates as a Fino, the producer marks the cask with a single line—a "stick" if you will. When the flor dies, the distiller draws another line through that line, cutting the stick, as it were.

Sherry matures in American oak barrels via what's known as the solera method. It's a blending process whereby a fraction of a liquid from a barrel of a certain age is merged with portions of wines of other ages. The barrels are stacked on top of each other, with the oldest on the bottom and the youngest on the top. It enables a consistent average age in each bottle.

Okay, enough with arcane maturation techniques. Let's get down to drinking. An ideal introductory flight for sherry newcomers should begin with a Fino, as it's the most accessible for virgin palates. It wouldn't hurt to sample a Manzanilla next, as they're nearly identical and it would be instructive to taste the two side by side. A good exercise would be to try to detect the slight differences in body—the seaside terroir of Sanlucar usually results in lighter Manzanilla grapes. Fino's inland growing area is conducive to somewhat rounder character.

Immediately after sipping those, it's time to go big. Try an Oloroso and throw in an Amontillado while you're at it.

"Seeing the contrast between these styles becomes very illuminating," says Liem. "If you have a flight of wine like that, you can pair them all with different foods and see how different styles of sherry will interact with the same dish."

Week 26
PONDERING PORT

War. What is it good for? Actually, quite a lot, as far as classic libations are concerned.

It's hard to believe that for centuries prior to the back-to-back world wars, two of the greatest modern allies were constantly at each other's throats dyeing oceans red with their perpetual bloodshed.

During one of their many conflicts with the French, the British stopped drinking the fine Bourdeaux wines for which their sworn enemy was world famous. However, as complete abstention from grape-based imbibing was not an option, the Brits faced a formidable quandary: where to find wine equally suitable for their thirsty empire. It was in the Douro region of northern Portugal where their prayers were answered.

Soon, the English began shipping barrels of Douro's finest to the British Isles, but the primitive journey of the time did a number on the wine.

To make the beverage more seaworthy, Britain decided to fortify it with a bit of brandy, halting the fermentation process midway through and leaving a significant amount of residual sugar untouched by the yeast. The sweet libation that's noticeably stronger than regular wine—19 to 20 percent alcohol to be precise—came to be known as port.[66] Today, true port must be produced in Douro.

The word port is just the beginning though. The beverage is further delineated into several subcategories; the terms you're likely to encounter more than others include:

- RUBY: A reference to the port's color, the ruby tends to be the entry-level, mass-produced variety. It sits in concrete or stainless steel tanks to prevent any oxidative nuances characteristic of a wood-aged beverage. It's then blended with others of its kind to ensure consistent, if not particularly complex flavor, bottle after bottle.

- TAWNY: The label refers to the light brownish, sandy color of the port, achieved through barrel aging—a key distinguishing facet. Tawny port typically ranges from sweet to medium-dry and often exhibits nutty characteristics, making it an ideal partner for nuts, dark chocolate, and white, soft cheeses like brie.

- VINTAGE: As in wines sans fortification, vintage ports contain only grapes from a particular vintage year—and only a select few receive that designation (a vintage is "declared" only a couple times a decade). They spend some time in a barrel (usually around a year and a half to two years), but significantly less than the average tawny, and age primarily in the bottle after that. This enables vintage ports to retain their deep red color. The younger vintage ports go well with chocolate desserts, while the more mature ones, say ten, fifteen, or twenty year olds, are tasty with a Stilton or other blue-style cheese. Vintage ports usually are at the higher end of the category.

- LATE BOTTLED VINTAGE (LBV): LBVs aren't even bottled until four to six years after the vintage date, spending at least double the amount of time in wood barrels that vintage ports do. It's something of an accidental style; original LBVs initially were intended to be bottled as vintages, but that didn't happen until there was actual demand for them.

- COLHEITA: Sort of a cross between a tawny and a vintage—essentially it's a tawny from a single vintage year. What sets it apart from a vintage proper is the amount of time it spends in the wood; it could be decades before it even sees a bottle.

- WHITE PORT: Unlike ruby and all of the aforementioned port iterations, whites use white grapes instead of red. They're served primarily as aperitifs along with nuts and cheese prior to dinner.

Basic ruby and tawny ports will run about $12 to $15 a bottle and are good places to start, but to graduate to a slightly more refined experience, spend about $10 more on a special offering such as Broadbent

Auction Reserve. It rests somewhere on the continuum between ruby and tawny, but for categorization purposes it's technically a reserve ruby port.

Broadbent Selections, its Richmond, Virginia–based importer, is run by a respected authority in the fortified wine world, Bartholomew Broadbent. Upscale libations are in his blood—the British expat apprenticed for his father, renowned wine critic and Christie's wine auctioneer Michael Broadbent.

"Port tends to be a wine that you have with dinner parties a lot,"[67] observes Bartholomew Broadbent. "If you were planning a big evening where you were going to drink port afterward, plan to have your table wines during that dinner—along the lines of 12.5 to 14 percent alcohol—because then you can drink it and still feel the capacity to have something else to drink."

If the table wines paired with the succession of dinner courses are in the range of 15.5 percent, it's likely everyone at the party will be too tipsy to appreciate, much less even get to, the port round.

If you're part of a considerably smaller party, don't worry about polishing off a bottle in a single session. Most styles tend to remain in tip-top shape for months after they're opened.

"People who say vintage port has to be drunk immediately are wrong," Broadbent explains. "A young vintage port will actually benefit from being open several weeks. When people talk about drinking a vintage port within a couple of days, they're talking about something that is fifty years old, sixty years old, seventy years old—in which case you don't want to leave it open too long. It changes; it loses its freshness a bit."

Another tip: be very mindful of the serving vessel. Broadbent prefers his port in a standard white wine glass; anything sold as a "port glass" is just a marketing ploy. Serving in a traditional wine glass enables the drinker to fully experience the aroma, as the usually modest, two-ounce pour has plenty of room to breathe. The much more compact serving area in one of those purpose-forged receptacles doesn't allow for this.

Also, stay away from brandy snifters. Those are designed to accentuate the smell of alcohol, forcing all of the other aroma notes into the back seat. It will diminish the tasting experience.

When you're ordering one at a bar or restaurant, don't be shy about demanding the appropriate glassware. More than likely, the establishment will be tempted to serve the drink in one of those so-called port glasses; they think it looks like they're giving you more when a tiny container is filled to the brim versus a mere splash in a wine glass. But you're the one paying for it (and you're likely spending $9 or $10 for a couple of ounces), so you're well within your rights to politely request that you get a white wine glass.

Since I'm a big fan of ritual, I want to recommend going full-on Portugal if there's a decanter at your table. The Portuguese pour their own and then pass the decanter to the person on the left—don't pour for that person, only for yourself (the host is the only one immune to this; he or she can pour for the person on the right and then pass to the left).

"It's a big faux pas to pass it the wrong way around the table," cautions Broadbent.

It frequently makes for some amusingly awkward moments, but that's part of the fun. For instance, let's say your friend, Jack, is so lost in conversation that he doesn't notice the decanter sitting in front of him and another companion, let's call her Jill, is waiting for a top-up. It wouldn't be uncommon or even bad form for Jill to make playfully sarcastic comments to alert Jack to the fact that he's the weak link.

Such theater rarely occurs outside of Portugal, but why not be part of a movement to reinforce the protocol in North America?

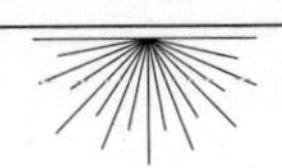

Mad About Madeira

I saved Madeira for last because the twenty-seventh week of the year coincides with Madeira Day, traditionally celebrated on July 1 to commemorate the day back in 1976 that Portugal granted autonomy to the fortified wine's namesake archipelago.

Despite its Portuguese origins, the history of the drink called Madeira is far more enmeshed with the history of America than it is with that of its Iberian ancestors.

As far as American inventions go, the one that most people don't usually think of as American is Madeira. And why should they? It sure doesn't sound American. It's not typically produced on American soil, save for some pale imitations. But for all intents and purposes, it would not exist were it not for the mysterious, exotic New World that later would come to be known as the United States of America.

The creation of this particular fortified wine—fortified, like port, with brandy during the fermentation process—was something of a happy accident. Between the fifteenth and eighteenth centuries, Madeira, situated off the coast of Morocco, served as a popular port for shippers to pick up wine and other rations. When Europeans started to colonize America, barrels of wine produced on the islands had quite a lot of ocean to cover before they got there. And many of them actually had to make a round trip because the barrels were used as the ship's ballast. When merchants made it back to the islands and sipped the barrels' contents, they discovered that the fortified wine had changed quite considerably into something that was surprisingly amazing. For a while after that, there was actually a law in effect that stated that no Madeira wine could be sold before it had made it around the world twice.[68] (That proved fairly impractical in modern times. Now producers just heat it to 115 degrees Fahrenheit to simulate the voyage.)

It soon became one of the most popular drinks in the American colonies, making rabid fans out of the likes of Thomas Jefferson and George Washington. It was so beloved that it became one of the first American tax loopholes. During the "no taxation without representation" days preceding the Revolutionary War, anything under the sun coming out of Europe had a tax imposed on it. Since Madeira technically wasn't coming from Europe—though from islands controlled by a European country—it dodged the levy.[69]

After the signing of the Declaration of Independence and the ratification of the US Constitution, the Founding Fathers sealed both deals with Madeira toasts. Legend has it that Betsy Ross kept a full glass of the stuff on the table next to her favorite sewing spot.

The beverage remained fashionable in the states until Prohibition, when the floor fell out from underneath it. After Repeal, it was virtually nonexistent in the country until about the late 1980s, when importers started making a concerted effort to bring it back. The man who is widely credited with its stateside reintroduction is, yes, our friend Bartholomew Broadbent. And in the quarter-century-plus since, American drinkers have been belatedly rediscovering the amped-up wine.

Now, in the twenty-first century, those who have grown to love the drink recognize that it has one distinct advantage over port: culinary versatility. "You can have it with soup, you can have it with cheese before dinner, you can have it with salad," raves Broadbent. "There's no other wine that can go with salad."

The reason for that is its relatively high natural acidity, enabling it to hold up against things like balsamic vinegar and citrus-based dressings.

It's also extremely flexible as a dessert wine, far more so than port. "It's probably the only dessert wine that goes with dessert, rather than being the dessert itself," Broadbent notes.

That's primarily due to the fact that, while it is on the sweet side, it has a dry finish. It doesn't clash with the sweetness of pie, cake, tart, or ice cream. Try doing that with a sweet Sauterne or a late-harvest Riesling and it's just going to be cloying sugariness from end-to-end.

This might sound like common sense, but make sure the Madeira you buy actually is from Madeira. More often than not, you'll encounter the real deal—especially if it's at the type of restaurant that would have the drink on the menu. But the bottom shelf of a wine aisle at an average retailer likely will be dominated by cheaper imitations produced on American soil.

Madeira doesn't have protected appellation status, but producers are working on making that a reality. It's not just a terroir issue. Usually the lesser, US-made Madeiras aren't even produced the proper way; makers often don't bother to heat them to replicate the optimal Madeira-creation conditions.

Most of the time those imitations are marketed as cooking wine, but even then they're doing a disservice to whatever dishes are being prepared. If a recipe calls for Madeira, the whole point is to get that flavor. With the inauthentic ones, the flavor burns off quickly during the cooking process.

Like port, a bottle of Madeira is typically 19 or 20 percent alcohol by volume, or roughly six or seven points higher than an average unfortified wine. Sure, a 750 mL container of Madeira is going to get a person drunk a lot faster than the same quantity of wine, but the desire to remain lucid shouldn't deter a drinker from cracking open a bottle. There's absolutely no pressure to finish it in a single sitting, as, in a fashion similar to port, it lasts, full flavor intact, for many months, even years. A $15 or $20 bottle is a pretty thrifty investment when it's getting consumed in occasional two-ounce snorts before or after dinner.

And, if you have the chance, line up a couple of Madeiras against flights of port and sherry. Those flights might look something like this:

SHERRY

- LA GUITA MANZANILLA (LA GUITA/GRUPO ESTÉVEZ): The winemaking family behind La Guita has been making sherry since the mid-nineteenth century. La Guita is an old slang term for cash (according to company legend, the founder insisted on being paid in cash), but it also means "twine"—to this day each bottle has a string attached to it. La Guita averages between five and six years old when bottled, and it's characteristically light and nuanced.

- VIÑA AB (GONZALEZ BYASS): Gonzalez Byass, one of the best-known sherry houses, makes this well-regarded 100 percent Palomino grape-based Amontillado that's amber in color, very dry, and full-bodied with a nutty nose.

- OLOROSO TRADICIÓN VORS (BODEGAS TRADICION): The youngest sherry in this Oloroso is thirty years old (average age is forty-five). The time in barrels has imparted some toasted, roasty notes, and it bears a mahogany hue. It's made with 100 percent Palomino grapes.

PORT

- SANDEMAN FOUNDERS RESERVE (SANDEMAN): Sandeman selects the finest grapes from each vintage in this five-year-old ruby port, bursting with the fruitiness characteristic of the style.

- FERREIRA DUQUE DE BRAGANCA 20 (A.A. FERREIRA): The twenty-year-old tawny port offers a full-bodied interplay between fruity and nutty. A. A. Ferreira's wine-making heritage spans more than two and a half centuries.

- QUINTA DO CRASTO LBV (QUINTA DO CRASTO): A good example of the late-bottled vintage style, Quinta de Crasto spends four to six years in oak vats before being bottled unfiltered. You'll detect the typical red fruit aromas characteristic of LBVs.

- DOW'S 2011 VINTAGE (SYMINGTON FAMILY ESTATES): The vintage Dow's is noteworthy for the fact that it was named *Wine Spectator* magazine's 2014 Wine of the Year, the first fortified wine to top the list.

MADEIRA

- BROADBENT 10-YEAR-OLD MALMSEY MADEIRA (BROADBENT): Malmsey typically is one of the sweeter styles of Madeira; the ten-year-old from Broadbent fits the bill, but is also well balanced, with a touch of dryness and just the right amount of acidity.

- BLANDY'S 5-YEAR-OLD DRY SERCIAL (MADEIRA WINE COMPANY SA): The Sercial is a light-skinned Portuguese grape and the base for this very dry style of Madeira. Nuts and toffee are the dominant notes.

That should be a fairly varied cross section and it at least scratches the surface on the complex world of fortified wines. Remember that sherry, port, and Madeira all go best with food, so pair accordingly!

Week 28

Cracking the Cognac Connoisseur Code

We're going to leave the Iberian Peninsula and head to France—just in time to celebrate Bastille Day (July 14). And why not wash down that generous serving of French history with an unmistakably French beverage?

But as we toast the revolution, let's overthrow any aristocratic pretensions that might be associated with Cognac.

The trouble with connoisseurs of any kind is that they can be a fairly exclusive bunch, protecting the mystique of their chosen beverage as if they're firewalling the Pentagon. I won't go so far as to use the word snob—though it certainly applies in a great many cases—but if they were a bit more open with the transmission of information, particularly about what makes the drinks they enjoy superior to others, they might be able to make a few new friends. That, in a nutshell, has been my relationship with Cognac. Full disclosure: It was very likely the last spirits style I ever managed to get my head around because its appreciators seemed so frustratingly insular.

I'm happy to report, however, that such an assessment was purely the product of my insecure mind. I soon learned that once you get a Cognac aficionado to talk to a mere layperson about the traditional French tipple, expect to engage in a lengthy yet scintillating conversation.

Most people usually operate under the assumption that Cognac is just brandy produced in a specific region of France that earns it the fancy name. It's an appellation d'origine controlee (AOC henceforth because anything else sounds pretentious and, well, French), much like

Champagne is for sparkling wine. If it's not produced in Champagne, you can't call it Champagne. Similarly, if it's not produced in Cognac, you can't call it Cognac. Brandy can be made anywhere in the world. Cognac can be made only in an area of about three hundred square miles.

That's a tremendous oversimplification. It's more than just by luck of geography that a distilled grape-based liquor gets to be part of an exclusive club. For one thing, any fruit base can result in a brandy. When it is made of grapes, there's no restriction on which parts of that fruit can be distilled into the finished product. In that sense, some brandies can more closely resemble Italian grappa in their distillation of pomace. Distillers of finer brandies are a little more selective about which parts of the grapes they use.

By contrast, the law limits Cognac makers to not only the best parts of the grape but only three actual grape varietals. About 97 percent use the Ugni-Blanc grape. The other 3 percent are Folle Blanche and Colombard[70]. Ugni-Blancs are known for their fairly high yield compared with traditional wine grapes. It takes a relatively long time for Ugni-Blancs to become ripe; but when they do there's usually a significant level of acidity and lower sugar content. Not only does the acid contribute to a wine's crispness, it acts as a necessary antioxidant; it protects the wine and, ultimately, the Cognac from the harmful effects of oxygen. Common table wines use sulfites to help preserve the flavor from oxygen's destructive wrath. Cognacs legally cannot. Such compounds could ruin the distillation and impart some distinctly unpleasant, not to mention potentially illness-inducing, flavors to the resulting spirit.

Another key distinguishing factor for Cognac is that it must be distilled twice in a copper pot still. And that is just the beginning, as, like with fine whiskey, time is arguably the most important ingredient.

If you've had any level of exposure to Cognac, even if you have, on occasion, walked past it in a liquor store and noticed it out of the corner of your eye, it's extremely likely you've encountered labels that have read either V.S., V.S.O.P., or X.O. Prior to my introduction to the spirit, I just thought it was some esoteric code that snooty, in-the-know aficionados used to communicate with one another at the exclusion of all others. You know, kind of like Klingon for high-end spirits fans. But if I had taken a moment to ask a store manager or bartender, I would have learned that there's a really easy, accessible explanation:

- V.S.: "VERY SPECIAL." Seriously, that's it. V.S. Cognacs must be aged a minimum of two years.
- V.S.O.P: "VERY SPECIAL OLD PALE." This one's a bit older, usually aged for at least four years.
- X.O. "You will kiss and hug this one." Kidding. It's actually, believe it or not, just "Extra Old." The youngest Cognac that goes into the blend must be at least six years old. There are often far older Cognacs in the blend.

Similar to whiskey, when Cognacs of different ages are blended, the declared age must reflect the youngest barrel in the blend. Some Cognac houses can go absolutely bonkers with the number of different barrels that end up in the blend—not because they're mad scientists but because they have a meticulous adherence to consistency. When a house packages the spirit for mass consumption, every single bottle must taste exactly alike, free of even the subtlest, most negligible deviation. Since it's virtually impossible—no, make that literally impossible—to replicate the nuances of a particular vintage from batch to batch, a blender must painstakingly siphon 7 percent from one barrel (say, a ten-year-old) 12 percent from another (maybe an eight-year-old), 11 percent from yet another (a fifteen-year-old) and so on. "It must have balance; it must have the same taste year over year,"[71] explains Manny Burnichon, who runs a company called Private Cask Imports that deals in higher-end Cognacs, among other spirits. "What the average consumer is looking for in a Cognac is to find a very particular taste with a specific brand. The V.S. of that brand should always taste the same, however, they're going to be different every year. So they have to keep blending different years to get a certain taste."

That means a brand might offer a V.S. expression that ostensibly is two years old, but it actually contains traces of a Cognac that's potentially decades old.

I'm going to go out on a limb and say that, save for the rare, experienced taster who can wax poetic about notes of dried tobacco and marzipan, most of us won't be able to zero in on such minuscule variations, vintage to vintage. However, when crafted in the hands of a Cognac house's seasoned master blenders, the flavor distinctions among V.S., V.S.O.P, and X.O. can be quite pronounced when sampled next to one another—especially a V.S. versus an X.O.

V.S. typically is an easy-drinking, highly mixable spirit with an aromatic fruitiness, but not much beyond that. The vast majority of mass-distributed Cognacs are of the V.S. variety. The average drinker might be combining it with Coca-Cola and couldn't really expound on the differences between brandy and Cognac.

Pass the V.S.O.P. threshold and hints of macerated cherry and other dried fruits, as well as toffee and coffee start to assert themselves on the palate. Aged a couple of more years and it enters X.O. territory; that's when a slight touch—but not too much—oxidation occurs, just enough to enable the wood in the barrel to impart dry nut and somewhat mushroomy notes. Occasionally, a taster might perceive a cigarish essence, even the cedar of the cigar box itself. There truly is a great deal going on once Cognac reaches six years old, and that's why the hardcore appreciators are willing to pay a premium for it.

"You have a bit more structure, a bit more elegance, a well-balanced smoothness," Burnichon says of X.O.

A notably good X.O. exhibits a markedly long finish, lingering like a fond memory of which the drinker refuses to let go. It still may be hanging around an hour after the sip. "This is the kind of talent that the distiller, the master blender brings," Burnichon points out. "He's been blending all of these different Cognacs, making sure it's superbalanced. It's like velvet, and it stays there forever."

In a perfect world, everyone who tastes Cognac with any regularity should be on a path to becoming an elite connoisseur. However, the world is far from perfect, and most sippers, appreciators, enthusiasts—whatever we want to call them—will never reach that extremely rarified air (I certainly won't). Nor need anyone strive for such an achievement. But some of the biggest names in the category are making it easier and easier for common folk like us to know what we're tasting and use some fundamental vocabulary to get us through a conversation with even the most insufferable pontificators.

Courvoisier, one of the best-known Cognac brands whose portfolio runs the gamut from crowd-pleasing, mass-marketed V.S.'s to ultra-über-high-end luxury expressions that would set a drinker back somewhere in the high five figures, works with everyone from professional chefs to perfume makers to make the flavors and aromas of their Cognacs as tangible as possible.

"The one thing that we try to explain right away is that they don't need to be connoisseurs necessarily to appreciate Cognac,"[72] says Courvoisier's global brand ambassador, Rebecca Asseline. "We try to break that cliché."

The brand, owned by global spirits conglomerate Beam Suntory, employs a tool called Le Nez (literally, "the nose"), which illustrates all of the key sensory elements that a taster may be experiencing.

"Working with perfumers and scent developers, we use key scents that resemble the key aromas of our Cognacs as developed and talked about by our master blender," Asseline explains.

In much the same way that perfume developers would workshop their scents, the Courvoisier team uses tiny bottles of essential oils for Cognac aroma comparison.

More likely that not, you won't have a cache of essential oil bottles on you when you're heading to a Cognac tasting. There are plenty of other less hardcore ways to appreciate the experience. First, if possible, taste it before lunch or dinner. It may seem counterintuitive (on a weekday, that prelunch tipple's especially hard to come by), but that's when your body is primed to connect with food or drink; your palate is much more attuned to what's happening if it's not already overloaded with flavors and aromas. Asseline recommends using an eight-ounce tulip versus the large balloon glass, when tasting. The smaller glass with the smaller rim brings your nose closer to the liquid, enabling you to experience the bouquet fully.

Despite the tendency to dilute the flavor of the base spirit in a mixed drink, it is possible to experience Cognac's complexity in a cocktail—if it's the right one.

In fact, some of the classic cocktails that traditionally have been bourbon or rye cocktails, such as the Old-Fashioned or the Sazerac (often credited as America's first cocktail), are making a comeback as Cognac cocktails. Many such creations started out as Cognac—or at least, non-AOC French brandy—drinks before whiskey took over.

They would have remained so had it not been for the phylloxera epidemic of the mid-nineteenth century, which pretty much obliterated

French grape vines and, therefore, wine and grape-based spirit exports to the United States. No one would argue that the relatively spare ingredients in a bourbon Old-Fashioned mute the character of the whiskey, and the same is true for Cognac. (To Wisconsinites, brandy is the only true base for an Old-Fashioned. In the Badger State, your server will give you the stink eye if you try to order a Wisconsin Old-Fashioned and ask, "What kind of bourbon do you use?")

Then, of course, there's the famous French 75, which combines Cognac with Champagne.

"Because people are a lot more interested in cocktails at the moment, we have been able to tap into our heritage and reintroduce Cognac as a spirit that has been, and can continue to be, enjoyed in the classics," Asseline reveals. "Because it is very, very aromatic, it is a fantastic base for cocktails. Over the past several years, we have been educating people that Cognac is far more than a digestif."

On the flipside of the cocktail curious, there's a small but growing contingent of drinkers who are gravitating to specialty expressions that are best experienced neat. As with other high-end spirits, not to mention beer categories, much of the credit goes to the foodie movement; people want to experience new flavor sensations and are willing to be a bit daring along the way. In the same way that they're embracing single-malt Scotch or single-barrel bourbon, they're seeking out spirits like single-cask or limited edition Cognacs. They're not expecting every release of a specific brand to taste exactly the same, year to year, bottle to bottle. In fact, they're hoping for the exact opposite. The thrill of the journey is comparing and contrasting a 2007 and a 2008 Cognac barreling, for instance. That dynamic is commonplace in wine, and serious drinkers want to apply it to other fine beverage categories, as well.

Such a mind-set is bringing a new wave of excitement to Cognac, with distillers daring to say, "Our products will not taste the same from year to year. If that's what you're looking for, go drink something else."

"Why," Burnichon posits, "do we have to blend it all the time to make it plain, to make it vanilla?"

Those artisanal leaps of faith will do little to augment mass sales, but they'll move mountains where buzz, creative momentum, and overall electricity are concerned. That's the future of Cognac, in a nutshell.

To help crack that shell a bit, try this flight.

REMY MARTIN VSOP (REMY COINTREAU)

For an introduction to V.S.O.P. level Cognacs, it never hurts to go with a dependable, widely distributed (i.e., easy to find) brand that's a solid representation of the style. Vanilla is quite apparent on the nose; on the palate, it's mostly fruit.

COURVOISIER CONNOISSEUR COLLECTION 12 YEAR OLD (BEAM SUNTORY)

It's a bit of a departure from the usual Cognac nomenclature (V.S., V.S.O.P., X.O., etc.), as it features, much like a fine whiskey, an age declaration. Twelve is the age of the youngest Cognac in the blend, which goes great with sweet desserts and chocolates.

PIERRE FERRAND RÉSERVE (COGNAC PIERRE FERRAND)

Fine confections come to mind when sipping the Pierre Ferrand Réserve. There's some really intense vanilla here, along with a few hints of cinnamon and baked apple.

MARTELL X.O. (PERNOD RICARD)

Come for the arch-shape bottle and deep amber-to-copper color; stay for the toasted oak, caramel, raisin and mildly spicy notes.

WEEK 29

PUCKER UP

THE SOUR SIDE OF BEER

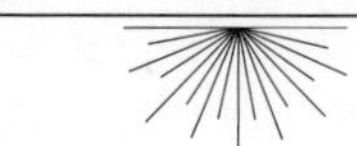

A BELGIAN SUMMER

We're not quite done celebrating European national holidays. France's Bastille Day undoubtedly gets most of the spotlight, but just a week later a neighboring country gets a significant observance of its own. July 21 is Belgian National Day and equally worth celebrating with some fine beverages—this is one of the world's great beer cultures we're talking about, after all. Since Belgium's stylistic contributions are many—and often emulated, as you'll discover, by some amazing US brews, I can't really do it justice in a single week. So we'll be extending the celebration across three whole weeks. We'll start things off on a sour note.

Pop culture wouldn't be pop culture if some influential medium or trendsetting pundit (the folks that marketing gurus like to call "tastemakers") wasn't deciding that "X is the new Y." (There's even a TV show called *Orange is the New Black*, for crying out loud). The craft brewing industry has not been immune to this phenomenon. On more than one occasion, someone in the know has declared, "Sour is the new hoppy." Without a doubt, hoppy brews—India pale ales (IPA) and the like—have represented the dominant flavor profile among craft drinkers for at least the past decade and a half or so and continue to do so. However, sour ales have come into their own as enthusiasts look for other ways to assault their palates with extreme flavors. And I mean that in the best possible way.

Where the IPAs of the world descended from the ancestral English style, sours are of Belgian extraction. Some of the greatest sours the world has ever known have emerged from the American craft scene;

the likes of Sonoma, California's, Russian River Brewing, and San Marcos, California's, The Lost Abbey turned sours into an American art form and get a lot of the credit for putting pucker-inducing potables on the map in the states.

Usually such New World breweries have been responsible for resurrecting styles long extinct, or at the very least, endangered in their countries of origin, but with sours, the styles were alive and well in Belgium long before the Yanks got their hands on them. And I say "styles," because "sour" is more a confederation of categories than a single variety—one of which we'll explore next week.

We'll focus this week on the flavor profiles for which no word other than sour does them justice.

My own personal entrée into the wonderful world of beer was through Belgium. I, like everyone else exposed only to mass-marketed macroproducts for most of their lives, thought of "beer" as the yellow, fizzy stuff I tried to buy as cheaply as possible ($8.99 for a twenty-four-pack of Busch Light was a frequent go-to in my formative years). That was until some friends invited me to a bar in Manhattan's West Village called Vol de Nuit, which sold only Belgian brews, paired with a very limited menu of Belgian cuisine—the national dish, moules frites (mussels and fries), was pretty much all you could get (the bar was generous enough to let you deconstruct it and make it an either/or proposition). At the time, I was so naïve, my reaction to the very existence of such a place was "They have beer in Belgium?"

After that, my world changed forever. It took me years to get a handle on the diversity of regional flavors and brewing traditions that have existed in Belgium for many hundreds of years. Sure, many of them died out in the late nineteenth or early twentieth century as multigenerational family-owned breweries realized they had to survive in a market that favored a single style that had become all the rage across Europe at the time: the lager known as pilsner, which maintains its lopsided hegemony across the globe today. But those local styles were reborn around the early 1960s when those same independent operators discovered that the next wave of survival meant differentiating one's products from those of the emerging megabrewers that had grown exponentially by scooping up smaller producers. Belgium became Belgium again—or, rather, this loose merger of French-speaking Wallonia and Flemish (Dutch) Flanders that we've called Belgium for nearly two hundred years. Among those were the sours, which achieved such acidic bite with the help of microorganisms like

Brettanomyces (or simply "brett"), the most commonly used "wild" yeast, and lactobacillus bacteria, which ferment sugars to lactic acid.

➳ Duchesse de Bourgogne (Brouwerij Verhaeghe-Vichte):
It's very likely that the first brand for anyone whose introduction to sours was by way of Flanders (like me) and not via American brewers was Duchesse de Bourgogne, the quintessential example of the Flemish brown. Despite its unmistakably French-sounding name, this Duchess of Burgundy is very much rooted in Flanders. Duchesse, the product of Brouwerij Verhaeghe-Vichte, whose family brewing history dates back to 1885, pours a reddish-brown. One's immediate impression on both the nose and palate is vinegar. It's striking for someone completely new to the style, but it has a way of growing on a person and ultimately becoming quite irresistible.

➳ Cuvée des Jacobins (Bockor Brewery):
Another Flemish brew with a Walloon name, Cuvée des Jacobins is a relatively new addition (2010, to be exact) to the portfolio of the 1892-founded Bockor Brewery. The reddish ale benefits from spontaneous fermentation (allowing ambient yeasts to get down to business and impart some intensely wild sour notes), as well as aging in giant wooden barrels known as foeders (made in France, where it's spelled foudre, but assembled at the brewery). It's a real treat being in the damp room that houses the foeder array. On a recent visit of my own, I couldn't get enough of inhaling the air, whose scent alternated between fruity sweetness and salad dressing acidity. My hosts had to drag me out of there.

➳ Rodenbach (Palm Breweries):
If Duchesse de Bourgogne isn't an American drinker's first taste of a genuine sour from Belgium, that honor probably belongs to Rodenbach. There are several iterations of the Flanders red ale, including Rodenbach proper (the most approachable for those new to the style), which has a fair heaping of tart cherry or cranberry notes. Rodenbach Grand Cru is a blend of less mature and old beer matured in foeders/foudres. The time spent in oak imparts some distinct woody notes, balancing some of the more vinegary elements. The holy grail within the Rodenbach line (only a very limited quantity makes it to the states) is Caractére Rouge, which spends two years in oak, followed by another six months aging with fresh cherries, raspberries, and cranberries. The fruit tempers the sour with a touch of sweet. Rodenbach, a brand that's nearly two hundred years old, is now owned by Palm Breweries, whose repertoire

also includes not just the eponymous Palm line, but Brugge Tripel, as well. Its home base is quite the vision; it's a castle-like stone manor complete with a stable of live horses.

»→ Monk's Café Flemish Sour Ale (Brewed Under Contract by Brouwerij Van Steenberge): Monk's bears mentioning because at the time of its release in the early 2000s, it was the product of something that didn't happen too often: a brewery in Belgium making a product for a bar in Philadelphia. Monk's, which has been a part of the beer scene in the City of Brotherly Love since 1997, was one of the pioneering establishments to embrace the wonders of Belgian beer. Cofounder Tom Peters is an icon of the local beer community. Such has been the bar's commitment to the traditions of Flanders and Wallonia that Brouwerij Van Steenberge began producing this Flemish sour brown under contract with Monk's. It's got all of the requisite—sour cherry notes and vinegar-like acidity, and you don't have to go to Philadelphia to get it. It's available all over the country in shops, bars, and restaurants that sell better beer.

Since I name-checked them earlier, here are a couple of prime examples of sours made on American soil:

»→ Supplication (Russian River Brewing Company): Russian River is a rare craft brewer that gets to have the best of many worlds as far as stylistic flavor profiles go. It has the hoppy thing all buttoned up with two of the most famous, if not the most famous, beer offerings: Pliny the Elder Double India Pale Ale and the extremely limited Pliny the Younger Triple IPA. The latter of those two is available at its Sonoma pub for only two weeks and in select distribution accounts each February. Russian River is equally famous for its range of sour varieties, notably Supplication, a seasonal ale aged for twelve months in Pinot Noir barrels with sour cherries. Brett, lactobacillus, and pediococcus microbes go to work on the sugars during that time, resulting in a 7 percent ABV treat that pours a reddish amber and sports a healthy dose of funk.

»→ Red Poppy (The Lost Abbey): Another California brewery, this one in the southern part of the state outside San Diego, The Lost Abbey is about as experimental as they come. Cofounder and brewery operations director Tomme Arthur is considered one of the great masters of the craft. The brewery calls its Red Poppy "a veritable celebration of sour cherries," and the very first whiff of it reveals that such a statement is no hyperbole. It starts as a brown ale, which hangs out in oak barrels for six-plus months with the usual wild microcritter cast of characters, giving it the signature tart and vanilla notes. The name comes from a flower indigenous to Flanders, from where this brew draws its obvious inspiration. Its alcohol content is a more modest 5.5 percent, so if you like this one, it's perfectly okay to have another.

***

We've focused this week primarily on reddish-brown ales from or inspired by the great independent brewers of Belgium. Next week things get considerably wilder.

Week 30

And So It Gueuze

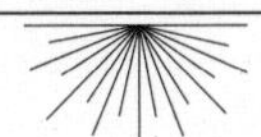

I've always found it intriguing that one of the first entry-level brands that introduces drinkers to Belgian brewing and often beer in general is Lindemans Framboise. The raspberry brew is extremely fruit and sweetness-forward, which makes it a suitable bridge for the "I don't like beer" set—those whose exposure to the beverage has been mostly through mass-marketed macrolagers .

What makes Lindemans such an odd gateway is that it's a lambic, one of the most challenging styles to come out of Belgium, if not the entire world. Where most brewers use carefully cultivated yeast strains to work their alcohol- and bubble-producing magic, lambic producers rely on whatever funky microfauna Mother Nature can muster (there's that spontaneous fermentation concept again). The most game of these wee-beasties are particularly abundant in the greater Brussels area; that's why the country's lambic brewers are concentrated in that region.

A tour of one of the most revered of this type, Cantillon Brewery, reveals dank, dusty, cobwebby fermentation chambers. No, they're not just lazy and no, the cleaning staff hasn't taken the year off. Such conditions create the right sort of party atmosphere for these wild yeast and bacteria to get really crazy.

When it's ready to be drunk, "tart" doesn't even begin to cover the taste of unadulterated lambic beer. That's like calling a ghost pepper "spicy." And it's for that reason that international markets primarily have tasted the fruitier varieties. Raspberry is the most popular, but peach, apple, black currant, and blueberry aren't uncommon. They'll include either real fruit or a syrupy extract, which dramatically tempers the lambic funk, making them as inoffensive as possible for the untrained palate.

Fruit beers, as polarizing as they can be, at least can be credited with introducing the word lambic into the mainstream consumer lexicon. By extension, we can thank lambics for expanding the vocabularies of more seasoned beer drinkers with the addition of another term: gueuze (combine "good" and "lose" and that's the closest you'll get to the pronunciation). In its simplest form, gueuze is a blend of lambics. Generally, a brewer will combine a younger with a more mature, oude (old) lambic (specifically, blending a one-year-old with a two-year-old and a three-year-old). The less mature lambic would be less dry than the older one since enough time hasn't passed to ferment away most of the sugars. The residual sweetness facilitates a secondary fermentation once the old and the new are married, giving the beer its natural carbonation. The resulting liquid is a feast of funk that is greater than the sum of its parts.

Gueuze actually owes a great deal of its blending method to Champagne and a certain Benedictine monk named Dom Pérignon—yes, that one—who inaugurated the era of modern bubbly by combining different nonsparkling white wines.

Not long after, brewers started doing the same thing. They'd taste a wide range of lambics before they settled on the five or so that would make the cut to become gueuze. Forget what the ads used to say about Miller High Life. Gueuze is the real champagne of beers (in fact, there was a time when it was called "The Champagne of Brussels").

Strong in flavor does not necessarily translate to strong in alcohol content. Most of the better gueuzes one would encounter range between about 5 and 7 percent ABV. If the aggressive boldness doesn't keep you from getting to the bottom of your glass and you're primed for another, it won't knock you off your barstool.

CANTILLON GUEUZE 100% LAMBIC (CANTILLON BREWERY):

Cantillon makes what is perhaps the gold standard of gueuze. The brewery hasn't changed its production methods since its founding in 1900—except for its designation as 100 percent organic in 1999.

OUDE BOON GUEUZE (BROUWERIJ BOON):

Ninety percent of Brouwerij Boon's Oude Gueuze is a mild eighteen-month-old lambic, 5 percent is a strong three-year-old, and the remaining 5 percent consists of very young lambic, which kick-starts the secondary fermentation. The flavor alternates between vinous sourness and gingery cooking spices.

TIMMERMANS OUDE GUEUZE LAMBICUS (MARTIN'S FINEST BEER SELECTION):

Timmermans says its family's first foray into gueuze commenced more than three centuries ago. The tradition continues as part of the portfolio of Britain's Martin's Finest Beer Selection, which acquired the brand in 1993. Timmermans Oude Gueuze evokes yeasty Champagnes, citrus fruit, and dry, pungent ciders.

LINDEMANS GUEUZE CUVÉE RENÉ (BROUWERIJ LINDEMANS):

It's a minor tragedy that in the United States Lindemans has become nearly synonymous with "that sweet raspberry beer." Brouwerij Lindemans offers so much more than its fruit lambics, and its gueuze, Cuvée René, is a stellar testament to its brewing prowess. The hazy, golden pour reveals an orchestra of flavors, from grapefruit, to deeply acidic cider vinegar, to sour apples and even a bit of strong cheese thrown in for good measure.

The fact that many of those breweries are better known to a larger slice of the legal-drinking-age population is not something those producers spend too much time lamenting. Berry, cherry, and apple brews may not be every consummate beer geek's cup of tea, but they've proved to be an effective survival tactic for the brewers in the Brussels region—one that essentially has kept their often intimidating styles alive over the centuries. And the producers are grateful to have those more accessibly crowd-pleasing brews as a means to an end. Most of the market demands the sweet beers and the sale of those beers has been supporting the production of the far less mainstream ones.

If you've got friends to whom you're preaching the gospel of beer and trying to convert them to the world of fine fermentables, gueuze is not likely the style that is going to win them over. It's a flavor to which one must graduate and it's not going to happen overnight.

There's really no rush, though. Gueuzes have an epic shelf life of about two decades. Buy those bottles now and store them in the basement so they're out of sight and out of mind. Remind your friends three, five, ten, or even twenty years into their beer journeys that something's waiting for them downstairs. In the meantime, next week's brews should give everyone's palate a nice workout.

Week 31

All the Trappist Trappings

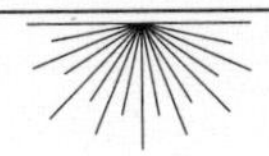

A funny thing happened on the way to Belgium. Somewhere along the line, the world went topsy-turvy and beer just went completely, barking mad. What other explanation is there for the fact that in just the past handful of years—though it seems to have happened overnight during the redeye to Brussels—the country that has been the Shangri-La of drinking pilgrimages for American beer enthusiasts is looking more and more like the place those travelers just left. That's because growing numbers of Belgium's most traditional breweries increasingly have been taking a cue from US craft beer producers and incorporating decidedly twenty-first-century American traditions into their portfolios. Who would ever have thought there'd be such a beer as Belgo-style IPA? Let's try to get our minds around that for a moment, shall we? The English invented what became known as India Pale Ale some three hundred years ago. Late twentieth-century American craft brewers reinvented the hop-forward style, putting aggressively floral and citrusy US-grown hop varietals on the map. By the beginning of the twenty-first century it had become the most popular craft beer style in the United States, if not the world. And now, the Belgians, whose own styles have been venerated by American brewers and drinkers alike—indeed, Belgium's beery bounty was my entry point to that world—are adopting and tweaking a style from the Americans, who previously had adopted and tweaked the style from the British.

That being said, they're all fine beers, with more than enough Belgian personality shining through the overabundance of hops (Belgium previously had been known for its brewers' sparing use of the bitter green flowers).

But call me a purist and a romantic. When I think Belgium, I think Saisons, Flemish Sours, Witbier, and, of course, Abbey Dubbels and Tripels.

Brewing, in most parts of Europe, began with the monks in the Middle Ages. And when it comes to those latter two styles, there's still a chance to drink some handcrafted by the holy robed fellows. The ones that are monastery-made are pretty easy to spot; they all bear the "Trappist" designation on the label.

Belgium still boasts the largest number of operating Trappist breweries—six—but their non-Belgo ranks are starting to gain on that tally. There now are five outside of Belgium: two right next door in the Netherlands, one in Austria, and one—ready for this—in Massachusetts. The first Trappist producer in the United States, the St. Joseph Abbey, commenced its brewing operations in 2013. The newest to join the ranks is Italy's Tre Fontane, which received its official designation from the International Trappist Association in May 2015. [73]

Others were fairly recent additions as well. In 2012, Austria's Stift Engelszell received its approval as a Trappist brewer. In 2014, Brouwerij Abdij Maria Toevlucht fired up its brew kettle, joining fellow Dutch operation, Brouwerij de Koningshoeven.

It is, of course, their Belgian elders that come up most when the conversation turns to Trappist beer. Before I list those, you need to bone up on your Dutch. Well, two words anyway. Abdij means "abbey" and brouwerij, if you haven't already guessed, is the word for "brewery." Lesson over. The six legendary Belgian Trappist brewers are as follows.

- Brasserie Chimay
- Brasserie de Rochefort
- Abdij St-Sixtus (better known as Brouwerij Westvleteren)
- Brasserie d'Orval
- Brouwerij der Sint-Benedictusabdij de Achelse Kluis (mercifully known simply as "Achel")
- Brouwerij der Trappisten van Westmalle

Each is famous in its own way, but some are better known for one style over another. Actually, style is a very loosely defined word in this case. When the Trappist Brotherhood started making beer, it originally was for their own consumption. Sometimes it was their only food source, especially during those fasting periods when they shunned solid sustenance. There were no stylistic guidelines; they brewed what they could with what they had. If it was strong, it was a dubbel (double). If it was stronger, it was a tripel (triple). Any categorical specifications came much later, applied by connoisseurs—the outsiders looking in. However, more often than not, dubbels tend to be on the darker side. Tripels often are considerably paler. Some of the brewers take things a bit further, crossing into quadruple territory, which usually are above 10 percent ABV (sometimes upwards of 11 and close to 12), dark, and very malty in character. The Trappists rarely make a bad beer; if you see the Trappist label—Chimay has the most widely available brews—buy it. But there are a few specific beers that are worth noting (going to stick with the Belgians):

WESTMALLE TRIPEL
(BROUWERIJ DER TRAPPISTEN VAN WESTMALLE)

It's up for debate, but in my humble yet educated opinion, the gold standard of Trappist Tripels is Westmalle Tripel. The brothers at Abdij der Trappisten van Westmalle first brewed the iconic Tripel in 1934, fine-tuned it for a couple of decades, and ultimately settled on a recipe that hasn't changed since 1956. It's 9.5 percent ABV (markedly more potent than its older Dubbel, which registers at 7 percent) and is quite dry, yet pleasantly fruity. When poured properly into the correct serving receptacle (the wide-mouthed, stemmed goblet), it sports a thick, creamy head that's retained for the bulk of the drinking session.

ROCHEFORT 8
(BRASSERIE DE ROCHEFORT)

The Rochefort abbey's brewing roots can be traced back more than four centuries, but Rochefort 8 goes back only about sixty years.

The dark, malty ale is north of 9 percent ABV and pours on the dark side—somewhere between dark amber and full-on brown. Flavorwise there's quite a bit of darkness as well—dark fruit that is, things like dates, raisins, and figs come to mind. Also worth trying, if you can find it, is the lighter-in-alcohol Rochefort 6, which registers a 7.5 percent ABV. The problem is the 6 accounts for only a tiny fraction of the brewery's output. The monks only brew it about once a year, while the 8 is a year-round offering. If you want to go in the stronger direction, there's Rochefort 10, which is a hefty 11.3 percent ABV.

ORVAL TRAPPIST ALE
(BRASSERIE D'ORVAL)

One of the most attractive attributes of the Trappist ales is that, despite their reputation as being alcoholically oppressive, there really is something for everyone. Some, dare I say, even border on sessionable.

Orval Trappist Ale fits that bill. It's got an ABV in the mid-6 percent range, sometimes as low as 6.2, sometimes approaching 7. (The lack of definitiveness is due to the bottle conditioning, typical of Belgian ales. The brewers drop live yeast in the bottle to get the secondary fermentation going. That's what naturally carbonates the beer. Depending on how hungry the yeast is, it might eat more of the fermentable sugar, resulting in a dryer, slightly higher ABV brew.)

Though it might seem strong by conventional standards, it's fairly mild by Belgian monk standards. If one were to put a label on it, Orval would fit most comfortably in the Belgian pale ale category. There's actually a notable hop aroma, thanks to its dry-hopping, which sets it apart from the other Trappists.

To taste a genuine Trappist-brewed session beer, a trip to the monastery is mandatory. That's the only place to find Petite Orval, a 3.5 percent pale brewed only for monk consumption but available for purchase in limited quantities at the abbey and its nearby café.

That's actually quite typical, by the way. Monks usually brew variations of their flagships that have much lower alcohol content for their own regular consumption. It makes a great deal of sense since it would be impractical for anyone to drink a 7, 8, 9, or 10 percent beer daily.

WESTVLETEREN 12
(ABDIJ ST-SIXTUS/BROUWERIJ WESTVLETEREN)

Now for a little bit of controversy: As with any passionate, rabid subculture, there on occasion can be, dare I say, a bit of a hive mentality. That dynamic rears its ugly head when it comes to one Trappist brewery in particular, Sint-Sixtus, aka Westvleteren (Westvleteren is the Flemish town the abbey calls home). Many beer geeks (I use the term lovingly, as I myself wear the label with pride) deemed one brew in its portfolio, Westvleteren 12, the best beer in the world. Stylistically, it's been called a quadruple by the categorization-obsessed (it's 10.2 percent ABV), but it's equally at home as a tripel. Westvleteren's most widely available is its 8, which is a dubbel, and there is no tripel per se in its bag of tricks.

The debate lies not in whatever stylistic taxonomy one should apply to Westvleteren 12, but on whether a beer, when experienced through the filter of rarity, automatically achieves mythical status. And whether it lives up to the hype.

Here's the thing about Westvleteren. It's almost never available for sale outside the abbey; those who want it usually have to trek to the small rural town after which it's named and buy a case. I say almost never because for a very limited time in 2012, 3,750 cases (fifteen thousand six-packs) of 12 (the year is just a coincidence), were shipped to the United States for sale in legal channels to help pay for an abbey renovation project.

Sure, plenty of beer fanatics have procured it through unsavory methods—scalpers make repeated trips to the abbey and mark it up exponentially for sale on the Internet—but the only officially sanctioned point of purchase is the brewery (a unique facet among Trappist breweries, as the rest distribute outside their four walls). And it's gotten harder to buy it even there. On my first trip to Belgium in November 2005, my wife and I were able to roll up in our rental car unannounced and buy a case. These days, don't even think of going anywhere near the place without calling ahead and making an appointment first.

Sounds like a pain, but it adds to the romance and sense of scarcity. It also feeds the white whale worship that surrounds the brand. Social media has only added fuel to that fire with Instagram pics and tweets that boast, "Look what I'm drinking!"

That's not to say Westvleteren 12 isn't a good beer. It's a great beer. Fantastic. World class, even. But it's really no "better" than—though arguably as good as—Westmalle Tripel, Orval, Rochefort, Chimay, or many other Trappist and non-Trappist ales.

Defining what's "good" is an incredibly subjective task anyway. The best advice is to like what you're going to like and don't succumb to the hive mind that too often runs rampant among the beer-loving population.

Week 32

Make a Bee-Line for Modern Mead

Remember how moonshine and gin got their own designated holidays? Well, it seems like there's an official occasion for just about everything: mead, the fermented honey-based beverage, gets its own special day, typically observed on the first Saturday in August.

The first time most of us ever had any sort of exposure to mead was, rather tangentially, in high school literature class when we were studying Beowulf (and/or Grendel, if you prefer), with all of its references to the "mead hall." A more minute number of us may then have actually sampled some of the honey-based beverage that a group of sword-and-sorcery cosplay folks were pouring at your friendly neighborhood renaissance faire.

Increasingly, however, curious imbibers have been able to taste the real deal out in the real world, as there are some two hundred or so operating commercial meaderies in the United States alone[74]. Okay, around fifty of those also make wine and/or beer, but that still leaves one hundred fifty whose sole business is the alcoholic fruits of honeybees' (and yeast's) labor. Some of those meaderies even have formed their own trade group, the American Mead Makers Association (AMMA), officially incorporated in 2012, though a less formal confederation of producers existed for years prior.

The advent of mead dramatically predates medieval times—as well as the Roman Empire and, hell, even the Moses-y antics in the Book of Exodus for that matter. Some archaeologists place its origins at around 6000 BCE[75]

There's such a diversity of mead styles that it's sometimes hard to believe that it's just one beverage category. To be classified as mead, more than half of the fermentable base should be honey (there are sometimes exceptions). AMMA lists forty-one official styles of mead as of the publication of this book, but given the volume of innovation that's starting to kick up in the segment, I wouldn't be surprised if that number's already past fifty.

Some of the key styles, as defined by AMMA[76]:

- **Traditional** is as basic as it gets, nothing but honey, water, and yeast.
- **Acerglyn** is likely to be quite popular in Vermont and eastern Canada, as it blends honey with maple syrup.
- **Braggot** is a honey/beer hybrid; it was originally brewed with honey and hops and later with honey and malt (with or without hops).
- **Cyser** is with apple juice added and, for obvious reasons, popular with cider drinkers.
- **Hydromel's** literal translation (from Greek) is "water honey," but it's most commonly used to describe a lighter traditional mead.
- **Melomel** is the umbrella term for any mead made with fruit; cyser would fit under that broader heading.
- **Metheglin** is kind of like "mulled mead;" it's made with spices like cloves, vanilla, cinnamon, and certain teas.
- **Pyment** is the style with which it wouldn't be technically wrong to call it "honey wine;" it blends honey with red or white grapes. AMMA notes that pyment made with white grape juice may be referred to as "white mead."
- **Sack** is to mead what "extra cheese" is to pizza; more honey than normal is used, often achieving higher alcohol contents.

»→ **Frankenmel** is mead makers' sense of humor at work. It's just as it sounds: an experimental creation—a monster mead, if you will, that doesn't fit neatly into any of the established style categories

Depending on the style, meads can range from about 6 percent (cysers and braggots and such) to 18 percent (traditional meads) ABV.

One of the largest producers of mead and many of its variants has been Sunnyvale, California's, Rabbit's Foot Meadery, which was also one of the pioneers of the modern movement. Michael Faul, who founded the company with his wife, Maria, in 1995, has become one of the nation's leading authorities on the beverage; he's even published an online guide to mead making.

Despite the fact that more drinkers are becoming hip to what mead actually is, the way to entice newcomers, Faul reveals, is with anything but the traditional honey, water, and yeast version. "I don't start off by trying to explain what mead is, I usually start off trying to say, 'here's something you probably already know, and let's work backward from that.' I usually introduce them to two other versions of mead: cyser, which is honey cider, and braggot, which is honey ale. They usually understand what those two things are and then I'd say, 'well, if you just took the malt out or took the apple juice out, you'd have mead." [77]

One of the most visible of the relative newcomers to the category—the operative word being relative, as the company officially launched in 2008—is Michigan's B. Nektar Meadery, founded by another husband-and-wife duo, Brad and Kerri Dahlhofer. B. Nektar has gained a bit of a reputation as the irreverent badasses of the fermented honey world.

While B. Nektar produces some traditional meads, both still and sparkling, they really grabbed the headlines and earned a cult following with the likes of Zombie Killer and Kill All the Golfers. (Lots of killing! Anger issues much?)

Zombie Killer is a riff on the cyser style of mead, but takes it a step further and adds some cherry juice to the mixture, post-fermentation. The label features a disturbing illustration of an anthropomorphized cherry, and an angry one at that, taking a katana sword to the head of an equally anthropomorphized cherry, spilling some deep-red blood . . . er, cherry juice.

Interestingly, what turned out to be B. Nektar's flagship was only ever meant to be a one-off, extremely limited batch offering.

"I will not say it was an accident,"[78] Brad Dahlhofer tells me during my visit to B. Nektar's Ferndale, Michigan, production headquarters, "but it was not planned to be our big best seller."

A distributor in North Carolina had requested that B. Nektar make a draught cherry mead, as one of that wholesaler's restaurant customers made cherries a central part of its identity. Dahlhofer and his team had to wing it, as they didn't have the appropriate equipment to make draught mead at the time. "We didn't have the bright tanks, the counter-pressure bottle fillers, keg cleaners, and that sort of stuff," Dahlhofer recalls. "We were putting it in kegs, putting it on CO_2 and just mixing it up to get the carbonation. We whipped up like ninety gallons of it."

It happened to be fall, so that's where the apples came in. The lower ABV was more out of necessity than anything else: To do something in the neighborhood of 14 percent ABV would have been too cost-prohibitive from a fermentable sugar raw material standpoint, especially on a batch that small, and the restaurant in North Carolina would have been none-too-pleased to have to absorb that extra expense.

"We called the distributor to tell them it's ready," Dahlhofer notes, "and they're, like, 'What?' The cherry mead in kegs you wanted. 'Oh, that restaurant went out of business, so, yeah, we won't be needing that anymore.'"

B. Nektar managed to talk the distributor into taking two of the kegs, but the mead makers had to figure out what to do with the rest of them. One member of the B. Nektar team, an avid fan of the graphic novel and now blockbuster TV series *The Walking Dead*, ("We're all geeks," Dahlhofer points out) suggested calling it a fairly unintelligible grunt that hungry zombies emit—something along the lines of "Raarrrrgh."

"We figured people wouldn't be able to read or pronounce it, so we settled on Zombie Killer," Dahlhofer reveals. "And it just took on a life of its own."

So much so that there were lines out the door of people waiting to make their two-bottle-maximum purchase.

The Dahlhofers and their staff knew they were on to something, so they took out a bank loan and invested in all the requisite equipment to scale up the production run of Zombie Killer.

Another unplanned twist of fate resulted in a limited-release, barrel-aged riff on Zombie Killer called Zombies Take Manhattan. It started off as a normal batch of the former, but, for some reason, the B. Nektar crew couldn't get it to stop fermenting.

"[The yeast] just kept eating everything we would throw at it," Dahlhofer explains—apropos, considering that's not unlike the type of behavior one would expect from undead walking corpses. The meadery's production manager conceded that they were very likely going to have to dump the batch.

"So I said, let's not be hasty, let's sit down, let's think about it," Dahlhofer says. "We all sat there smelling it. I'm kind of smelling bitters, and we're getting cherry coming through."

Those, they realized, were components of the classic cocktail, the Manhattan. All that was missing was the rye whiskey. So they threw it into some used rye whiskey barrels, aged it a bit and, lo and behold, it ended up tasting quite good. Thus, Zombies Take Manhattan was born.

B. Nektar's beat-of-a-different-drummer approach has earned praise, as well as a few jeers from its mead-making peers. "I get everything from people loving it to people saying it's not real mead because it's not sweet enough, it's not 18 percent," Dahlhofer admits. "But overall, the majority of people have been receptive to it."

Now, go forth on your fermented-honey adventures. It would be a shame for all of the bees' hard work to go unappreciated. Here are a few more, fresh from the hive:

RABBIT'S FOOT SWEET MEAD AND DRY MEAD

(Rabbit's Foot Meadery)

In its sweet, traditional offering, there's plenty of residual sugar giving it its sweet profile. It's 12 percent ABV and great with dessert.

By contrast, Rabbit's Foot Dry Mead has less residual sugar and a slightly higher ABV (13 percent).

SWEET MINT JULEP

(Kuhnhenn Brewing Company)

Michigan brewer Kuhnhenn is known for its beers, but it also makes a couple of well-crafted meads. Sweet Mint Julep, which falls under the metheglin heading, takes its original Sweet OB hydromel-style mead, adds spearmint tea, and ages it in bourbon barrels.

KILL ALL THE GOLFERS

(B. Nektar Meadery)

Did someone say tea? Kill All the Golfers is B. Nektar's alcoholic take on a classic Arnold Palmer (hence, the name that would make everyone in the PGA cringe), mixing honey with black tea and fresh-squeezed lemon juice. If the name sounds familiar, it's not déjà vu. It was part of a Carl Spackler (Bill Murray) line from *Caddyshack*. In fact, the label features all sorts of *Caddyshack* Easter eggs: the notorious Bushwood Country Club gopher, wearing Spackler's trademark hat, is driving a golf cart on an exploding green. Kill All the Golfers fits most comfortably under the Frankenmel umbrella.

REDSTONE BLUEBERRY

(Redstone Meadery)

Boulder, Colorado's, Redstone Meadery offers this melomel brewed with blueberry puree. The sweet mead has a cranberry hue and is 12 percent ABV.

Week 33
The Wine Taster's Blues

Blueberry Wine

Sometimes you've got to work with what you've got. That seems to be the overarching ethos for folks who want to make wine, but through some geographic twist of fate, don't get to live in climates similar to Napa or Bordeaux. If you've ever visited the wine countries in colder parts of the country and you've tasted a glass of a relatively high-volume product, chances are a good chunk of the grapes in the glass came from somewhere else. (This isn't some dirty little secret. The wineries are usually upfront about it.) Yes, they've got the vines out back with real grapes growing on them, but do the math.

Though grape-based wines are always going to be the bread and butter no matter where a winery falls on the latitude/longitude grid, some have gotten quite adept employing secondary fruits, those with which Mother Nature is far more forgiving. Since August typically marks the tail end of the North American blueberry harvest, let's focus on those sweet little spheres.

With a color and consistency similar to many types of grapes, blueberries have fed a veritable wine category of their own. It doesn't hurt that blueberries have been labeled a "superfruit" for their high antioxidant content (whether you buy into that sort of thing or not).

Bartlett Winery

If there's one agricultural product with which Maine is nearly synonymous, it's the blueberry. It should come as no surprise then that the Pine Tree State hosts some fairly robust blueberry wine business.

The berry is the main attraction at Bartlett Winery in Gouldsboro, Maine. In fact, it foregoes grapes entirely—every one of its reds is blueberry-based. When founders Bob and Kathe Bartlett moved to Maine from Michigan back in 1975, they were keen to open a winery and had every intention to use grapes.

"We planted a small, experimental vineyard, thinking we might have a microclimate where we could do that because we were close to the coast,"[79] remembers Bob Bartlett. But the severe winters in those first few years had other plans for them.

The weather didn't shake the Bartlett's resolve to make high-quality wines, so they started playing around with various fruits. At the time, however, nongrape fruit wines didn't have the greatest reputation. They were often sweet and completely unbalanced (many still are).

"They had never been taken seriously, but for us it was what we had to work with," Bob says. "We didn't want to bring in grapes or juice from other states. It was all about Maine agriculture."

The Bartletts, therefore, sought to defy convention with wines tilting toward the dry end of the spectrum.

A combination of oaks help age the aptly named Blueberry Dry, whose discernible tang makes it an ideal companion for cold-weather stews, lamb, or anything seasoned with generous helpings of rosemary, sage, and thyme.

Meanwhile, Bartlett's limited-release Blueberry Winemakers Reserve is aged in French oak barrels and is rich and full-bodied enough to hold up against wild game. The reserve scored a major coup in 1996 when Wine Enthusiast magazine named it among the one hundred best wines, sharing the spotlight with traditional grape-based reds.

Even the most seasoned aficionados have been stumped by how closely the flavor and structure of Barlett's blueberry brands resemble vineyard-grown red varietals.

Several years back, the winery teamed up with a grape wine distributor to conduct a blind tasting. The Bartlett blueberry range was pitted against traditional European reds. "We listed them on a sheet and had the public try to pick out what's what," Bartlett notes. "What was interesting was that a lot of times our wines were thought to be the

European grape wines, which was really bizarre. There was a reserve Chianti against our Dry Oak Blueberry, and they thought our blueberry was the Chianti."

The Bartlett portfolio also includes some fruit blends. Coastal Red, for instance, combines blueberries with Maine apples for a drink that could be classified as a wine/cider hybrid. It's light and fruity and quite versatile with a range of foods.

Additionally, the winery produces some grape blends, such as a Blueberry Zinfandel and a Blueberry Sangiovese. Those two, incidentally, are sold only in Maine, thanks to an inexplicable federal law courtesy of the Alcohol and Tobacco Tax and Trade Bureau (TTB); TTB doesn't allow the blending of grapes with other fruits. Bartlett also operates a distillery.

SAVAGE OAKES VINEYARD

Another of Maine's key players is Savage Oakes Vineyard in the town of Union. For a New England winery, Savage Oakes boasts an impressive range of products composed entirely of Maine-grown grapes, but it wisely has supplemented that business with brands derived from the state's fruitiest bounty. Its Blue Moon is a dry offering made with the winery's estate-grown wild blueberries aged in oak. For the sweet-tooth inclined, there's Blueberry Pi, a full-on dessert wine that's satisfying enough to make a drinker forego the actual dessert.

BOYDEN VALLEY WINERY

In a neighboring New England state, Vermont's Boyden Valley Winery is known throughout the region for its fruit wines, particularly its Blueberry. Boyden Valley gathers low bush Vermont blueberries for a semisweet, full-bodied experience perfect for those after-dinner sipping occasions. It's actually the rare wine to come in a cobalt blue bottle, for those who like to hang on to such things. Boyden also makes wines from cranberry and rhubarb, as well as some more traditional grape creations.

TOMASELLO WINERY

A few hundred miles south, the Tomasello Winery in Hammonton, New Jersey, also makes plenty of wines made from grapes grown on its estates—Southeastern Jersey's Outer Coastal Plain is a bona fide appellation, with a longer growing season than the rest of the state. But it also has a celebrated portfolio of alternative fruit wines. The flagship of the lot is the semidry Tomasello Blueberry Wine, made entirely of high bush blueberries cultivated in the region. Tomasello also produces a sparkling 100 percent blueberry wine designed as a bubbly aperitif or after-dinner cheese or dessert pairing, as well as a Blueberry Moscato blend. The estate doesn't stop at the blueberry; it boasts a vast array of wines made from blackberries, raspberries, pomegranates, and cranberries.

BEAR CREEK WINERY

Remote doesn't even begin to describe Bear Creek; it's in Alaska after all, and that's just the way its owners like it. Obviously, when wine happens up in the forty-ninth state, a hell of a lot of improvisation is involved. Bear Creek has a popular (for Alaska) wine made entirely of blueberries, but it also has some multifruit blends that marry the blues with strawberries, rhubarb, and raspberries. Despite the fact that grapes and near-arctic conditions don't mix well, Bear Creek does market some combos that blend grapes with some of those other fruits.

Undoubtedly there are purists out there who probably believe it is a prosecutable offense to write this sort of love letter to wines born of anything other than the precious grape. Further, it's likely that many of them insist any fermented nongrape fruit beverage be called anything but wine. Personally, I'll make that concession for apples and pears; if apples and pears are fermented (but not distilled), it's a cider, pure and simple, despite the fact that many label their products "apple wine." But berries are kind of grapes' cousins and, therefore, worthy of the "wine" designation.

Week 34
ANDEAN ALCOHOL
PISCO

Let's get back to grapes for a moment.

The most remarkable thing about those little vine-grown oblong spheres of fermentable juiciness is that they enjoy a spirited afterlife that transcends world cultures.

As we've explored, Italy has its grappa, France has its Cognac, and most of the rest of the world has its brandy. South America, though, has a grape-derived spirit of its own that was, until relatively recently, barely on the radar of the neighboring continent to the north.

Native to Andean cultures, pisco ("pea-sco") enjoys a regional history that's said to span close to four centuries.

"We have a five-hundred-year tradition of grapes in Peru,"[80] says Peruvian-born Melanie da Trindade-Asher, who, with her sister, Lizzie, launched the Macchu Pisco brand. "The Spaniards brought the grapes to the Viceroyalty of Peru, and the Jesuits were the ones who started making pisco."

It is, therefore, yet another world-class drink we can credit to the clergy; religion and imbibing are inextricably linked through history.

As the story goes, Spain's King Felipe II in 1641 banned Peruvian wine production to fend off competition Spanish producers faced from imports of New World wines. To dodge the ban, Peru's wine makers distilled their grapes into pisco. Despite those centuries of tradition, pisco is still relatively obscure in the post-Prohibition United States. But that's gradually changing.

One of the largest hurdles US pisco importers face is explaining exactly what it is. Many North American drinkers assume its Latin American heritage makes it a close cousin of tequila. While it's perfectly acceptable as a tequila substitute, the two share very little in common.

"I always say to people, pisco gives you much more than vodka, which is completely neutral,"[81] explains Lizzie da Trindade-Asher. "And it's less affronting than would be a tequila or gin with all of the juniper notes. You would get a similar and yet different cocktail—a surprising twist on whatever your expectations were."

Peru and Chile are engaged in a bit of a pisco tug-of-war, each distilling the spirit and each laying claim to its origin and legitimacy.

Peru asserts that it has exclusive ownership of the term, as a protected appellation. The country in 2009 petitioned the European Union to register "pisco" as a geographic designation, given that much of its export business is European. Indeed, much of Europe now recognizes Peru as the place of origin, but there are still countries on the continent that allow Chilean products to bear the pisco label. The United States also allows Chile's products to be categorized as such—as long as they adhere to certain alcohol content requirements, which align more closely with Peru's pisco definition: between 40 and 43 percent ABV (some Chilean products are as low as 29 percent).

There's even a debate over the linguistic origins of the term. Peruvian linguists say that pisco derives from the word for "bird" in Quechua, the ancient tongue of the indigenous peoples of the region. Those supporting this theory say it's a nod to the robust ornithological population in the pisco-producing valleys of Peru.

Chilean scholars, not surprisingly, reject that interpretation, noting that the term likely derived from a word that refers to a clay-and-mud container, a typical vessel for early pisco.

It's a little above my pay grade to be mediating a debate clouded by five hundred years of fuzzy history like some Renaissance-era referee. It's especially murky considering that on early maps, the Viceroyalty of Peru included Chile.[82] For the sake of harmony, let's just say "it's complicated," but, were a gun at my head, I might say I tilt slightly toward the Peruvian side. And, good or bad, both countries' piscos have a right to exist.

That's not to imply Chilean and Peruvian piscos are exactly alike. Each has country-specific guidelines for its production, though Peruvian standards and their enforcement are significantly more rigid. The biggest restriction is that it must be made from one or a combination of eight specific grape varietals: Quebranta, Negra Criolla, Mollar, Uvina, Italia, Torontel, Moscatel, and Albilla.

Three classifications exist, as per the Peruvian government:

Pisco Puro: Puro, meaning "pure," refers to the use of only one grape varietal in production

Pisco Acholado: A blend of any number of the designated grape varietals

Pisco Mosto Verde: These are on the sweeter side because they're distilled from a wine that hasn't been completely fermented. There's still a high concentration of sugar left.

Peruvian pisco may be distilled only once, thereby retaining much of the character of the original fruit. Once distillation is complete, Peruvian piscos must undergo a maturation period of at least three months. And it can't be in wood; aging must take place in either stainless steel or glass, neither of which has any influence on the flavor or color. Flavor and aroma cannot be augmented in any way post-distillation. Peruvian distillers can't even add water once it enters the aging vessel.

While Chilé, by comparison, has standardized pisco production to some extent, it mandates no minimum maturation period. What's more, there are no restrictions on the number of distillations it goes through. The more rounds through the still, the more it's neutralized; in that sense it can approach vodka in character.

Another key difference is that where Peruvians can use one of eight grapes, Chilean producers generally stick with three: Moscato (the dominant varietal), Torontel, and Pedro Ximénez. Additionally, Chileans are allowed to barrel-age their pisco; Peruvians are not.

And those who already are familiar with it are more likely to default to its best-known drink, the pisco sour: pisco, lime juice, simple syrup, egg white, bitters, and ice. It's a fine cocktail and considered the national drink of Peru, but kind of yesterday's news. To explore the spirit a bit further, there is a wide array of classic, pisco-specific mixed drinks that are still pretty far from mainstream in the United States:

PISCO PUNCH

A fairly distant second (to the pisco sour) in its modern popularity, this one's actually of American origin. Pisco Punch was born in San Francisco during the great Gold Rush of the mid-nineteenth century and remained in fashion in Northern California until Prohibition. Like many early mixed drinks, it's relatively minimalist in its preparation: 2 parts pisco, 2 parts pineapple juice, 1 part fresh lime juice, 1 part simple syrup. It's a fairly easy drink to riff on if you're so inclined to make it a bit more complex.

CHILCANO

Chilcano: It's not every cocktail that gets its own official week. The second week of January belongs to the Chilcano. The Andean answer to the Moscow Mule typically means topping off 2 parts pisco, 1/2 part fresh lime juice and a few drops of bitters with ginger ale or ginger. Sometimes, to make it a bit more relatable for Anglo audiences, bars will dub it "Peruvian Mule" or "Peruvian Llama."

CAPITAN

O Capitan, mi Capitan, you are the Peruvian equivalent of the Manhattan: 2 parts pisco, 1-1/2 parts vermouth, a splash of fresh lime juice, a few drops of bitters and an optional teaspoon of simple syrup. As is the case with the Manhattan, there are plenty of variations.

PANAMERICANO

Those familiar with the Negroni should gravitate to the Panamericano. It has most of the usual trappings of that Italian cocktail (1 part Campari, 1 part vermouth, orange peel), but it replaces the one-part gin with the same quantity of pisco.

ANDEAN DUSK

Modern-day mixologists have fallen in love with pisco for its versatility and have been having a lot of fun testing its limits. New York–based bartender Meaghan Dorman created the Andean Dusk, a delightfully innovative grape-on-grape concoction: pisco, three red grapes, fresh lemon juice, and simple syrup, topped off with sparkling rosé wine.

Cocktails have been the preferred method of pisco appreciation and a good gateway to the spirit, but it's complex enough to enjoy neat or on the rocks, especially if it's a higher-price-tier reserve offering. It also goes well alongside Peru's national dish, ceviche. At the bottom of a plate of ceviche is a broth of sorts that Peruvians like to call leche de tigre (tiger's milk). It forms when the lime, fish juice, onion, and other marinades settle to the base of the dish. After finishing the ceviche, one would sip la leche de tigre, followed by a shot of pisco. Very few practices are able to encapsulate Peruvian culture and cuisine as thoroughly as that deliciously simple ritual.

As for which brands to try, Peruvian brands are easier to find (and, therefore, recommended), but you should definitely see for yourself how Chilean pisco measures up.

- MACCHU PISCO (MACCHU PISCO, LLC): The flagship Macchu Pisco variety derives from the traditional nonaromatic quebranta grape. The Peruvian company's La Diablada uses a blend of grapes, balancing aroma, body, and flavor. Finally, the company offers a reserve product, Ñusta, made from Peru's rarest and finest aromatic grapes. It actually comes in a nifty, limited edition brown ceramic bottle that you're likely to want to keep.

- BARSOL SELECTO ACHOLADO (BARSOL PISCO): The blend of Quebranta, Italia, and Torontel grapes gives Peru's Barsol Selecto Acholado a balance of fruity and floral aromas. Definitely worth sipping neat.

- PISCO PORTÓN (HACIENDA LA CARAVADO DISTILLERY): Hacienda La Caravado in Peru's Ica Valley says it's the oldest distillery in the

Americas, having opened its doors in 1684. Pisco Portón itself isn't quite so old, as it was first introduced in 2010. The brand blends four grape varietals, giving it some citrus and floral notes.

- KAPPA (HOUSE OF MARNIER LAPOSTOLLE): Here's a Chilean one for you. Kappa uses Moscato grapes from the country's Elqui Valley and pure Andean mountain water. From sip to sip, you'll get everything from earthy and spicy to fruity and floral notes. It took a double gold medal at the San Francisco World Spirits Competition in 2012, so it definitely can hold its own against Peru's finest.
- PISCO ABA (PISCO ABA): Pisco ABA is another Moscato-based spirit from Chile's Elqui Valley; the gently sweet and fragrant pisco also has a couple of medals under its belt.

Week 35
PULP NOVEL
Solbeso

I've tried to avoid including any "definitive," historically unassailable origin stories throughout our journey. As you witnessed in the pisco section, history can be a dicey business. Anytime someone tries to offer something that's supposedly conclusive about the birth of any sort of alcoholic beverage, there's always going to be someone else out there champing at the bit to say, "No, that's not how that happened, you tool!" When we're talking about drinks that have existed for hundreds, even thousands, of years, provenance is more a leap of faith than a documented fact. However, that gets exponentially easier when a tipple can trace its origins back exactly half a decade.

That's the case with Solbeso ("sole-bay-so"), one of the rare new spirits categories to be created in the twenty-first century. It, too, is of South American parentage—Peru to be exact—but it's no pisco. It's distilled from neither grapes nor sugar cane, but from cacao. Now, before anyone jumps to conclusions, know this: There is not even the remotest hint of chocolate in Solbeso. Chocolatiers make one of the world's favorite confections from cacao beans. Solbeso distillers use the grossly underappreciated, usually forgotten fruity pulp that surrounds those beans.

One aspect it does share with its South American peers—and just about every fermented or distilled drinkable in the world—is that its creation is anchored in happenstance. Entrepreneur Tom Higbee, whose background is in product innovation of many sorts, was trying to help a Peruvian cacao farmer launch a chocolate brand. What struck Higbee the most during his exploratory process was how wasteful cacao procurement was. Harvesters would cut through the pod to get to the beans and then just toss the rich, pulpy fruit into the river like last week's trash.

Part of the problem with the fruit was that it oxidized pretty quickly—think the brown nastiness that forms on a sliced apple or avocado after it's been sitting untouched for several minutes. Having worked with the Bacardis and Diageos of the world, Higbee's heart was in spirits production. It was only natural that he immediately thought, "Why don't we distill the pulp?"

There are historical instances of locals drinking juice from the pulp, even in fermented form. But no one, to Higbee's knowledge, has ever brought distillation into the equation. Naturally, he had to perform a trial run to see if it was even worth distilling. Because of that oxidation issue, as well as the fact that the humid temperatures are breeding grounds for ambient yeasts that kick-start the fermentation process immediately, Higbee has kept the production sites fairly close to the source. Unfortunately, the nearest stills were a good ten or twelve hours away in major metro areas like Lima, so he had to make do with whatever he could get his hands on locally. So, he traded some chickens and beer for a copper pot, affixed a bamboo neck to the pot, and had a very crude still.

"It was total moonshine,"[83] he remembers. "Just to see if it was possible."

The end product exceeded his expectations. It also challenged his preconceived notions about flavor profile and how drinkers would choose to consume it. "I actually took it back to one of my clients and said, 'Hey, what do you think?'" Higbee continues. "He accused me of taking rum and tequila and mixing them together—that's the flavor profile that he took away from it."

Initially, Higbee's thinking was that it would fit in among other Latin spirits like pisco and tequila, performing well in old-standby cocktails like mojitos and pisco sours. During Solbeso's first year in operation, Higbee's local bar surprised him with his go-to drink, a rye Manhattan. But it had a notable twist. "I said, 'This doesn't taste like a Manhattan,'" he recalls. "And they said, 'It's not; it's your product.' We discovered that it had, as a base spirit, a tremendous amount of versatility. I wasn't thinking Negronis or Old-Fashioneds when I created it. If one hundred bars are serving it in New York, they're serving it with vermouth, in sort of boozy cocktails. We never saw that coming."

The easiest way to experience the spirit and get a sense of what its flavor is all about is to pour it over some ice and squeeze a fresh lemon in it. Tasting is a fairly subjective thing, but common notes include hints of honeysuckle or orange blossom on the nose, tangy citrus midpalate, and a long, smooth finish without much of the bite most would expect. Higbee says it's that taste profile that has made it more gender-democratic than a spirit like tequila, which tends to skew more male.

Solbeso volume is still extremely small as spirits go. Give it some time because it's not every day someone creates a new category, much less one that supports rural South American economies by turning what was once considered trash into a potentially lucrative cash crop.

There's no denying that it has come a long way from the makeshift still that first brought it into the world. It's now distilled in three different regions and some rougher edges come off of it when it's tidied up and bottled in Bardstown, KY. But Higbee insists that the more refined product that it has become isn't that far off from the one that first came out of that cobbled-together copper bowl and bamboo tube.

"It doesn't taste too dissimilar," Higbee insists. "It's a testament to the fruit."

Week 36

Chicago Is... Malört's Kind of Town

Kentucky has bourbon. Its neighbor to the south has Tennessee whiskey and moonshine. Those are usually the two states that immediately come to mind when someone says, "Quick, associate a spirit with a particular area within the United States." But now try this: Name an American city and the liquor with which it is most inextricably intertwined. That one might take a minute. Here's a hint: Windy. Okay, so, Chicago. Those from outside Cook County might take a bit longer to generate the answer. However, a significant percentage of those in the greater Chicagoland area, even those inclined to be teetotalers, likely will muster a common response: Mälort ("muh-lort").

The bitter, wormwood-based take on the Swedish spiced bësk spirit—a cousin of absinthe—is the stuff of legends on the shores of Lake Michigan. It gets its name from its core ingredient (Malört means "wormwood") and was widely consumed in Sweden in the early twentieth century. Swedish immigrants subsequently brought it with them when they settled in the Midwest. Among those transplants was a man by the name of Carl Jeppson, who, during Prohibition, made a living producing legal alcohol for "medicinal" purposes—the medical marijuana of its time, purported to cure at least as many "ailments." By the time the states ratified the Twenty-First Amendment ending the fourteen-year not-so-Noble Experiment, Chicago's Swedish population knew to ask for Jeppson's Malört by name at their neighborhood taverns. Jeppson already had sold his recipe to local distillery Bielzoff Products Company, whose owner, George Brode, is credited with making it a household name beyond just the Scandinavian enclaves. In 1934, Brode incorporated The Carl Jeppson Company, which exists to this day under the leadership of Brode's former secretary, Patricia Gabelick, to whom Brode bequeathed the company upon his passing in 1999.[84] It maintains its cult following among Chicagoans to this day and continues to enjoy volume and revenue growth even though it's no longer distilled within the city limits—The Carl Jeppson Company licenses production to a Florida-based distillery.

Many hardcore locals are extremely passionate about it, but I am skeptical that anyone actually loves—or even likes—Malört, regardless of what they may say. That's neither here nor there. It's a spirit that transcends the worldly concerns of mere mortals—like flavor.

I was first exposed to Jeppson's Malört when a visiting acquaintance had smuggled a flask of it on his flight east. "I want you to try this and then I want to take a picture of your 'Malört face' the moment you do," he said. That's actually a thing, the "Malört face." There's an entire Flickr group devoted to photos of the expression on the faces of sippers from all walks of life. The faces range from puckery grimaces to visages of pure befuddlement. Mine was closer to a hybrid of the two.

It's a drink that elicits strong reactions. I doubt that anyone in the history of the spirit has ever been nonchalant in a "Hmm, interesting" kind of way. If you ever encounter such a person, do yourself a favor and never play poker against that highly gifted con artist.

The taste? Imagine sucking on a grapefruit into which pure ethanol has been injected (and to think the stuff's only 70 proof/35 percent alcohol). That's about as close a comparison as can be mustered. But I say that with the utmost affection. These days, I'm in Chicago at least three or four times a year and I can't leave before I've had my obligatory pour (and watched someone else have it for the first time). It's more than just a liqueur; it's the perfect metaphor for the city that birthed it. "Chicago is kind of a rough place to live; it's a very beautiful place and it's got a lot going for it, but it's kind of dangerous sometimes, it's kind of cold and kind of bitter, and I think in a lot of ways Malört is a reflection of that,"[85] muses Sam Mechling, marketing director for the Carl Jeppson Company.

And, while "marketing director" may be his official title, Mechling actually is much more than a shill for a product. How he ended up on the Malört payroll is quite possibly the craziest episode in the brand's saga. Back in 2010, while he was bartending and living above the beer, booze, and bacon paradise that is Paddy Long's, he created (completely unauthorized) Jeppson's Malört Twitter and Facebook accounts.

"It started out as a way to make my friends laugh, kind of like this weird little experiment," he tells me over a drink at Paddy Long's, where he continues to tend bar. "We'd gotten so recognized that people assumed it was real. We had the readership or whatever you want to call it of an actual account."

Malört sales spiked about 15 percent for the full year after he launched the social media presence, which, he felt, was no coincidence. At the prodding of family and friends, he decided to monetize that presence by selling T-shirts at Paddy's. Of course, he had absolutely no authorization from Gabelick to do so, but it wasn't for lack of trying. Mechling attempted to contact her but was unsuccessful. Then, when he started generating impressive revenue from the branded merch sales, he mailed her a check. "It was like in a mafia movie when the young guy goes up and punches a made man, just to let people know he's there," he explains.

But that too was to no avail. The envelope was returned to him marked "deceased."

Only, she wasn't. She only had moved across the street; the buildings housed predominantly older individuals and thus had a higher mortality rate than most other residences (the postal service was just playing the odds). One day, the very-much-alive Patricia Gabelick showed up at Paddy Long's, attorney in tow.

"I knew I was pretty much screwed," Mechling recalls.

The conversation was mostly civil until the lawyer chimed in and asked, "When were you going to tell us about those T-shirts?" Fortunately, Mechling had held on to the returned check and letter, which he quickly ran upstairs to retrieve.

"She saw the words I had written to her, and I saw the expression on her face change," he continues. "Rather than suing me, they ended up hiring me instead. It was a very, very touch-and-go situation."

Malört sales have continued to increase steadily, though it's still an incredibly small niche product, moving around five thousand cases annually.

The start of Mechling's tenure with the company—both officially and unofficially—and its Twitter and Facebook identity was arguably a turning point for the beverage.

"I was just giving it away as the 'fuck you' shot,"[86] admits Paddy Long's owner Patrick Berger. "Either you were fucking with a tourist—'you've got to have this Chicago-only liqueur, Malört'—or it was a twenty-one-year-old Trixie who was saying, 'It's my birthday, do I get a free shot?' and you were like, 'Sure, here you go.' To me, it was a miracle when people started to order it on their own."

Another quintessential Malört bar has to be Chicago's Old Town Ale House. Calling it a dive bar is doing the Ale House a grave disservice (though it wears the distinction with pride, calling itself "Le Premiere Dive Bar" on its own website). It definitely fits the profile—scuffed wooden bar, general dankness, fiercely loyal townie clientele of all (legal drinking, I think) ages—but it also transcends that concept. It's right around the corner from Second City, so you can imagine how many comedy legends have sipped their Malört there. The wall art features portraits of all sorts of Chicago glitterati, including erstwhile Second City alum like John Belushi, Dan Aykroyd, and Bill Murray and other Windy City legends like Roger Ebert, who, shortly before he passed away in 2013, blogged that it was "The Best Bar in the World That I Know About." There's also a nude, full-frontal painting of Sarah Palin holding an assault rifle, if that gives you any idea of Old Town's attitude.

The hipster craft cocktail set has been serving Malört to a new, more ironic generation and taking things to entirely new levels of eye-popping insanity. For instance, there's the Lone Wolf in the über-trendy West Loop. It's one of those dim, candlelit great-place-for-a-first-date kinds of venues, with a handful of mixological master strokes. Among those is B.A.F., which, cover your ears, stands for "Bitter As Fuck." It's a gonzo mixture of Malört, Suze (French bitters brand), Campari, Yellow Chartreuse liqueur, and Rittenhouse Rye whiskey. I'm not sure how bitter "fuck" is, but I'd bet money on the fact that "fuck" is not one-tenth as bitter as the B.A.F. The bite still lingers on my palate, and I feel like it's something that I'll carry with me to my dying day, like the tinnitus I developed after standing too close to the sound system at a Ramones concert.

I'd often wondered whether locals were still drinking the stuff or if it's mostly tourists who hear it's something one's supposed to order when visiting Chicago, not realizing that no one who actually lives there even touches the stuff (sort of like deep dish pizza). "We did the math on it and if people drank only one shot and never drank it again, we'd never be selling as much as we have," Mechling points out. "It's a very versatile thing. As a bartender, I can weaponize it to mess with an unruly customer, or I can pour a shot to help somebody celebrate. It's about the drinker and what they're looking for."

The neighborhood clientele inhale the stuff at Scofflaw, another of the city's popular cocktail spaces, with a decidedly gin-centric orientation. Malört's such a popular attraction there that it's offered on draft, with a Jeppson's-shaped bottle as a tap handle.

As was almost destined to happen given the sense of local pride that accompanies the drink, Jeppson's ceased to be the only game in town just a few years ago. The competition is thanks, once again, to the craft distilling movement. In 2012, Robby Franklin Haynes, bar manager of Chicago cocktail hotspot The Violet Hour, worked with the city's Letherbee Distillers to develop R. Franklin's Malört. Meanwhile, FEW Spirits, based in the Evanston suburb, created what it called Anguish and Regret Malört, and popular Louisiana bitters producer Bittermens released a product named Bäska Snaps med malört. Note the lowercase in the latter. That "med malört" component, which simply means "with wormwood," proved crucial for the brand when The Carl Jeppson Company filed with the US Patent and Trademark Office to essentially own the trade name "Malört" once the imitators started crawling out of the woodwork. Gabelick had argued that when drinkers speak of Malört, they mean Jeppson's. The brand, she asserted, had put the very concept of a wormwood spirit on the map and, therefore, it should be the only one to bear the name. After an initial rejection, The Carl Jeppson Company secured the trademark on appeal and the others had to remove Malört from their names—with the exception of Bittermens, as all parties ultimately agreed that "med malört" was merely a descriptor and not part of its proper name. (Case sensitivity exists for a reason, folks!)

Imitation being the sincerest form of flattery and all, it's not a major leap to suggest that the market is in the throes of a mini-Malört renaissance, not unlike the resurgence of Fernet among San Franciscans. They're both famous for their strong, off-putting (to most) flavors and they're both linked to grittier times in their respective local drinking cultures' histories. And they're both the drink of choice among bartenders, cooks, and servers.

The key difference, though, is that there's much more hyper-locality involved with Malört. You're now nearly as likely to find a Fernet devotee in New York as you are in the Bay Area. The same really can't be said about Malört. Its celebrity (or, more accurately, notoriety) seems to begin and end at O'Hare International Airport.

And that is more of an asset than a liability. The most rewarding drinking experiences are those that foster a clear sense of place. Many wear that hometown pride on their sleeves, or more accurately, on their actual arms and legs. "I've lost track, but I think there's in the neighborhood of fifty or one hundred Malört tattoos on people in the city," Mechling observes. "I'm sure there are a couple of Jack Daniel's tattoos out there, but that's more the person celebrating being a drunk. Malört is a very personal thing. It's a tribute to where they came from, it's not just about alcohol."

Week 37
Cachaça—Rum's Brazilian Cousin

For global business types, Brazil is the B of the "BRIC" countries; Russia, India, and China are the remaining letters. A few years back, it was impossible to have a conversation with an international beverage marketer without that acronym coming up. For a while, those offered the greatest opportunity for growing a drink produced in mature markets. For, say, a Scotch whisky or French Cognac, Brazil has been the gateway to the emerging markets of the Americas. It hasn't been a one-way transaction, however. Brazil has had a spirit of its own to offer in exchange: cachaça ("cah-chahssa"). It's that country's number one spirit; it's such an institution there that it joins the ranks of other distilled beverages that get their own holiday. Brazilians celebrate National Cachaça Day on September 13.

Bit by bit, cachaça has been taking over the rest of the world, most visibly in Brazil's national cocktail, the caipirinha: cachaça, lime, simple syrup poured over ice.

Cachaça is most closely associated with rum as it, too, is based on sugar cane. The critical distinction between the two is that rum typically is distilled from molasses—a sugar byproduct—while cachaça is produced from the juice extracted from pure sugar cane (a few rums have been known to be made this way as well).

As is the case with many of the other beverages we've discussed, it's impossible to declare a particular date when cachaça was born. And it can be quite tricky to separate the myths from the hard, verifiable facts.

Most historians agree that cachaça's origins date back to around the 1530s, which means it actually predates rum by a good hundred years and is the first spirit of the Americas. The legend associated with it—the part that falls squarely in the myth column—relates to its unexpected discovery. When the early colonials were processing sugar cane by boiling it, the steam would condense back to water on the roof. It would drip off the ceiling and sting the badly scarred backs of slaves. It supposedly got its nickname, "pinga," that way. It was the "ping, ping" from the ceiling; probably not a legend on which makers of cachaça (or the slangish "pinga," if you prefer) really would want to hang their hats. Slavery's not something that a brand would proudly market as its heritage.

In any event, cachaça soon became ubiquitous throughout Brazil and, for centuries, was produced in traditional pot stills. But, inevitably, tradition was no match for progress and by the 1950s, column distillation technology conquered Brazil, as it had so many other spirits-making regions before it. And that's when everything changed for the strong Brazilian beverage. Mass production virtually erased any trace of cachaça's artisanal past. Distillers were able to make extremely high volumes of it at very low cost. That's also when the caipirinha became all the rage. You can learn how to make your own in the back cocktail section.

Unfortunately, as is common with the indigenous spirit of an emerging market—think China's baijiu—the vast majority of the output of the ten thousand-plus producers is, how shall we say, not of the most impeccable quality. Fortunately for Brazil and much of the rest of the world, though, there are several producers that have brought it back to its artisan-crafted roots and are making significant inroads across international markets. One of the best known of those is Leblon, which, in only a decade of existence, has helped put the spirit on the North American radar. "We have two focuses,"[87] says Leblon's New York–based founder, president, and CEO, Steve Luttmann. "Bring cachaça to the world and then in Brazil, ironically enough, reintroduce artisanal pot still cachaça. It's a huge category, but the majority of it is industrial, cheap cachaça. Our mission there is kind of like the craft movement."

That's no small task, considering how firmly entrenched the fast and cheap variety is in the country. It's been somewhat easier for newer, craft-minded marketers to introduce their finer offerings to a market like North America where cachaça awareness previously had been somewhere around zero.

"Nobody knew what it was and the very few who did associated it with the industrial production rocket fuel—and the headaches,"

Luttmann observes. "And if they did know it, it's because they spent time in Brazil."

But a mere ten years later, at least a third of serious cocktail enthusiasts now are quite well acquainted with the caipirinha and roughly 25 percent of adult drinkers in general have at least heard of cachaça. It's still not anywhere near where tequila is in the collective American consciousness—probably in the 95 percent range—but it's a sizable jump in such a short time from complete invisibility. The category will be getting considerably more exposure; as of 2015 Leblon is a wholly owned subsidiary of Bacardi.

Lovers of connoisseur-magnet beverages likely will find appeal in more refined, aged versions of cachaças that are coming on the market. Leblon, for instance, has a reserve bottling whose contents have been aged for two to four years in new French oak barrels. That's the type of spirit that should be consumed neat—no caipirinhas here.

"Our approach to making cachaça is exactly the same as Cognac—we don't use grapes, we use sugar cane," says Luttmann.

A big boost for the product, internationally speaking, occurred in 2013 when the United States agreed to recognize cachaça as a product specific to Brazil. If it's not made there, it may not be labeled as such in the US market. It also no longer has to be classified as "Brazilian rum," which confused a lot of drinkers because cachaça doesn't taste like rum.

There's a considerably different dynamic at play in Europe. It's as recognizable to the nightlife set in countries like France and Germany as tequila is in the United States. Europe traditionally has had a closer connection with Brazil; it historically has been much more of a tourist destination for Europeans than it has for Americans. The northeastern region of the country is particularly popular with German travelers.

In most of the more cosmopolitan European cities, it's fairly common to find caipirinhas on the menu. It's a great gateway drink, but there are far more applications worth trying. The craft cocktail movement has been playing a key part in expanding its role in many a mix. Some up-and-coming mixed options include the Antiquado (a Brazilian spin on an Old-Fashioned, substituting cachaça for whiskey—recipe is in the back!) and the rum-forward Mr. Wilson (cachaça, rum agricole, Jamaican rum, orgeat, vanilla syrup, and lime). Mr. Wilson is the brainchild of mixologist Jesus Diáz of New York's WeatherUp.

As for which cachaça to use in these cocktails or to drink, simply, neat, or on the rocks, you can't go wrong here:

- AVUA PRATA (AVUA CORP.): Prata is Portuguese for "silver" and Avua's unaged variety is a nice introduction to handcrafted small-batch cachaças. The eighty-four-proof spirit has some distinct vegetal, earthy characteristics.

- MAISON LEBLON RESERVA ESPECIAL (LEBLON CACHAÇA) The flagship Leblon is great too, but the Riserva is a prime example of how to enhance the spirit with some good, old-fashioned barrel aging. Matured for up to two years, it combines the flavor of cane sugar with some of the caramel elements of French oak.

- NOVO FOGO CACHAÇA ORGANICA (BOM DIA IMPORTS LLC DBA NOVO FOGO): Novo Fogo is certified organic and touts its unique terroir—the ocean, a rainforest, and mountains all play a role. There are plenty of bananas growing around there and hints of the fruit's influence can be detected on the nose. Novo Fogo also markets a barrel-aged cachaça that turns the aroma of banana into banana bread.

Week 38

CERVEZAS Y MAS

CHAVELAS AND MICHELADAS

It's kind of disappointing how undercelebrated Mexican Independence Day (September 16) is among the general US population and how it gets eclipsed by Cinco de Mayo—which marks an important battle in Mexican history, to be sure, but not one as monumental as an entire war for freedom. In honor of the historic Grito de Dolores—the cry in the town of Dolores commemorated as the start of that war—let's celebrate our independence from played-out margaritas and watery beers with limes stuffed down their bottle necks.

"But," you'll say, "it's just what you order at a Mexican restaurant." It doesn't have to be.

What if you took one of those beers and jazzed it up a bit with, oh, I don't know, tomato juice, hot sauce, or even Clamato? Stay with me, now. Sounds gross on paper, but actually, it can be pretty tasty.

I was certainly intrigued enough to order one for myself when I saw this gargantuan stemmed fishbowl of a glass arrive at the table next me at a no-frills, authentic Mexican joint in Santa Cruz, California. It was filled maybe two-thirds to halfway with red liquid; there was a special slot for a bottle of beer to rest and empty its contents into the glass. Around the rim of the glass? Picante spices mixed with salt, margarita-style. And chilled, cooked shrimp. Yep. It was essentially a shrimp cocktail with beer.

That was a chavela, one of the more extreme examples of cerveza preparada (prepared beer). Chavela (sometimes written "chabela") ingredients may vary. The base could be V8, straight tomato juice, or Clamato, on the rocks more often than not. There's usually a few shots of hot sauce in the juice; feel free to add more. Shrimp is a common garnish, but it's not unheard of for it to be something simpler like crudité.

Not feeling particularly peckish? A michelada is a little less involved, ditching the crustaceans, adding some lime juice and, perhaps, Cholula, El Yucateca, Tabasco, or local artisan hot sauce or two. Sometimes Worcestershire is involved, which results in something along the lines of a Bloody Mary with beer instead of vodka.

For the indecisive who are torn between this concept and the old-standby margarita, there's a sort of hybrid known as a Negro y Marron (black and brown). Clamato, hot sauce, and a dash of lemon or lime juice fill the salt-rimmed glass, but the beer shares the alcohol spotlight with tequila. One thing to keep in mind is that these are really just loose guidelines. There are no hard-and-fast recipes, and even the nomenclature is debatable. Michelada and chavela/chabela often are used interchangeably from venue to venue.

The most attractive element is that anything on the cerveza preparada spectrum is fairly customizable. The beer used is up to the drinker, so the more extensive the list the better. I wouldn't recommend using a craft beer; those are just fine on their own. Light lagers are best; Dos Equis Lager Especial is the wiser choice than its sister, Amber. Remember, there are tomatoes involved and sometimes even clams, so the crisper and less complex, the better.

Cervezas preparadas could be having their moment, as there's been a spike in interest for beer cocktails. A particular global brewing behemoth that shall remain nameless tried to jumpstart the concept in the early 2000s, and I remember a particular retch-inducing concoction it served at a media lunch designed to get the world to think differently about beer. An A for effort, but the mix just wasn't right.

Today, however, mixologists are getting involved and staying true to the original Mexican traditions while adding a bit of creative flair. The best are those who make it their own and don't phone it in—house-made sauces versus cracking open a can of V8 or Clamato, are more likely to win people over immediately.

It's been an especially welcome development for drinking establishments that have licenses to serve wine and beer, but not spirits. Cocktail culture is extremely hot these days, and those who don't have the resources or are forbidden by local zoning ordinances to serve anything stronger than fermented grapes don't get to join in the fun.

Mexican beer cocktails represent at least a partial opportunity to play in that sandbox.

New York's pulqueria tries to cover all of the classic Mexican bases—not just its namesake beverage—and offers its own hand-crafted twist on the michelada: beer, fresh-squeezed lime juice, Valentina hot sauce, a proprietary blend of spices and other sauces (including Worcestershire), and a chili salt rim.

Pulqueria bartenders pick the beer, which is usually Modelo Especial, sometimes Tecate. Both work well because they are kind of blank canvases that interact appropriately with the flavor profiles imparted by the rest of the ingredients without eclipsing the carefully orchestrated recipe. They're not rigid about it, though. If someone requests a preferred brew, the bar team will incorporate it (sometimes reluctantly).

"Modelo Especial and Tecate are definitely a little softer,"[88] Pulqueria's Mishi Torgove explains. "However, some have asked for it with Negra Modelo, which definitely has a stronger flavor presence. We want the house mix to shine, not be overshadowed."

For those who really need that spirit component for it to qualify as a cocktail, a lot of bars will offer add-ons like tequila or mezcal. Mezcal works best because it gives it that smoky component that only mezcal can. When combined with a peppery sauce, it's like an instant chipotle.

Mixing beer with tomato-based juices and spices may not sound like the most appetizing combination to a lot of people—hell, most people. Until recently I felt the same way. But the concept of a cerveza preparada has really grown on me, and when I'm in the right mood and I've encountered the right house recipe, I'm more than eager to pop the cap on that Dos Equis and watch it disappear into a spicy sea of red.

Week 39

No Filter

Coffee Beer

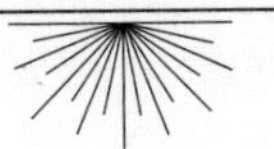

Your calendar should be pretty marked up by now with all of the drink-specific holidays that have popped up in recent years. Here's another one for you: September 29, better known among caffeine fanatics as International Coffee Day.

The rise of craft brewing over the past few decades in a lot of ways paralleled the Starbucks-ization of coffee. Beer drinkers were tired of guzzling the watery, characterless output of the world's megabrewers in the same way that coffee lovers demanded more than Taster's Choice and Folgers crystals. It was only a matter of time before consumers demanded both beverages at the exact same time, in the exact same glass.

Brewers have been happy to oblige, as coffee beer is one of fastest growing styles to emerge in the past ten to fifteen years.

It was a natural progression for darker brews, as the roasty malts they use echo some of the flavor and aroma characteristics common in a good cup of joe.

In fact, "coffee" has been one of the default descriptors for some darker beers like porters and stouts, even when there's nary a bean to be found. And how would one accentuate those flavor notes? Why, adding actual coffee, of course!

Brewers have been so keen to get their roast on that coffee beer is now an official category in all of the major beer competitions, including the Great American Beer Festival awards and the World Beer Cup.

The craft revolution has been, in some respects, influenced by the "buy local," "eat local," "think local" movement; despite a large number of brewers having a multistate or even nationwide presence, they are, at their hearts, local or regional businesses. Many of the ones producing coffee beers remain true to that ethos by collaborating with roasters in their own backyards.

SCHLAFLY COFFEE STOUT
(THE SAINT LOUIS BREWERY)

It's not easy running a brewery in St. Louis when its name isn't Anheuser-Busch. But the St. Louis Brewery, the official moniker of the company behind the Schlafly brand, has been doing just that for more than a quarter century. One of its colder weather offerings has been its Coffee Stout, which blends its oatmeal stout with beans from its local roaster, Kaldi's Coffee. The story the brewery likes to tell resembles the old Reese's Peanut Butter Cup ads from the 1970s and 1980s ("Two great tastes that go great together!") Back in the 1990s, the Kaldi's staff had been frequent visitors to the Schlafly Tap Room, often asking for a pint of stout and a shot of espresso. An enduring partnership was born.

BELL'S JAVA STOUT
(BELL'S BREWERY)

Kalamazoo, Michigan's, Bell's, which knows its way around a stout, uses a custom blend of beans roasted by the nearby Water Street Coffee Joint. At 7.5 percent alcohol, Java Stout is quite warming during the winter months in which it is available.

FOUNDERS BREAKFAST STOUT
(FOUNDERS BREWING COMPANY)

Grand Rapids, Michigan, is barely fifty miles from Kalamazoo, and there seems to be a bit neighborly one-upmanship going on when it comes to alcohol content in coffee beers. Grand Rapids' Founders Brewing Company clocks in at 8.3 percent ABV and features a blend of Sumatra and Kona beans, combined with flaked oats and bitter chocolate. For a touch of bourbon with the morning cup, there's one of Founders's most sought-after brews, the barrel-aged Kentucky Breakfast Stout (more on that in the barrel-aged section).

MOBCRAFT BATSHIT CRAZY
(MOBCRAFT BEER, LLC)

The business model for Madison, Wisconsin's, MobCraft seems as batshit crazy as its coffee beer: Its recipes are crowd-sourced. Fans submit their ideas for a beer and MobCraft lets the public vote on those. Whatever wins that month gets brewed. In 2014, the English-style brown ale brewed with milk, sugar, and coffee from the local co-op, Just Coffee, won a silver medal at the Great American Beer Festival. Now who's crazy?

CAPPUCCINO STOUT
(LAGUNITAS BREWING COMPANY)

Petaluma, California's, Lagunitas sourced its beans from Hardcore Coffee in nearby Sebastapol. It's an amped 9.2 percent ABV brew available from January to March. Good thing Lagunitas opened another brewery in Chicago in 2014; such a boozy concoction is just what the doctor ordered for those dealing with those not-so-mild winters on Lake Michigan.

JAVAHEAD STOUT
(TROEGS BREWERY)

Hershey, Pennsylvania–based Troegs uses Kenyan coffee beans courtesy of St. Thomas Roasters in nearby Linglestown. Troegs tweaked the recipe of its original Oatmeal Stout for this jet-black 7.5 percent brew. After the boil, the hot wort (the pre-fermentation liquid containing all of the sugars to be converted to alcohol) flows through the brewery's hopback vessel, which the Troegs' gang say is not unlike using a gigantic French press. The process accentuates the coffee nose.

CAFÉ CON LECHE
(CIGAR CITY BREWING COMPANY)

Tampa, Florida, may not experience much in the way of winter, but that doesn't mean the locals don't like a good roasty pick-me-up. Cigar City's Café Con Leche infuses a milk stout with Cuban espresso; its aroma evokes not only the beans, but the faint essence of dairy cream, as well.

FUEL CAFÉ
(LAKEFRONT BREWERY)

Milwaukee has built its reputation on being one of the great beer cities in North America—its Major League baseball team certainly would agree. One of the finest breweries to come out of the Wisconsin city is Lakefront. And one of Lakefront's finest beers is Fuel Café, named after the local coffeehouse that supplies the beans. The stout reveals flavor notes alternating among toffee, chocolate, malt sweetness, and, of course, black coffee.

NO MIDDLE GROUND
(SIERRA NEVADA BREWING COMPANY)

Not all coffee beer has to be dark, as counterintuitive as that may seem. A prime example of an against-the-grain (and bean) java brew was actually the product of a collaboration among the second-largest craft brewer in the country (behind Sam Adams), Chico, California-based Sierra Nevada, Durham, North Carolina's, Counter Culture Coffee, and the team behind the popular Durham-headquartered enthusiast magazine, All About Beer. The result: the limited edition No Middle Ground, which, get ready for this, is a coffee Imperial Pale Ale (IPA). American IPAs, as you may know, are known much more for their citrusy hop bitterness than for anything even remotely resembling roastiness. And, with the operative word in IPA's name being "pale," they're not typically dark like conventional coffee beers (with the notable exception of the rise of "black IPAs"). No Middle Ground is pale in its truest sense.

Sipping it, a drinker expects a heavy hit of hops, but instead, there's that morning blend, wafting through the nasal passages before landing gracefully on the palate.

REGULAR COFFEE
(CARTON BREWING COMPANY)

Those who grew up in the New York Tri-State area (like I did) are more than familiar with the concept of ordering a coffee "regular"—milk and two sugars. Carton Brewing in Atlantic Highlands, New Jersey—part of the New York City metro market—emulates that tradition in this imperial cream ale brewed with a blend from Fair Mountain Roasters. It's got a hefty ABV of 12 percent—something that requires extra fermentable sugar to achieve, of course—and pours a hazy pale orange.

None of these bean-forward brews is likely to keep you bright-eyed, bushy-tailed, and alert throughout the day, so don't go canceling that Starbucks appointment. But they're still the best part of waking up.

WEEK 40

HOW 'BOUT THESE APPLES?

Apple-Picking Season!

We've reached that time of the year when the apples have fully ripened and significant others everywhere get coerced into romantic apple orchard weekends. As a reminder that autumn's bounty is responsible for far more wonderful things than just pies and juice, we're going to spend a few weeks with some more offbeat varieties of cider. Now that the cider renaissance has revealed itself to be more trend than fad, keep an eye out for some of these stylistic offshoots. Adult drinkers finally have gotten their head around what this cider thing is (after some false starts in past generations)—fermented apples, as opposed to fermented barley malt in beer—and they're eager to explore within the category.

Mention the phrase "Old World wine" and most people will have the same short list of countries: France, Italy, Greece, and Spain. Then bring up cider and those countries rarely are uttered in casual company; invariably, the likes of the United Kingdom and Ireland will enter the conversation. That's why when someone includes "Spain" and "world-class cider culture" in the same sentence, the predictable response is something along the lines of, "Surely, you mean wine culture."

True, Spain is far better known for its viticulture—and probably always will be, considering how much of the country's geography and economy it occupies—but head to the northwest of the Iberian nation and discover a region whose culture is so rooted in cider that its signature product has earned Protected by Designation of Origin (PDO) status from the European Union. The autonomous, self-governing Principality of Asturias boasts stunning vistas, courtesy of the surrounding Cantabrian Mountains and the sea on the northern coast. Its variable elevations result in some climatological swings, getting quite cold in some parts during winter months. It is therefore far more conducive to growing apples than grapes.

Hence, Sidra (Spanish for cider) de Asturias has been able to thrive, offering a range of tastes and aromas that challenge the common notion of cider. The region, which accounts for 80 percent of Spain's cider production, is the fourth-largest European producer of the beverage, behind, predictably, the United Kingdom, Ireland, and France.

Economically, cider is Asturias's third most important food industry, behind milk and meat. As of its most recent industry census, the number of commercial cider producers in the principality was closing in on one hundred.

It's clearly not new to the region; there's a great deal of historical and archaeological evidence to suggest that cider making was a regular occurrence during the Middle Ages. Sidra de Asturias producers also hypothesize that it may even extend back to the pre-Roman period, as historians claim that the ancient Hebrews, Egyptians, and Greeks had a certain degree of familiarity with the apple-based drink. (Why not, there reportedly are plenty of references to apple orchards, so it's not too much of a stretch to conclude that fermentation was happening.)

Okay, enough with the history lesson. Let's drink.

Tastewise, Sidra de Asturias is, in many cases, far more reminiscent of a funky, sour, yeasty Belgian or French farmhouse ale than the sweeter stuff (sometimes cloyingly so) Americans are used to in the mass-marketed varieties. Love it or hate it; there's no in-between. Its flavor is brazen and aggressive and will not tolerate lukewarm, fence-sitting reactions.

Its stewards are very protective of their local drink (remember what that P in "PDO" stands for) and extremely fastidious about quality control. Sidra de Asturias may only be made from the twenty-two apple varieties indigenous to the region and must bear a minimum ABV of 5 percent.

The hundreds of products that bear the prized Sidra de Asturias seal fit three styles:

- NATURAL (TRADITIONAL): Still and unfiltered, produced from twenty-two different Asturian apple varieties; it's typically straw yellow and cloudy, of medium intensity, intense astringency, and subtly sweet.

- NATURAL (NEW EXPRESSION): Lightly carbonated, made from five of the twenty-two apple varieties; it's clear with a lemon yellow hue and hints of green and gold. It's characterized by its tiny bubbles, medium intensity, fruit, vegetable, and floral aromas, with notes of apple and apricot. Ciders of this type are strikingly acidic with a lingering bitterness on the finish.

- SPARKLING: Filtered, more strongly carbonated and, like Natural (New Expression), produced from five of the twenty-two different apples; it's pale yellow with golden tones and slow-forming bubbles that form a pronounced head. It's also of medium intensity—not too mild, not too pungent—and fruity, with some subtle oak notes.

Many producers will market expressions that fit into each, or at least two, of those stylistic categories. Here are some of the top Asturian artisans, most of whose products are exported to the United States:

- LLAGAR HERMINIO: The Zythos label offers both Natural Traditional and New Expression styles. Zythos Tradicional features an intense, fruity aroma and an equally intense flavor. The New Expression offers a little more sparkle and a dry astringency on the finish.

- SIDRA CANAL: El Santu's the one to look out for, with its distinctly tart flavor, dry mouthfeel, and yeasty sediment.

- SIDRA CASTAÑON: Val de Boides (Natural Traditional) is Sidra Castañon's cider that qualifies for the Sidra de Asturias PDO label. It's pale yellow, with a fruity aroma and is a good companion for seafood and meat.

- SIDRA TRABANCO: Drinking Pomma Aurea (Sparkling) is like sipping Champagne, except with apples. Trabanco bills it as the first brut cider to earn the Sidras de Asturias PDO. Its close resemblance to the French bubbly grape beverage makes it an equally good accompaniment for cheese and fish.

Locals tout their rustic cuisine as the perfect accompaniment for the strongly flavored cider. It often combines the best of both land and sea; it's not uncommon for the rich stews to include sausage, beans, and whatever the fishermen may be hauling in that day. And then there's the cheese. Pungent is frequently an understatement. Such an assertive assault on the senses demands a beverage that's up to the task, and any number of Sidra de Asturias brands brings its A game.

Now, about those senses. We're not just talking about the ones associated with taste buds and olfactory nerves. There's a great deal of optical splendor as well. The pouring ritual for some styles is a little piece of theater in itself. The pourer holds the bottle aloft, about five feet above the traditional serving vessel, a wide-mouthed glass. At twelve centimeters high, nine centimeters across the mouth, and seven centimeters across the bottom, it's a bit shorter and more cylindrical (though not perfectly so) than a classic shaker pint. The liquid then cascades down the full distance in a steady, linear stream, never missing its intended receptacle (which takes some practice, of course).

"The canonical method for pouring cider tells us that the posture should be straight without being rigid,"[90] explains Reyes Ceñal, manager of the Spanish regulatory council for Sidra de Asturias. "The arm holding the bottle must be stretched up straight over the head."

The protocol doesn't end there. "When the bottle is tilted to pour the culete, or shot, it should be held with the index, middle, and ring fingers around the body and the little finger underneath the bottom of the bottle," Ceñal continues. "The fingers holding the bottle should not move toward the bottle's neck."

And that's just the bottle; we haven't even gotten to the glass.

For the drinking vessel, proper etiquette dictates that it be held with the thumb and forefinger, with the server's middle finger supporting the bottom of the glass while the ring finger and pinky are retracted into the palm.

"The glass must not move from the center of the body, which means that it is the stream of cider that has to find the glass," Ceñal is quick to point out. "The cork can be grasped with the ring and little fingers of the hand responsible for holding the glass."

It's not all for spectacle's sake. There is a practical purpose to it. The pouring method actually aerates the bottle-conditioned, naturally carbonated (i.e., from the fermentation process alone, sans added CO_2) cider and cuts some of the sourness, making it more pleasing on the palate. Asturias cider makers call the gas stirred up by the pour the estrella (star).

Connoisseurs identify the mark of a quality cider by its aguante, the bubbles that remain in the cider after foaming.

The other qualitative component is its pegue or grano, which essentially is the same as the beer drinker's concept of lacing—how well the post-drink foamy remains adhere to the sides of the glass.

If it's really good, the impression a Sidra de Asturias brand leaves on the drinker will last far longer than its bubbles and lingering foam.

Next week we leave Spain behind for less-temperate climes.

Week 41
FROZEN FRUIT
ICE CIDER

For most people involved with an agricultural product of one sort or another, cold weather is the devil. Most, but not all.

In southern Quebec, a place not exactly known for mild winters, some cider producers have openly encouraged Jack Frost to do his dirty deeds and created their own unique beverage style in the process.

Ice Cider, or Cidre de Glace as it's called in the French-speaking province, makes the most of the local climate and abundance of apples, turning the region's frigidity into a profit-making asset.

There are essentially two methods for producing Cidre de Glace, each with a technical name that sounds as stark and chilly as those long Quebecois winters: cryoextraction and cryoconcentration.

Let's tackle the former first. During the cryoextraction process, growers leave the apples on the trees during the bleakest parts of winter and let Mother Nature do a number on them. No surprise that it ultimately results in frozen and dried fruit. And that's exactly what the cideries want. They're usually picked when the nip in the air is somewhere between about five and eighteen degrees Fahrenheit. (Did I mention it's cold?) The apples then are pressed while still frozen and the juice ferments for a good eight (!) months at low temperatures. The ultra-long fermentation period and relatively low yield make this the pricier of the two options and the reason most Cidres de Glaces—95 percent or so—rely on cryoconcentration, rather than cryoextraction (though the method Canadian ice wines employ more closely resembles cryoextraction).

Cryococentration involves what sounds like substantially less insanity. Cider makers harvest the apples in the fall—a far, far more logical and common practice in the orchard-growing world—and then press the juice before things get too frosty. However, when the big chill does come, producers expose the juice to the elements and let the deep freeze take its toll. The process adds flavor complexity with a pronounced, crisp apple taste and often, notes of caramel and toffee.

The ice concentrates the sugar and most of the flavor, similar to the way it works on the grapes in ice wine. When pressed, all of the concentrated juice flavor gets squeezed out of the fruit. Freezing also concentrates the acidity, imparting a light crispness that pairs well with certain foods. The acid helps cut through the fat on strong cheeses, for instance.

Typically, ice ciders range between 7 percent and 13 percent alcohol by volume, all from the fermentation process. Quebec regulators forbid the addition of supplemental alcohol or sugar in the process. The provincial authority also prohibits artificial freezing; the ice must be a product of the climate alone.

Cider production in Quebec dates back to about the mid-seventeenth century, around the same time the practice commenced in Colonial America. Commercial ice cider making, though, has been going on for just over two decades. Today there are about sixty commercial cideries in Quebec making the ice style. Many of those pride themselves on using the type of apples one would find in the produce aisle of their supermarket or at farmers' markets—the kind people actually eat as opposed to those designated as "cider apples," which generally aren't sold for consumption raw or in baked confections. Cider apples tend to have considerably higher sugar content to facilitate the fermentation process. Cidre de Glace producers tout the more apple-forward flavor that results from their use of traditional eating apples.

"When people taste it, they're like, 'Wow, this is an apple juice for grownups,'"[91] says François Pouliot, president of La Face Cachée de la Pomme (The Hidden Side of the Apple), the ice cider segment leader in Quebec.

La Face Cachée inaugurated the ice tradition quite unintentionally. Pouliot, who worked outside the beverage world prior to the late 1980s, decided to plant a vineyard on his grandparents' farm. "I didn't know anything about wine or wine production," Pouliot remembers. "My mentor had said if you're going to do wine in Quebec, do ice wine."

A few years later, when it came time to move to another site, Pouliot purchased an orchard with the aim of removing the trees and planting the vines. For purely logistical reasons, the company for the first season chose to make apple ice wine with the fruit already growing there and expected to transition to grape wine production for all subsequent seasons. But the apple product turned out to be so good that all plans for grape growing were scrapped. "[We said], let's forget about the wine," Pouliot recalls, "and call it 'apple ice wine' or 'ice cider.' That was 1995." The product in question was called Neige and remains popular to this day.

Quebecoise Cidre de Glace is easy enough to find in the United States, with just a small caveat: In many cases it is marketed as "ice apple wine" on the south side of the Canadian border, mainly to forge a mental connection with the more-familiar ice wine. It's also promoted for the same drinking occasions as dessert wines.

But as the US cider market continues to explode—at the moment it's the fastest-growing alcohol beverage segment in the country—that will gradually change. There are plenty of American producers who already have imported the concept and begun making their own ice ciders. Unsurprisingly, such activity is particularly robust in one of Quebec's neighbor's, Vermont. In fact, there's already a Vermont Ice Cider Association, which boasts about fifteen member companies.

If you're ready to embrace the cold, here are some Quebecois ice ciders you definitely should try.

- **Neige Premiére (La Face Cachée de la Pomme):** Few would argue that there even would be an ice cider industry in Quebec without Neige Premiére. Not only is it the "first snow," it also was Cidre de Glace to be in the 1990s. La Face Cachée de la Pomme produces it in collaboration with its creator, Christian Barthomeuf, a prominent personality in the province's wine community. Neige marries the juices of McIntosh, Cortland, and Spartan apples in the cryoconcentration process, resulting in a 12 percent ABV golden yellow cider with aromas of freshly picked ripe apples.

»→ Cryo Prestige (Cidrerie Cryo):

The aptly named Cryo cidery employs both the cryoextraction and cryoconcentration methods for its portfolio. This particular offering uses cryoextraction, harvesting its apples from the frozen trees at the foot of Mont Saint-Hallaire in mid-January. The 10 percent ABV cider uses only Cortlands in its recipe.

»→ Val Caudalies Cidre de Glace Réserve (Cidrerie La Pomme)

Cidrerie La Pomme blends a total of five different varieties to achieve its desired flavor: Cortland, McIntosh, Empire, Liberty, and Spartan. The result is a complex affair, with prominent notes of sweet apples, as well as a certain nuttiness. It pairs well with foie gras and strong cheeses.

»→ Brise-Glace (Cidrerie Saint-Antoine):

Its name means "Icebreaker" and it's just that—a good introduction to the ice cider category. Aromas of the 9.5 percent ABV beverage suggest baked apple and wintery cooking spices like nutmeg and cloves. Cidrerie Saint-Antoine produces this offering, which pairs well with dark chocolate cake.

I wouldn't want to leave the Americans out in the cold—pun very much intended—so here are a few from cideries south of the Canadian border.

»→ Eden Ice Cider Company

Newport, Vermont's, Eden boasts a fairly extensive portfolio of the frost-forward ilk. Among those:

• Heirloom Blend, Eden's flagship, blends McIntosh, Empire, Russet, Calville Blanc, Esopus Spitzenburg, and Ashmead's Kernel apples. The complex concoction is a potent 10 percent ABV and is an ideal partner for artisanal cheeses, wild game, or a range of desserts.

• Where Heirloom features six apple varieties, Honeycrisp includes just the one in its name. It balances a honey-like sweetness with just the right touch of acidity for a balanced flavor experience. It, too, is 10 percent ABV and recommended for pairing with cheese or maple crème brulee.

»→ Hall Home Place

Located in Hall's Orchard in Isle La Motte, Vermont, Hall Home Place is another cidery in the Green Mountain State with a fairly vast ice cider portfolio.

• Sweet Six includes, you guessed it, six different apple varieties. McIntosh, Cortland, Golden Delicious, and Northern Spy are the mainstays, but with each harvest a different pair rounds out the sextet. It's 12 percent alcohol and pairs with spicy and salty meals.

• Pure Cortland is one of those single-apple creations, with 10 percent alcohol, designed to accompany cheese and fruits. This one tends to sell out pretty quickly and the cidery doesn't always commit to making it every year.

Vermont Ice

It's not uncommon for cider to be just one trick up a multiple beverage producer's sleeve, and that's just the type of environment in which Vermont Ice was born. A product of the Boyden Valley Winery, Vermont Ice combines Vermont-grown Northern Spy, McIntosh, and Empire apples and then ages the fermented mixture in French oak barrels, complementing the apple notes with a touch of vanilla.

Angry Orchard Iceman (Boston Beer Company):

Angry Orchard, the cider division of Boston Beer (better known by the name of its flagship brand, Samuel Adams) and now the largest cider producer in the United States, produces this appropriately monikered creation. The 10 percent ABV beverage, cork-finished in a 750 mL Champagne-style bottle, is aged in oak, giving it some of those subtle hints of vanilla.

It's fitting that we end our icy expedition with a cider-making beer brewer. Next week we look at ciders—and, as an added bonus, whiskeys—that infuse one of beer's most critical ingredients.

Week 42

Worlds Collide

Hopped Cider and Whiskey

Whiskey is making a return guest appearance this week as it shares a particular alternative ingredient trend with cider.

It has been said that craft distilling and cider are riding the coattails of craft beer. That's a fairly unfair statement, as it does a disservice to those smaller but faster-growing beverage segments. Make no mistake; the craft-brewing phenomenon most certainly has created the opportunities for similarly handcrafted ciders and spirits. Neither would be enjoying as much of the spotlight if drinkers hadn't finally started getting on board with better beer. Keep in mind, though, that both are rooted in traditions that date back centuries.

The terms "cider" and "hard cider" are used interchangeably, and I tend to avoid the latter unless I'm talking about companies that use "hard cider" as part of their names. Americans have added the "hard" prefix to the drink because we've grown accustomed to applying the cider label to those jugs of unfiltered apple juice we get at green markets and those apple picking farms our significant others drag us to on fall weekends. We can thank Prohibition for that. Prior to the not-so-Noble Experiment, cider was cider. Then, in January 1920, cideries suddenly found themselves with an overabundance of apples and had to do something with them. They continued to sell the unfermented version of their product as "cider." Prohibition ended and the name stuck around, even as the alcohol-based apple product returned. But the hard stuff that we won't call hard has been made in the United States since Colonial times.

As has whiskey, for that matter. It's no surprise that whiskey has become the go-to spirit of the craft segment, despite the fact that the aging required for the finer ones usually makes it cost-prohibitive for small distillers to put all of their eggs in that basket. That's why you'll see many whose flagships are vodka, gin, and rum. When it doesn't have to be aged particularly long, it can be bottled and sold more or less fresh out of the still.

Another reality that small producers have to deal with is that the big guys actually do a damned good job making the stuff they make, so why should drinkers pay a few bucks extra for a bottle from a little guy without the same history or heritage? Dave Pickerell, a legend in whiskey circles and former master distiller of Maker's Mark who now has his fingers in about twenty-five pies (pies of the commercial whiskey-making kind) through his Oakview Consulting, frequently points out that "you can't out-Maker's Mark Maker's Mark."[92] Never a truer statement has been uttered. So why does anyone even bother trying?

The successful ones know they have neither the time nor the resources to surpass what most of the venerable legacy brands are doing by testing the limits of whiskey with nontraditional grains and other ingredients.

— CORSAIR ARTISAN DISTILLERY —

Nashville, Tennessee's, Corsair Artisan Distillery is one such whiskey producer that has produced an entire range of spirits that incorporate the same variety of hops that craft brewers have been working with. It makes sense since Corsair's owner, Darek Bell, brings a brewing background to his distilling efforts. Corsair's Amarillo is a bourbon that's distilled with the hop varietal of the same name, known for its pronounced floral, citrus, and pine aromas. It also produces a whiskey called Hopmonster, which in addition to Amarillo, distills with the Saaz, Hersbrucker, and Strisselspalt varietals. The distillery also has created one called Citra Double IPA, whose dominant hops, as the name suggests, are the Citra varietal. Citra hops, as you probably could guess from their name, are known to be highly fruity in nature, with notes of passion fruit, grapefruit, lime, pineapple, mango, and papaya, as well as some nontropical produce such as peach and apricots.

Given that whiskey is really just beer that's been taken one step further—through distillation—it should be pretty easy to give the former the same kind of hop character that an India pale ale or other lupulin-forward brew has. Not so fast! The Corsair team went through a lot of trial and error before the distillery settled on what it calls its hopped whiskey library—encompassing some eighty different single-hop or hop-blend spirits.

"If you were making craft beer and you were wanting to just distill and imagine it would be a good whiskey, you would probably be disappointed by the results,"[93] Bell warns. "There is this translation through the still and a lot of times the hops just don't react how you think they're going to. "

For instance, sometimes certain aromas one would expect from a particular type of hop are lost in translation, while other flavors are amplified. And, when alcohol that is a much higher proof than that found in beer enters the equation, so does a great degree of volatility. "Alcohol evaporates so rapidly and it's so volatile that it really picks up aromas, which are much more intense on the nose," Bell explains. "I can open a hopped whiskey across the room and someone else will be like, "Whoa, is there a Christmas tree in this room?"

The hopped-up offerings provide a nice tractor beam for beer geeks who may or may not be considering dipping a toe in the whiskey world. Bell made a similar journey, which he considers a natural progression from beer to whiskey. Really, whiskey just takes beer one step further and distills what's been fermented.

"We have a lot of hardcore beer drinkers who come into our facility," Bell reveals. "They're not that big on whiskey, but when they try our hopped whiskeys, they really get into it and they love it. If they're a hardcore hophead, they're going to love hopped whiskeys."

It might be relatively easy to win over the craft beer aficionado, but the classic whiskey drinker is an entirely different story. Craft beer drinkers, for the most part, discovered their favorite beverage because they're explorers; they sought out new taste experiences beyond what the multinational macros have commoditized as "beer." Many whiskey drinkers, by contrast, can be a more old-fashioned lot.

"There are some more traditional whiskey drinkers who look down on beer as some kind of lesser thing, and they think whiskey is the greatest thing ever," Bell concedes. "They think we've bastardized the whiskey. But for us, there's room to be influenced by all kinds of drinks."

Bell literally wrote the book on off-the-beaten-path spirits-making, Alt Whiskey. He also authored the follow-up, Fire Water: Experimental Smoked Malts and Whiskeys.

Cider perhaps has a closer kinship with beer, as there's no distillation involved with either. There also are far fewer purists than there are with whiskey, especially since cider is still such a relatively small category, and the vast majority of adult beverage drinkers are in the process of just figuring out what this sparkling apple-based libation is in the first place.

And, typically, cider volume is usually lumped in with that of beer when market research houses and pundits are measuring the overall market. The clear distinction, however, is the source from which each derives its fermentable sugars (grains versus apples). The growing interest among cider producers to infuse their products with hops is blurring the lines a bit between the two worlds. And that's definitely not a bad thing.

— REVEREND NAT'S HARD CIDER —

Reverend Nat's Hard Cider offers a whole line of hopped-up apple offerings, which is not a huge shocker since the company is nestled in the heart of Hop Heaven, the Pacific Northwest—not to mention the brewing capital of North America, if not the world, Portland, Oregon. One of its year-round bottled brands is Hallelujah Hopricot, which boasts Oregon-grown Cascade hops and a drop or two of apricot juice. It also just happens to be the cidery's flagship product.

The good Reverend also has a rotating roster of limited edition hop infusions, including one fermented from Bartlett Pears (pear cider often is referred to as "perry," by the way). Bartlett Simcoe is a medium-sweet concoction that incorporates Simcoe hops for some earthy, piney, citrusy flavor notes.

Another pear-based creation is D'Anjou Mosaic, whose pear of choice is of the French d'Anjou variety. It gets the second half of its name from the Mosaic hop, known for its tropical fruit qualities. It also used the French fruit for its D'Anjou Nelson, whose namesake hop produces aromas of white wine and berries.

"You can look at it as either taking it to a logical extreme or an illogical extreme,"[94] says founder and namesake Nat West. "I don't really care if it makes sense or not. It tastes good and people are buying it. I make ciders for Portland palates."

And many of those palates have converged on his headquarters in the City of Roses for Reverend Nat's Hopped Cider Festival, an annual spring event that has been known to violate a few fire codes. "We had eight hundred people at the cider fest—it's impossible to fit eight hundred people in our place," West notes. "They were physically shoulder-to-shoulder for a little over four hours, with really long lines crisscrossing each other." The second edition, held in the spring of 2015, had to move outside with a street closure. It more than doubled the number of hop-infused offerings over the first year; it went from twenty-one to forty-four ciders from around the world—many not available in the state of Oregon.

Doc's Draft Dry Hopped
(Warwick Valley Winery & Distillery)

Another cider that gets an extra hit of those bitter little flowers originates in one of the most unlikely of places: a winery that's also a distillery (and, of course, a cidery). The Warwick Valley Winery & Distillery is the company behind the Doc's Draft cider line, one of whose popular offerings is Doc's Draft Dry Hopped Hard Cider. Dry hopping refers to the practice of adding hops to the fermenter (in addition to during the boil stage) to enhance the aroma of the final beer or, in this case, cider. The dry hopping in Doc's comes courtesy of Centennial and Chinook hops, imparting citrusy and spicy/piney notes to the beverage.

Dank Hop (Swift Cider)

Swift Cider is another Portland, Oregon, operation that makes full use of the region's hop bounty. Three hop varieties (Columbus, Centennial, and Chinok) combined with organic pineapples give Dank Hop its flavorful character, which alternates between pine and tropical fruit.

GRASSHOP-AH (COLORADO CIDER COMPANY)

The one state that rivals Oregon in craft brewing acumen is Colorado—and now the state is holding its own with cider as well. Hops aren't the only star of Colorado Cider's apple-based curiosity. Grasshop-ah throws in some lemongrass for some additional botanical zest, counterbalancing the citrusy hop bite. The team at Colorado Cider likes to think of it as the gateway cider for beer drinkers.

WOODCHUCK HOPSATION (VERMONT HARD CIDER COMPANY)

Even a relatively mainstream brand like Woodchuck, the first cider the average consumer is likely to have encountered, launched Woodchuck Dry Hop in 2013 as part of its higher-end Cellar Series. But that was just the beginning. The following year it introduced Hopsation, a core, year-round cider that's semidry, with a touch of sweetness and just enough of the pine-needle-y hints drinkers have come to expect from American hops.

Hopped ciders and whiskeys are still small niches within niches, but with the greater experimentation that's taking place among cider and whiskey producers large and small, a little bitter, earthy, floral, citrusy kick in an otherwise traditional alcohol is becoming a sensory experience that's easier to come by for the curious drinker.

Week 43
Revitalizing Vodka

Brace yourselves; I'm about to get controversial.

Vodka, despite its enormous cultural significance, impeccable mixability, and general ubiquity, often can be a bit of a scam. By definition, it's supposed to be colorless, flavorless, and odorless. Producers actually set out to achieve those three objectives. Part of the reason there's no real mandate dictating the source from which it must be distilled—any given bar might stock ones made from potatoes, wheat, rye, corn, and many other starchy bases—is that there's no distinguishable grain or spud character left after it's gone through its multiple distillation rounds. What difference would it make, anyway?

That's what makes the advent of ultrapremium vodka all the more remarkable. Drinkers pay considerably more for cocktails mixed with Ciroc or Ketel One than one with Smirnoff or Wolfschmidt, mainly so they can get a lot more of that zero flavor, color, and aroma. Business schools should make vodka-marketing classes mandatory because there's no greater case study in stellar branding than the rise of the high-end of that category.

This may sound like the cynical rant of a curmudgeonly consumer, but full disclosure: This ranter happens to actually enjoy vodka very much. It's a combination of that aforementioned mixability and ubiquity that makes it so appealing—it's an empty vessel that begs to be filled. It's particularly delicious when it's combined with savory ingredients; sometimes there's nothing better than a well-built Bloody Mary. But even then, it's more about covering up the vodka than transforming it.

That's where infusions come in—not those flavored vodkas with artificial berry or cloying breakfast food flavors (yes, there are waffle and doughnut vodkas on the market), but proprietary, steeped-with-care creations that bars and restaurants with a pronounced Eastern European bent serve to their discerning patrons.

There really are few limits to the types of natural flavors that can be infused, though some admittedly work better than others. But the ones that do work? Wow! Especially the salty and spicy options. Nothing goes better with the smoky, briny, stewy dishes typical of Russia and its neighboring countries.

The most eye-opening component of dining at a Russian restaurant is not the exotic food, but discovering how many vodka brands there are that you weren't aware existed in the first place. Certainly, vodka has become nearly commoditized as every celebrity or opportunistic entrepreneur has tried to slap a label on a neutral spirit and make it trendy as possible. But most of those have either cutesy or luxury-sounding names and at one time or another, they showed up at some nightclub in New York City, Chicago, or LA, if only for a week. The brands you're likely to encounter at a Russian restaurant are hardcore Eastern Bloc brands, which very well may have resulted in the maiming of the would-be defector who smuggled them in at the height of the Cold War. They're an adventure in and of themselves without any adulteration, but with the right infusions, they're on another plane of existence all together.

The Russia House in Washington, DC, is one of the premier vodka lounges this side of the Black Sea, boasting a formidable list of some two hundred different vodkas, most with names barely pronounceable to the average Westerner. Its infusions rotate frequently, and they're always available in $40 tasting flights of six, carefully arranged in a circular tray atop an ice bucket, with various briny and citrusy munchable/garnishable accompaniments in the center. Sound steep? For one person maybe, but keep in mind each of these so-called shots is a generous, filled-to-the-brim pour in a slim, two-ounce glass. Do the math. If you still think that's an acceptable quantity of an eighty-proof spirit for a single human being to consume in a solitary sitting, you should maybe consider forgoing the twelve ounces for twelve steps.

A typical flight balancing the sweet and fruity with pungent and savory begins with a mango/orange/pineapple infusion, continues with a berry blend, and then transitions into "pickled" (dirty martini-ish), cucumber and dill (not tremendously unlike the pickled, though noticeably crisper and fresher), and horseradish (a classic). It's always good to save something sweet for the end. That could be either a cherry-vanilla or honey option, depending on availability.

New York's Anyway Café's steeped savories are so insidious that you'd swear that it's an actual cocktail occupying most of the real estate in your martini glass. Instead, it's almost all vodka, incognito thanks to the crimson tint from infused tomatoes. Even the strongest Bloody Mary has nothing on that one.

Sadly, in recent years, it's only been in these ethnic eateries that one could get a quality infusion. The concept was hot in the early to mid-2000s, but then, like all good things, it veered into over-the-top territory and overstayed its welcome (enter: those aforementioned artificially flavored breakfast-confection and Twinkie-inspired concoctions). Meat-market nightclubs started getting in on the trend, and it all went to hell. Our friend, mixologist extraordinaire Ben Paré, laments that unfortunate turn of events.

"People were just throwing stuff in and it became a gimmicky thing,"[95] Paré explains. "That's when you started to see things like 'Swedish Fish vodka.'"

The more craft-minded cocktail bars started to back away from infusions, but Paré believes such creations will have their moment once again in those venues. Especially with the rise of molecular mixology—turning liquids into solids like gels and semisolids like foam—bartenders have a lot more tools at their disposal to perfectly capture the essence of fresh-from-the-garden ingredients. The iSi whipper works especially well. The nitrous-oxide pressurization enables liquid and solid ingredients to marry far more quickly than the standard steeping method. What normally would entail six days of waiting for nature to take its course can be accomplished in barely half an hour with an iSi.

"For example, if you want to infuse roasted butternut squash, cut it up, fill it into the iSi, pressurize it three times, let it sit for thirty minutes, and let the air out," Paré says. "You basically have an infusion."

Until the rest of the cocktailing world forgives the transgressions of gimmicky brand owners and less quality-minded nightspots and starts taking infusions as seriously as Paré does—and it will happen—you'll do well to brush up on your Russian.

Week 44

There Will Be Blood

Reinventing Mary

Halloween wouldn't be Halloween without a marathon of classic horror movies. And what would those films be without generous helpings of blood? It amazes me that the classic Bloody Mary isn't mined more frequently for its fright-inducing potential—it already has one of the scariest names in the entire cocktail world.

Instead, it's largely relegated to brunch as America's favorite "hair of the dog" to help mitigate the previous night's excesses.

Brunch restaurants make a killing mixing these relatively cheap cocktails, sometimes serving them as loss leaders for $3 to get week-end diners to shell out $15 or more for a glorified plate of bacon and eggs or the remnants of last night's dinner special that the eatery was going to have to dump anyway. Others promise bottomless refills for $10 or $11, letting the moderate drinkers subsidize the bingers. The problem here is that very little thought goes into these Bloodies, or roughly the same amount involved in mixing vodka and orange juice and calling it a Screwdriver or the latter with sparkling white wine and deeming it a Mimosa.

Even worse, try ordering a Mary on a plane, and the flight attendant will hand you a can of Campbell's tomato juice and a 50 mL bottle of vodka (if he or she likes you, you'll get two) and tell you to go nuts. I've since learned to travel with little packets of Tabasco sauce and pepper, but it's still not the same.

Fortunately we live in the age of the mixologist and no one has to settle for a subpar, dumbed-down Bloody. The tomato-based marvel has become as much of a canvas for the creative cocktail set as anything ending in -tini has. It's, therefore, time we start taking the Bloody Mary seriously and stop treating it merely as a component of an either/or proposition for those rejecting the sweet, citrusy option with their first meal on a Sunday. And who says it should be limited to brunch-time consumption anyway?

A word of caution: Elevating the Bloody Mary to new heights with nontraditional ingredients, unconventional garnishes, and general mixological know-how is something we all should embrace. Jumping the shark is a whole other story. (That term, with its 1977 Happy Days origins, no longer should be applied exclusively to television properties. It works in any medium or consumer product category where something that was once great lost its way and forgot what it was supposed to be).

For instance, the social media-sphere recently was abuzz with chatter about Sobelman's Pub in Milwaukee, creator of "The Chicken Fried Bloody Mary." The $50 monstrosity starts with a giant jar filled with eighty ounces of the tomato juice and vodka components and adds bacon-wrapped jalapeño cheese balls on skewers (it is Wisconsin, after all), cheeseburger sliders and, the centerpiece element, a four-pound deep-fried whole chicken. Before that, Sobelman's was known for what it calls "The Bloody Masterpiece," which includes a few modest tweaks on the classic Bloody—if you consider garnishing the drink with Brussels sprouts, shrimp, a cheeseburger, and about ten other dinner items to be still within the realm of classic.[96]

Those don't just jump the shark. They jump, ride, taunt, and take selfies with the shark. While they're amazingly indulgent and undoubtedly tasty, for our purposes, a Bloody Mary should be something a person enjoys with a meal. It shouldn't be the meal (a meal that feeds a family of six, at that).

The basic Bloody is one of mixologist Paré's favorite vehicles for innovation. At his base, SoHo's Sanctuary T, he's drawn upon some of the freshest ingredients Mother Nature has to offer to challenge the public perception of what the drink could be without resorting to cheap, gimmicky, headline-whoring stunts. Even when it's the most basic iteration of the classic, it's not something he or the rest of the staff are phoning in. For the standard Bloody, it begins and ends with the quality of the juice. In Sanctuary T's case, fresh liquid from world-famous San Marzano tomatoes is the go-to base of choice.

Those plum-shaped Italian legends are known to be a bit on the sweet side and, to temper that, Paré frequently sprinkles in some pinewood-smoked Chinese black tea. "If it's just regular tomato juice, it would stand out and be very abrasive," Paré notes. "But when combined with San Marzano tomato juice, it kind of all makes sense."

When San Marzanos aren't available, he recommends, for the most standard of Bloodies, using V8 rather than tomato-only juice, given the former's multiveggie complexity and lower acidity.

Make no mistake, though: regardless of how much backup it might have, the tomato is still the star of the show. "Tomato juice is such a versatile ingredient because it's seen in so many cultures."

That's what makes ethnic twists on the traditional concept—the most popular being the tequila-based Mexican variation, the Bloody Maria—so appealing to bartenders and drinkers alike.

Portland's Tasty n Sons offers something of a globetrotting Mary menu with international riffs on the savory classic, ranging from subtle tweaks to outright reinventions. Its Tasty Mary is as traditional as it gets: Sobieski vodka, tomato, Worcestershire, horseradish, lemon, Sriracha, celery salt, celery, and house pickles. Pretty standard save for the Asian hot sauce twist. For an even more Eastern influence, Tasty n Sons' Dim Summore combines vodka, tomato, and Sriracha with hoisin, lime, and ginger, and its Lady Vengeance (named for the Korean crime film) tosses the vodka altogether in favor of Old Overholt rye whiskey; it then pours in some kimchi juice, lime, fish sauce, and Korean chili salt.

Tasty n Sons also does a Mexican variation called the Chollollan that takes the Bloody Maria considerably further than simply substituting the core spirit; in addition to substituting vodka with tequila, it also mixes in some mezcal for a touch of smoke and combines the liquors with Cholula hot sauce, tomato, pimenton, and, for a slight touch of Italy, Calabrian chiles. Scandinavia gets its fair share of the spotlight in the Tasty Maiken: tomato, dill, pickle, and the Nordic spirit aquavit (more on that in week forty-nine).

Those are all great if it's a red Mary you crave.

What's this now?

Just because blood is red and Bloody Marys typically sport that sanguine hue, there's no law stating they must be that color. In fact, green works quite well (and, as any Trekkie will argue, Vulcans' blood actually is that tint). Paré makes what he calls a "twist on a twist:" a green Bloody Maria. Instead of tomatoes, he juices tomatillos, which give it its color. And, since tomatillos can be considerably thinner in body, pureed avocados come in handy, thickening the texture and adding a delicious dimension. Muddled cilantro and jalapeño fulfill the herbal and spicy duties, while a whole tomatillo and a couple of slices of the aforementioned hot pepper make for an attractive, chlorophyll-tinted (and potentially tongue-burning, head-sweat-inducing) garnish.

But who says you need any color at all? It's not unheard of to mix a Mary that's completely clear. Paré has achieved that end by infusing vodka with horseradish and combining it with tomato water rather than juice. To extract the water, juice the tomato (or tomatillo), salt it, and let it sit overnight. The clear elements will settle to the bottom and the pulpy, colorful portions will rise to the top. Strain it all through a cheesecloth and, voila! Tomato water!

The horseradish infusion phase actually helps even the most colorful of Bloodies. The shredded root has as many detractors as it does fans, and for many of those who can't stand it, it's more often than not a textural issue. Infusing horseradish retains its spicy pungency without what many find to be an off-putting, pulpy mouth feel.

Horseradish, no horseradish. Tomato, tomatillo. Red, green, or clear. There technically are no right or wrong ways to make Bloody Marys. But there are millions of downright lazy Bloody Marys and an equal number of truly inspired ones. Life's too short to settle for anything but the latter.

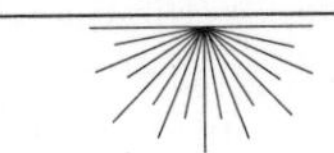

THE WALL COMES DOWN FOR BERLINER WEISSE

On November 9, 1989, that notorious concrete symbol of oppression, the Berlin Wall, finally came down. Though it may seem a frivolous ritual for an event of such global and historical significance, I like to mark the anniversary with a glass of the German capital's signature beer style, Berliner Weisse (pronounced "vice").

When what came to be known as craft beer just started to get going in the 1970s and 1980s, the big selling point for many of its pioneering participants was the notion that they were bringing to US consumers some classic beer styles that had gone all but untasted on the American side of the pond. There would be no American pale ales or India pale ales in the United States if no brewers had imported the original concept from England and made them their own with homegrown hops.

Berliner Weisse was one of those styles that had become nearly extinct (or at least a pale shade of its former self) in its home country. I like to think about it as a wheat beer for those who aren't crazy about wheat beers. Wheat makes up about a quarter to a third of its malt bill—in ages past it was significantly more—and it can be quite refreshing. That's why, in the states, it's frequently released as a summer seasonal. And that's a shame, because the style, characterized by its moderate tartness, is enjoyable throughout the year—even in . . . no, especially in November. Drinking adventurously, after all, means sometimes defying conventional wisdom.

Technically Berliner Weisse would fall under the sour beer umbrella, but it's such an experience unto itself that it deserves its own chapter. First of all, there's such a wild variation in ABVs among sours, from a sessionable 5-ish percent to the ultra-extremes in the teens. Berliner Weisses, on the other hand, achieve their tart complexity with a modest ABV usually south of 3 percent.

Like the Kölsch and Altbier styles, the Berliner Weisse is localized to its German city of origin. Visit Cologne and Düsseldorf and you're pretty much only going to get Kölsch and Altbier, respectively, when you ask for *ein bier*. It's a bit more complicated in Deustchland's capital city and Berliner Weisse's namesake. Like much of the rest of Germany (and all of Europe for that matter), Berlin largely is dominated by pilsners (though there's a growing US-influenced craft beer revolution beginning to take root in the capital, but that's a story for another day). Berliner Weisses are easy enough to find, but they're by no means ubiquitous. And Berliners tend not to drink them these days. In fact, I sensed a bit of silent judgment from the waitstaff any time I ordered one there. Male friends have told me they have been downright mocked at Berlin bars for ordering beers only drunk by the frauleins. (Despite the huge and growing percentage of beer drinkers that are women, libation-specific sexism is still rampant on just about every continent.)

Part of the reason is that relatively minuscule alcohol content. But, perhaps a bigger part of it is the shot of sweet syrup that's often squirted into the glass. If the bartender, waiter, or waitress is asking if you want it *mit schuss*, they're inquiring whether you want that shot—if they're even nice enough to give you a choice. In some bars, it's unthinkable for them to serve it schuss-free. Usually the question you'll get is *ein rotes*? (a red one) or ein grünes? (a green one). The rotes is raspberry, while the grünes is the herbal woodruff flavor. Berliners had developed a taste for the stuff, as it was designed to counteract some of the tartness. Servers deliver these day-glow crimson or lime-hued concoctions in short, wide, cylindrical glasses with a (gasp!) straw protruding from the liquid.

No disrespect to the good people of Berlin, but that is a rather unfortunate tradition. It's the equivalent of lobotomizing an artist for expressing him or herself.

It's also probably why the style was relatively endangered until American craft brewers rediscovered it and started adding it to their repertoires. The syrup remains a source of great controversy. Some US establishments offer it as an option, assuming they're giving consumers a taste of the old country. That's their prerogative. Personally, I prefer to experience Berliner Weisse in all its tart, naked glory. And

I'm sure I'm not the only one. Palates have adapted to IPAs, high-ABV sours, lambics, and a whole host of other previously unapproachable taste profiles. They don't need a sugary syrup to cut notes that aren't even close to offensive. But, that's for you to judge. And here are Berliners by way of America to help you get started.

- **Boiler Room (Saint Arnold Brewing Company):** Thankfully, Saint Arnold Brewing Company has made Boiler Room a year-round lineup and not limited it to a single season (then again, Saint Arnold's based in Houston, Texas, where seasons aren't quite as defined as in other areas). Boiler Room came into being quite inadvertently. Brewer Stephen Rawlings was in the process of making a batch of Lawnmower, Saint Arnold's popular German-style Kölsch (pale, malty, refreshing style native to Cologne), when half of the malt ended up on the floor rather than in the grain mill. It resulted in a wort that was half the strength it was supposed to be. Rawlings made the best of a bad situation and put ten gallons of it in a fermenting container (known as a carboy), topped it off with a bottle of a funky, bacteria-rich Belgian beer, and left it in the boiler room to sour for a couple of days. The 3.5 percent ABV creation, a nice balance of sweet and lime-like tartness, was quite the happy little accident.

- **Cape Codder Weisse (Night Shift Brewing Company):** Night Shift, of Everett, Massachusetts, offers an entire line of rotating brews loosely based on the Berliner Weisse style. Notable among those is the Cape Codder Weisse, aged with cranberries and infused with orange zest, amping up the tart-quotient considerably. It gets extra points for being released in the winter, proving that there's a Weisse for all seasons.

- **Cayuga Cruiser (Ithaca Brewing Company):** Upstate New York's Finger Lakes region has given us more wineries than we can count, but tucked amid all of those are some of the mid-Atlantic region's most prolific breweries. Ithaca's reputation spans far beyond its college town base, thanks to creations like its summer seasonal, Cayuga Cruiser (as well as a couple of others you'll discover throughout these pages). It's hazy on the eyes, but light and refreshing on the tongue and stays true to the German style it emulates with its über-sessionable 4.2 percent ABV. Lactobacillus gives it just the right amount of snap.

»→ Checkpoint Charlie (Newburgh Brewing Company): With a name that's a very obvious nod to a notorious component of Berlin's all-too-recent history, Checkpoint Charlie is the work of another up-and-coming New York State operation, Newburgh Brewing Company in the Hudson Valley region. At 3 percent ABV, it's even closer to what the original Berlin brewers intended. Those who visit the brewery can sample it with those polarizing syrups; in addition to woodruff and raspberry, it also lets drinkers douse it with blueberry. Newburgh recommends pairing it with shellfish and salads.

»→ Hottenroth (The Bruery): Here's a world-class option from the more temperate (in climate, not consumption) part of the country. Southern California's The Bruery, essentially a pun that incorporates founder Patrick Rue's surname, produces Hottenroth in memory of Rue's grandparents, Fred and Sarah Hottenroth. Like Checkpoint Charlie, it keeps things as close to Berliner Weisse's roots as possible, with a remarkably complex 3.1 percent ABV beer. A little bit of brettanomyces joins the requisite lactobacillus culture in imparting the sour bite.

»→ Amerikaner In Berliner Weisse (Pints Brewery): It wouldn't be fair to talk about American brewing without giving at least one shout-out to the brewing capital of the country (and pretty much the world), Portland, Oregon. One of the newer players in the city is the pocket-sized downtown Pints Brewery (whose taproom doubles as a coffee house in the morning hours), which opened in 2012.
I'm going to go out on a limb here and say Amerikaner in Berliner Weisse is perhaps the closest approximation of the original style that I've had. And its alcohol content is a staggeringly low 2.8 percent by volume. In the very small seasonal window that the taproom has Amerikaner on the board, it stocks plenty of woodruff and raspberry syrups for those insistent on kicking it old school . . . but you know my feelings on that.

Week 46
BRING ON THE BRINE
ENTER THE PICKLEBACK

Sweet syrups may not be my cup of tea, but one thing I absolutely cannot get enough of is a thoroughly pucker-inducing pickle. November 14 is National Pickle Day—yes, that's a thing—and it might as well be my birthday.

One thing I'm not crazy about, though, is a chaser, especially when whiskey's involved. Any whiskey that requires a chaser, for the most part, usually isn't worth drinking in the first place. However, sometimes the concept is so delicious—say, it involves pickles—that the chaser becomes the star of the show and the very reason one drinks the "chasee." Thus was born the pickleback, which couldn't get any simpler: It's a shot of briny pickle juice, which, if sipped properly, actually enhances the chased spirit, rather than neutralizes it. Think of it as a cocktail deconstructed into two parts.

It's actually a fairly new phenomenon, originating as recently as 2006 and credited to Brooklyn bartender Reggie Cunningham, who was working at a local watering hole called the Bushwick Country Club at the eastern edge of the hipster haven that is Williamsburg. Despite its name, it's not actually a country club; there aren't any argyle-clad elitists sipping chardonnay at the Bushwick, but there is, believe it or not, golf—six holes of putt-putt in the back of this dive bar, to be exact.

The bar's owner, John Roberts, says the birth of the pickleback was more a matter of hilarious synchronicity than any premeditated design.

Bob McClure, founder of the now fairly well-known artisanal pickle company, McClure's, happened to live two doors down from Roberts.

At the time, McClure was working out of his kitchen and needed a place to stash some of his inventory. Roberts had basement space to spare, so he was glad to help. As a token of his gratitude, McClure gave him a case of pickles to use in Bloody Marys and such at the Country Club.

One day, Cunningham was eating some of the pickles out of the jar to nurse a hangover when an out-of-towner popped in and eyed some of the brine.

"She had a gold tooth and was a redneck kind of chick,"[97] Cunningham recalls. "'Let's drink a shot of pickle juice,' she said. I said, 'That sounds kind of disgusting. I'm not even drinking tonight, anyway.' She demanded that we start throwing them back."

Cunningham was a bit taken aback by this request, but ultimately relented, suggesting they do the house shot before slurping straight pickle juice. The whiskey of choice was Old Crow bourbon, which the Country Club usually served as half of its beer-and-shot special. The beer, incidentally, was Pabst Blue Ribbon (this is Williamsburg, after all).

The Old Crow, immediately followed by the shot of brine, created an unexpected harmony that made an instant believer out of Cunningham. "John came in, and I said, 'We've got to name this thing, put it on our board, and start selling it,'" he remembers.

Roberts admits that when his then-bartender told him about it, he was mildly repulsed by the concept. But finally, after much goading by staff and regulars, he tried the Old Crow/pickleback pairing, and it made an immediate convert out of the bar owner as well.

Certainly, the idea of drinking pickle juice was nothing new.

"People had been drinking the brine forever,"[98] Roberts says, "but Reggie was the one who created the whiskey-shot-and-pickleback combination."

Originally it was just a means to erase a rather intense shot from the palate—Old Crow is not for the squeamish—but eventually bartenders started experimenting with sipping whiskeys that tend to taste fine on their own. The marketers of Jameson whiskey got wind of the fact that bars were pairing the Irish spirit with picklebacks and even started using the salty shot in its promotions.

"There's no wrong way or right way to do it, I guess," Roberts says.

However, that doesn't mean it's as simple as taking any old salty juice and chugging it down with liquor. McClure's worked as a good prototype because it's a well crafted pickle in an exceptional brine—the lingering spicy garlic dill character with a warming finish matches up well with the spirit. It's not something that's likely to be replicated by sipping the juice from one of those ubiquitous giant pickle vats next to a supermarket's deli counter. "I've had it with the deli pickle brine, that stuff that looks like antifreeze," Roberts cautions. "That's disgusting."

Let's just say, in this age of mobile apps and social media, the concept has gone viral.

The United Kingdom has been quick to embrace the trend, with a number of high-end hotspots adopting the pickleback and making it their own. Some have experimented with their own crafty concoctions. London's Rivington Grill created a version mixing olive brine with a touch of pickled onion vinegar.

About three hours outside of London in the seaside town of Sheringham, England, The Burlington Hotel takes things in a radical direction with shots ranging from pickled strawberry to pickled radish.

Picklebacks have popped up in some of the least expected places as well, as far away as Japan and as removed from civilization as the rainforests of Central America.

One of Bushwick Country Club's former employees was backpacking through the latter region and happened upon a bar inside a tree house that had picklebacks on the menu.

Back in the Country Club's more populous neck of the woods, Barcade, the Brooklyn-born pub and classic video game arcade hybrid that has expanded to Manhattan, Jersey City, New Jersey, and Philadelphia, showcased its craft beer cred with the introduction of the Hopback: bitter hops steeped in the savory brine.

It was only a matter of time before someone started packaging the idea, and now there's something of a cottage industry of entrepreneurs bottling the briny stuff and slapping on a pickleback label. A Wisconsin-based pickle company called Van Holten's decided to package the juice from its late nineteenth-century pickle recipe when, in late 2013, it started fielding calls from a United Kingdom–based start-up that was hoping to import Van Holten's brine for a brand it was launching.

The logistics of supplying the product made the partnership more trouble than it was worth for Van Holten's, but the discussions did pique the pickle company's interest about a burgeoning bar trend that previously had not been on its radar.

The company noticed that Spec's, the major liquor chain in Texas that had been carrying Van Holten's Pickle-in-a-Pouch, had on its shelves bottles of pickle brine that a store-brand manufacturer had produced for the chain, selling for $9 a pop.

"Spec's recognized the whole pickleback phenomenon and knew it was a big thing,"[99] Van Holten's vice president of sales and marketing, Eric Girard, remembers. "But they had a private-label margarita maker making it for them—they were having to buy the pickles, get them into a vat, and put the juice in a bottle."

Van Holten's, by contrast, already had the pickle brine infrastructure in place and when it floated the idea to Spec's management about possibly packaging its own pickleback and branding it at a significantly lower cost—about $5 at retail—Spec's only question was, "How soon can you get it here?"

"So," says Girard, "we're in the pickleback business."

An expat American entrepreneur living in the United Kingdom also branded and packaged the idea as, what else, Pickleback. Creator Byron Knight's version actually brings a bit of a farm-to-glass dynamic to its production: His company grows the cucumbers and pickles them with dill.

Cunningham, who now works at a craft beer bar called Mission Dolores in Brooklyn's Park Slope neighborhood, expresses no hard feelings toward those who've been capitalizing off the concept and name he created, nor has he been seeking a piece of the action. The subject has come up from time to time, but he doesn't think the pickleback idea would have caught on globally like it has if he and Roberts had tried to hold on to it for dear life.

"Would others be making combinations with the stuff if they were paying rights to it?" he ponders. "I doubt it."

When Cunningham sees people ordering the combo these days, he tends to keep his ego in check and doesn't even tell them that it all started with him.

And Roberts remains dumbfounded by the minirevolution that his humble little dive bar in Brooklyn unintentionally ignited.

"It just started as an inside joke," he muses, "and it's literally worldwide now."

Week 47

Pass the Sweet Potatoes

Sweet-Potato-Based Beer

Whether or not you're on board with a holiday like National Pickle Day, you're not likely to dispute the validity of this week's big event: Thanksgiving. And what would Thanksgiving be without a side of sweet potatoes.

For this most American of holidays, we have to give special props to . . . the Japanese.

You'll recall from earlier in the year that sweet potato–based shochu is the most popular style of the spirit in Japan. The varieties grown in Japan are a bit different from the bright orange ones we're used to in America. The Japanese variants usually have purplish or reddish skin and either off-white or yellowish flesh. On some varieties, the flesh can be purplish or reddish, as well.

— Beniaka (Coedo Brewery) —

The starchy spuds are so popular in Japan that they've also found their way into another beverage: beer. Coedo Brewery, part of the country's burgeoning craft beer scene that echoes the brewing revolution that's been taking place in the United States and most of the rest of the world, unleashed Beniaka onto the scene, and it quickly became the brewer's signature beer. The amber lager gets its name from the variety of bright red sweet potatoes grown in Coedo's home region of Kawagoe. It's got an ABV of 7 percent and contains less than 25 percent malt.

It technically falls under the umbrella of happoshu, a Japanese classification for beer with a low- or no-malt content (the threshold is 67 percent malt). Happoshu actually is taxed at a lower rate than mostly malt beer, so many producers, especially the large macroproducers in the country, often produce a subpremium brew with minimal malt to market it cheaply. That is not the case with Coedo. Beniaka's raison d'etre was not thrift, but flavor. It was an experiment to see if the brewer could produce a beer that was as flavorfully complex as the shochus made from the same vegetable. Needless to say, Coedo was quite happy with its results.

Now, purist beer geeks, especially on this side of the Pacific, might have initially cried foul that 75 percent of their beloved malt had been replaced by a starch source they'd consider an adjunct, but it's key to consider the brewer's true intention.

Beyond flavor, there's the added benefit that the sweet potato actually is a gluten-free food. However, I'd advise those with celiac disease not to rush out and hunt down a bottle of Beniaka, because it still has that 25 percent barley malt content.

For Coedo, creating Beniaka was akin to finding a home for all of the inhabitants of the Island of Misfit Toys. About 40 percent of sweet potatoes grown in Japan are considered substandard; the veggies are packaged based on size, and any potatoes that are deemed to be of irregular proportion are tossed out. Coedo witnessed this every day; before it got into beer, it was a vegetable distributor in the farm-rich Kawagoe region. One industry's trash is another industry's treasure and those misfit taters were the seeds of an entirely new business model (with the help of equipment and an expert brewmaster imported from Germany). Coedo created its potato-based prototype in 1996 and continued to tinker with it for about a decade before settling on the recipe used today. [100]

Since then, Beniaka has captured the imagination of the world and garnered multiple international awards to prove it.

It also made it okay for American craft brewers to dabble with the vegetable. After all, pumpkin beers have been all the rage in the fall from coast to coast, and sweet potatoes are kind of the gourd's cousin, right? At least that's the case when people try to convince me that sweet potato pie is just as good as pumpkin pie.

– CARVER (FULLSTEAM BREWERY) –

Among the earliest products to come out of the tank from Durham, North Carolina's, Fullsteam Brewery was a brand called Carver, which it brews with a colossal (for American brewers) two hundred pounds of the starch powerhouse. It's a nod to its own local terroir, as North Carolina's sweet potato crop is known to be quite robust. The "Carver" in question is none other than George Washington Carver. Wait, wasn't he the peanut guy? Why, yes, he was, but somewhat lesser known was that he was the consummate sweet potato aficionado.

Fullsteam was not taking a cue from the likes of Beniaka, but really wanted to ferment the soul of the South. "In our quest to make a distinctly Southern beer using local ingredients, it was just an obvious choice with how many farms rely on sweet potatoes for their income and how important it is in the state's overall agriculture industry,"[101] Fullsteam's "chief executive optimist," Sean Lilly Wilson, tells me.

Despite the volume of the vegetable Fullsteam puts in Carver, it accounts for only about one-third of its fermentable base, with traditional malt making up the rest.

Though the thought of a brew with such a base may initially appeal to the dessert-minded, Wilson is very adamant about there being no pie spices whatsoever in Carver. A disproportionate number of American pumpkin beers tend to be dominated by cinnamon, nutmeg, clove, and their ilk with very little actual pumpkin character showing though. Do not expect any such enhancements in a Carver. "It's smooth and well-balanced like a lager should be, with the absence of pie spices," Wilson says. "I think a lot of people's experiences with sweet potatoes are the olfactory memories created by cinnamon, nutmeg, allspice, burnt marshmallow, brown sugar, et cetera. But we're stripping all of that out and making it a smooth, easy-drinking lager; it's very subtle."

It doesn't actually work well with desserts at all. It pairs far better with earthy, savory dishes such as roasted chicken or game birds.

— GLUTENATOR —
(EPIC BREWING COMPANY)

Clear across a couple of time zones, Epic Brewing Company, with operations in Utah and Colorado, launched a completely gluten-free alternative that it named, rather fittingly, the Glutenator. Molasses complements the taters as the fermentable source, creating a recipe for which Epic often is credited for bringing actual flavor to gluten-free beer. Prior releases by other breweries have substituted grains less flavorful than barley and wheat and the final products frequently seemed like second-class afterthoughts. "We tasted a lot of gluten-free beers on the market and a lot of them had this strange, tart kind of twang at the end and we've come to know that to be contributed by the sorghum—95 percent of gluten-free beers contain sorghum,"[102] notes Epic brewmaster Kevin Crompton. "Sorghum is what we believe makes them taste kind of nasty."

Proof that all grains don't work in all beverages. Sorghum, remember, is quite indispensible in baijiu.

Epic fiddled around with other gluten-free bases like millet and brown rice until the team decided on sweet potatoes, which provide slightly less than one-third of the fermentable sugars. "Sweet potato really comes across like pumpkin—it contributes a mouthfeel and texture, which is something we're pretty happy about."

Sweet potato beers likely will never account for more than a fraction of a fraction of a percent of brewers' overall output. But it's nice to know they're there for an occasional change of pace.

Week 48

PUTTING THE 'BEER' BACK IN 'GINGER BEER'

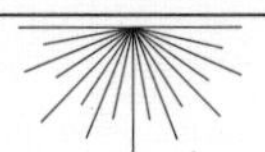

The fact that ginger ale and ginger beer exist is one of the most confounding mysteries a drinker ever will encounter. No, it's not because, in most cases, neither contains alcohol. It's because in the fermented world, ale resides under this larger umbrella we call "beer." So, wouldn't that mean that all ginger ales are ginger beers? (And, since we're going down that rabbit hole, ginger is a root. Wouldn't that make all ginger beers and, ergo, by applying transitive logic, root beers?)

Perplexing nomenclature aside, anyone who's tasted either will assert that aside from the word ginger the two have very little in common.

Ginger beer, which is ginger ale's great-granddaddy, originated in the eighteenth century, at least a century before what we traditionally think of as ginger ale came into being. While there are many claims on its exact origins some time in the nineteenth century, one of the first to actually market the golden-colored soft drink with which we're most familiar today was pharmacist John Vernor around 1870.[103] Vernor's creation was a more natural version of what we've come to accept as ginger ale: carbonated water flavored with a syrup made with ginger extracts. Today, most mass-produced ginger ales barely use any actual ginger, opting, instead for artificial flavorings. And don't even think of ordering from a fountain at a major restaurant chain. One of the first things waitstaff trainees learn is how to make "ginger ale" by mixing three parts Sprite (7Up or Sierra Mist work as well) with one part Coke or Pepsi.

The carbonation of true ginger beers, on the other hand, actually results from the fermentation process. Yes, that means there's some alcohol involved. The first ginger beers had considerably more than most of today's popular brands. Producers of the modern ones usually heat their products to not only kill the yeast, but also to boil off any sizable amounts of alcohol. As is the case with nonalcoholic beers like O'Doul's, there still is a trace of alcohol in the bottle, but it's usually under 0.5 percent, the legal threshold for marketing a beverage as "nonalcoholic."

Crabbie's (Halewood International):

And then there are those ginger beer makers that have no desire to halt the fermentation. In fact, they encourage the yeast to produce more alcohol. A leader in that world is the United Kingdom brand Crabbie's, which, in its current iteration, launched in 2009 but has spiritual roots in 1801. The early nineteenth century was a time of feverish entrepreneurial innovation and the time that the brand's namesake, John Crabbie, began utilizing Scotland's Port of Leith "to procure the finest spices and ingredients from far-off lands." He imported the finest ginger, and the best and most exotic herbs and spices from across the globe, he used his flair and imagination to conjure up adventurous recipes. Today, Crabbie's Original Alcoholic Ginger Beer is created using four secret ingredients, and steeps the finest ginger for up to six weeks to give the 4.8 percent ABV beverage its spicy character.

The brand's current owners, Halewood International, saw an opportunity to capitalize on cider and lager drinkers' desire for something different. "In the United Kingdom, ginger beer had been a nonalcholic drink,"[104] explains Crabbie's marketing director Richard Clark.

It was a doubly challenging proposition in the United States. Despite the fact that a substantial proportion of the stateside population already had fallen in love with ginger as an ingredient, ginger beer was nothing beyond a soft drink in the minds of most Americans. "We had to show that it was only for grownups," Clark reveals.

Now grownups are enjoying it across the United States. A great deal of the credit goes to a marketing campaign that romanticizes a bit of history (1801 is on every bottle) and promises a "Refreshingly Adventurous" experience. The two-word slogan captures everything Crabbie's strives to be: light, approachable, and an invitation (as well as permission) for cider and beer drinkers to live a little and expand their horizons. It's mostly those cider drinkers who are gravitating to it, though the beverage is drawing its fair share of beer (and even craft beer) drinkers. “Consumers are promiscuous,” Clark points out. “They like to try new things.”

And try new things you can, as the brand has since expanded to include Citrus Twist, Spiced Orange, and Scottish Raspberry varieties.

Ginger Grouse

Joining the gingery alcohol ranks is Ginger Grouse, which leverages the branding of its parent brand, The Famous Grouse Scotch Whisky, to market its own riff on the emerging category. The packaged product took its inspiration from a cocktail of the same name that the Scotch brand promoted to mixologists: 25 mL of The Famous Grouse, topped with ginger beer, served over ice with two freshly squeezed wedges of lime. (Sadly, there’s no actual whisky in Ginger Grouse). Its alcohol content is a slightly lower 4 percent, and it has very little presence in the United States. In the United Kingdom, it’s available at all of the major retail chains.

Hollows & Fentimans (Fentimans UK):

Fentimans British artisanal sodas are quite popular in the United States in trendy farm-to-table restaurants and upscale retail shops. The company also is marketing an alcoholic ginger beer, which draws upon a recipe more than a century old. (The “Hollows” in question is John Hollows, who married Fentimans founder Thomas Fentiman’s daughter in 1906). The company slowly ferments Chinese ginger root and a variety of handpicked herbs and natural flavorings. Hollows & Fentimans boldly displays the words “All Natural” on its label.

A key facet that sets alcoholic ginger beer apart from beer proper is that it’s okay to drink it over ice—Crabbie’s marketers are quite fond of the phrase “over ice with a slice” (insert favorite citrus garnish) as one of the recommended serving methods. It also works well in classic cocktails that call for ginger beer (the Moscow mule is the obvious option) or just plain neat in all of its effervescent glory.

It’s also pretty flexible from a culinary standpoint. It matches with traditional summer grilling staples like steaks and burgers and is equally compatible with richer cold-weather dishes such as those hearty stews one savors in front of a fire. And, as Brits have discovered, it’s a nice complement for what’s become their de facto national dish:

curry. The more soothing components of the ginger cut right through the heat.

Whether with food or without, on the rocks, in a mixed drink, or right out of the bottle, the reinvented, United Kingdom–born classic should have no trouble finding an audience when so many beer lovers are already expanding their repertoires to include cider, mead, and related refreshers. The sparkling spiciness of adult ginger beer will be right at home in such esteemed company.

WEEK 49

SCANDINAVIA'S WATER OF LIFE

AQUAVIT

Scandinavia boasts one of the world's great drinking cultures, which often is obscured by those of its closest regional neighbors. That's primarily due to the fact that one of the biggest contributions the Nordic countries have made to global beverage alcohol, up until relatively recently, was very rarely made outside of Northern Europe. And only a small fraction of North American watering holes are likely even to carry the stuff outside of Scandinavian enclaves and restaurants.

That's gradually changing as some American entrepreneurs are increasingly making their own versions of aquavit ("aqua-veet," "ock-va-veet" or sometimes "ock-a-veet"). In 2012, Portland, Oregon, bartender and writer Jacob Grier founded Aquavit Week[105]—celebrated in the first week of December, which should raise the profile of the spirit further.

Aquavit, usually spelled Akvavit in much of Scandinavia, traces its origins back to about the fifteenth century and, like just about every other alcohol produced on its native continent[106], the EU has set specific standards about what actually defines it. In a nutshell, as far as the European Powers That Be are concerned, aquavit is a "caraway and/or dillseed-flavored spirit drink with a distillate of plants or spices" and a minimum strength of 37.5 percent alcohol by volume.[107] Other natural or "nature-identical" (eek!) flavoring substances may be added but the dominant flavor must be attributable to the distillates of caraway and/

or dill. As long as aquavit makers follow those relatively modest guidelines, they're free to let their creative freak flags fly.

As with just about any strong liquid to originate in Europe, we can thank the monks for this particular contribution to the global drinking culture. And, in keeping with a common theme throughout this book, they began as medicinal agents.

"In those days there were a lot of roots and insects and snakes and herbs—you could mix it with anything and it was aquavit,"[108] restaurateur Håkan Swahn tells me at his famed Scandinavian fine dining establishment—called, what else, Aquavit—in Manhattan's Midtown East neighborhood.

Ingredients evolved over the centuries, of course, and distillers got fairly innovative with what they were infusing in their aquavits.

Given its northerly origins, aquavit, like many vodkas from that region of Europe, tends to be potato-based, but it wouldn't be wrong to distill it from another source.

Drinkers usually consume aquavit neat, often with food—it pairs particularly well with Scandinavian staples like pickled herring or smoked cod roe. Caraway is known for its palate-cleansing properties, which makes aquavit an ideal accompaniment with such intense flavors. Fish oils have a tendency to just latch onto one's palate without letting go, so it's always a good idea to have a small glass poured, ready to get scrubbing.

There's a common misconception that one should drink Champagne with caviar—primarily due to the high price point of both. ("This is some classy, fancy stuff, so I'd better drink something classy and fancy.") But it's actually a pretty terrible idea, unless you like your Champagne to taste like smoked fish eggs. Try it with aquavit. You're not likely to regret it.

You're also not likely to regret drinking it the way the Norse gods intended: in "snaps," small half-ounce shots (not to be confused with German schnapps—there's no sugar added to aquavit), the perfect between-bites serving.

However, if you were to ask Swahn and many other connoisseurs of the beverage, the standards that ostensibly sought to protect its heritage—first in Scandinavia in the 1950s and 1960s and then affirmed by the EU decades later—may have had the opposite effect; at the very least, it manifests itself as a bit of artistic censorship.

Requiring the dominant flavor components to be caraway or dill essentially neuters all of the other products that lack those ingredients entirely or spotlight other ingredients, savory or sweet. It's not that the distillers had to stop producing them, they just couldn't label them aquavit any longer.

Swahn contends that there's very little historical significance in producing with caraway or dill only, those were just the botanicals of choice among Scandinavian distillers at the time the industry started talking about standards. "Why should you be locked into those things when they have no historical meaning anyway?" he questions.

A more favorable course of action would have been to go the route of Cognac, Champagne, or Scotch whisky and strictly specify the region in which aquavit is manufactured—limiting production of anything labeled as such to Scandinavia—rather than what goes in it.

"They could've done that and probably gotten that through in the EU in Brussels," Swahn argues, "but instead we're going to protect our own current production and make sure nobody else gets in. I thought it was a fundamental mistake."

EU guidelines be damned; the restaurant has its own proprietary, white cranberry-forward brand (with a touch of caraway) simply called Aquavit (or, sometimes AQNY). It also sports an ABV of only 35 percent, a full 2.5 percentage points below the EU minimum. Its bar also showcases a rotating menu of house-infused creations (not unlike infused vodkas), which diners can enjoy individually or as components of mix-and-match tasting flights of three. They range from the basic (anise, caraway, and fennel; coriander and crown dill) to more off-centered riffs (blueberry and elderflower; grapefruit and lemongrass; mango, lime, and chili pepper; heirloom tomato). I was lucky enough to drop by at a time when the bar manager still had a store of Aquavit's limited-time-only rye bread infusion. The process begins with fennel and caraway in a canister of neutral spirit (aka vodka). After those seeds sit for a while, the beverage team toasts fresh rye bread and steeps that along with the fennel and caraway. The infusing process, which varies from style to style, takes about a month for the rye offering. The bread is immediately apparent on the nose; it's the rare expression the restaurant serves at room temperature, versus chilled, as the full flavor asserts itself under ambient conditions. It's also uncharacteristically brown, which lends itself to that Cognac or brandy-sipping occasion.

The restaurant is always happy to indulge its artistic side with such fanciful concoctions, but Swahn wishes he was able to offer more Scandinavian imports to help with some of the heavy lifting. Problem is, the number of brands being exported from the region has dwindled significantly over the years. For the most part, American consumers are likely to find only Denmark's Aalborg brand and Norway's Linie, both of which the New York Michelin-starred eatery keeps on the menu.

— LINIE (ARCUS AS) —

The Norwegian brand has one of the more offbeat histories in the global beverage market. The brand, launched more than two centuries ago in 1805, had been shipping oak barrels of the stuff to Southeast Asia in the hope of finding an untapped market. According to the story the Linie team likes to tell (and the company's sticking to it), no one was interested, so back it went across the then canal-less globe to Oslo. When it arrived home, the distillers were so enraptured by the unexpected smoothness imparted by the transoceanic aging process, that they made it a key component of the production process. It continues to be so to this day. That's right, even with the advent of modern production and aging methods and technology, the distillers insist on sending the spirit for a four-month sea voyage, replicating that original journey as closely as they can. The choppy waters help ensure optimal contact between liquid and oak. The "line" to which the name "Linie" refers is the equator, which each batch crosses twice on its coming-of-age adventure.

As with any origin story, certain assertions must be taken with a grain of salt, but this one's likely at least 75 percent true. Everyone's got a secret ingredient; in this case that ingredient is a mixture of time and sea legs.

It's a dynamic not unlike the mythical beginnings of the India pale ale beer style. That tale, which has its own set of fabrications comingled with truths, has the English over-hopping and upping the alcohol content of a traditional pale to survive the long journey around the globe to colonial troops stationed in India.

When all is said and done, separating the facts from the fictions is really a fool's errand. There's really one notion that's virtually unimpeachable: When a brand manages to survive for more than two centuries, it must be doing something right. And the high seas can't take all of the credit.

On this side of the ocean, craft distillers tend to stick with tried-and-true spirits like whiskey, vodka, gin, and rum, but there are quite a few that have tried their hands at replicating the flavors of Scandinavia. That's actually a positive development that has resulted from the EU's desire to dictate ingredients, not terroir, in its guidelines. It's enabled American distillers to experiment and actually label their end products aquavit. Swahn enthusiastically stocks those stateside spirits along with the imports and house brand.

Even though they're distilled as far as seven thousand miles away from the mother countries, US-distilled varieties tend to adhere a little more closely to the EU guidelines. They don't have the benefit of being a known culinary establishment on the scene since 1987 that has as much a claim to the word aquavit as the original Northern European drinks do.

Among those, and one of the more (relatively) popular American-made aquavits comes from Portland, Oregon's, House Spirits Distillery, best known for its Aviation Gin.

➸ KROGSTAD (HOUSE SPIRITS DISTILLERY):

Christian Krogstad can't remember a time when aquavit wasn't in his life. The House Spirits founder and master distiller grew up around it, as he's the grandson of Norwegian immigrants. "I grew up eating all of the pickled herring and the pickled cod roe, these very strong flavors, and getting to sip on some aquavit as well as a child," Krogstad recalls.[108] "It's just a fantastic flavor combination; they really complement each other."

Krogstad's heritage, combined with the relative dearth of American-produced versions of the Scandinavian spirit, ultimately led to the creation of the caraway and star anise–forward Krogstad Festlig Aquavit.

"I'd had a lot of aquavit in Scandinavia and other people in the company had aquavit in Scandinavia, but the variety and quality of aquavit wasn't available in this country," Krogstad says. "So we decided to make our own."

Krogstad Festlig is aged in new American oak barrels, which imparts a straw-like yellowish color to the final spirit. It also helps mellow some of those spices that otherwise might be a bit too intense pre-aging.

»→ NORTH SHORE AQUAVIT-PRIVATE RESERVE:
Another US-based producer that makes a version of the Nordic classic is the Chicagoland-area's North Shore Distillery. Cumin, coriander, and cinnamon complement the caraway in North Shore's Aquavit-Private Reserve. It, too, is aged in oak, which imparts traces of caramel to the straw-colored finished product.

While neat is the preferred consumption method, aquavit is not unheard of as a mixer; in fact, as aquavit's stateside profile improves, mixologists have gotten fairly creative with it. Some have used it in place of gin in classics like the Bee's Knees, a Prohibition-era creation that's typically a fusion of gin, lemon, and honey. Celebrity bartender Jim Meehan, owner of the modern-day Manhattan speakeasy PDT, devised the Golden Star Fizz, which mixes aquavit with sparkling jasmine tea, dill, pineapple and lemon juices, cucumber, and absinthe.

Aquavit often fills in for vodka when a bartender wants to give a traditional cocktail a bit more pizazz. The Bloody Mary fits the bill because of its savory nature—it's often dubbed a "Danish Mary" when aquavit is involved.

Drinks of that nature can act as a bridge for gin and vodka lovers to this new world. In Krogstad's experience, it's been easiest to convert vodka drinkers looking for something with a little more flavor and gin drinkers who want to avoid the big juniper hit.

"I tell them it's botanical-flavored vodka," Krogstad explains.

Mention of that b word automatically brings to mind gin.

"But [aquavit] doesn't have juniper," he points out. "Gin is defined as having juniper and aquavit is defined as having caraway. Aquavit is a cousin of gin, just different botanicals."

It's really just semantics. The important thing to remember is that whether it's called Akvavit in Scandinavian tongues, eau de vie in

French or, yes, "whisky" in ancient Gaelic, it all means "water of life." And the former lubricates the enjoyment of the latter.

WEEK 50

'TIS THE SEASON FOR GLÜHWEIN

The Christmas holiday season is great and all, but if you're like me and you live in the Northern Hemisphere—and the northern two-thirds, well above the Tropic of Cancer—it's only a modest consolation for the fact that winter is coming. I've always said the powers that be in the holiday-deciding business should move it to March so at least there's spring to look forward to when it's over. When we wake up with the postholiday malaise on December 26, we find absolutely no comfort in the fact that we're only five days past the Winter Solstice and at least ninety away from the air starting to feel the slightest bit tolerable. Suddenly, the effusive, "Ooooo, it's snowing!" declaration common between about November 30 and December 25 makes way for, "F$%k, snow?!" That's the magic of the holiday season. It puts us under its spell and hypnotizes us into believing that we've got a high tolerance for cold.

Most of us in the holiday spirit will shop outside at quaint little Christmas markets when it's twenty degrees Fahrenheit. It's a custom we imported from German-speaking countries where the Christmas markets are virtually a compulsory activity. Seriously, I've often envisioned that, on December 1, a Christmas market truant officer would show up at one's house if that person is found to be absent from the pop-up wooden gaiety.

Turns out there's no need for a cheer enforcer when there's glühwein ("glue-vine"), which, alas, seems to be MIA from the vast majority of North American, European-inspired faux villages of commerce. (We're a country founded by ascetic Puritans that banned alcohol for fourteen years, so what should we expect?)

Most legal-drinking-age Americans of the non-Humbug variety have probably tasted or at least smelled someone making mulled wine at a friend's holiday party, in the comfort of a climate-controlled home. And chances are it was a half-hearted imitation of those typically ladled out in tiny open-air huts. Cheap bottle of red? Pour it in the pan. Got a cinnamon stick? Toss that in and voila! Pass the cup of cheer!

The true artisans of the Christkindlmarkts pride themselves on not taking any shortcuts. They really can't, especially when there's a glühwein maker a few stalls down more than willing to poach a thirsty, chilly shopper.

A typical steaming cup includes the base wine—usually red, but there are white variations on occasion—and the requisite cinnamon and sugar. Add to that more intense, seasonally evocative spices like star anise and clove, as well as some citrus (usually orange, sometimes a little lemon as well) and that's pretty close to what one could expect to be drinking at the markets.

Wait, there's more. More often than not there's a bit of an added surprise, often in the form of a shot of brandy or rum.

Depending on the city and the particular market, there may be heat-lamp equipped, tent-like spaces where market-goers can sit down, sip, and converse for a little while (as others waiting for a seat eagerly hover over them), but that's rare. Most of the time, the best you're going to do is a chair-less highboy bar table—often little more than a barrel with a plywood platform resting atop it—and your parka, hat, and hugs from your neighbor for warmth. But few who toast over a mug or two of glühwein (loose translation: glow wine) would have it any other way.

Berlin has some of the most epic Christmas markets a traveler is likely to find. Nüremberg, meanwhile, is a far smaller city, but its Christkindlmarkt is likely the most famous in the world and one of the top, non-war-crimes-trial reasons tourists visit. Vienna, Austria, in my humble opinion, holds the title for single most visually stunning market. There are small ones in every corner of the city, but the one to behold is nearest the city's Rathaus, which, itself, becomes a joyous lightshow.

There really is no need, though, to hop a plane for Europe just to slurp some heated, spicy, boozy wine (though it should be experienced at least once in your lifetime). The local würsthaus or beer hall more than likely will have it on the menu when 'tis the season. If not, there's surely someone who works there who'll know how to make you a good one, especially if it's one of the old-school family-owned joints founded by German immigrants (those still exist in many towns, though sprawling hipster-magnet establishments launched by Wall Street investors are becoming the norm these days).

I'm focusing primarily on the German styles of mulled wines because, let's face it, Germany basically invented the modern concept of Christmas, so credit where credit's due.

However, most individual countries or regions of the continent offer their own local spins on the mulled wine concept.

You'll notice that the Nordics have come up on more than one occasion during the course of our adventure (hey, they really know how to keep warm way up north). And yes, Scandinavians have culturally specific mulled wines as well. They call theirs Glögg, which has all of the usual trimmings like cinnamon, cardamom, and clove, but tends to use fortified wine like port, as well as a local spirit like aquavit or vodka. It's also not atypical to find raisins, almonds, and ginger in Glögg (the Swedish spelling; Norwegians and Danes spell it Gløgg).

It's possible to bring semiauthentic tastes of German and Scandinavian Christmas to the comfort of your own home with bottled versions of Glühwein and Glögg. Most popularly, drinks purveyor Franz Stettner & Sohn packages its own recipe of red wine, cinnamon, cloves, oranges, lemons, and a bit of sugar under the label Christkindl Glühwein. Just add heat and you're good to go. (I've spotted the bottle behind the counter at some Christmas market stalls—as good as it is, the vendors are kind of phoning it in when they're defaulting to a ready-made version.)

Blossa is one of the go-to brands in Sweden for prepackaged Glögg, offering a host of flavor innovations (lavender and elderflower among those), as well as vintages(!) for the holiday season.

Another product, Geijier Glögg Liqueur, takes wine out of the equation entirely, infusing the spices of an old family recipe into neutral spirit. Heating it still imparts the requisite magic, though its distilled base technically makes it a hot toddy.

Traditionalists, of course, will swear glühwein and glögg must be homemade. After all, Christmas is a time of traditions, and why would we want to sacrifice the last remnants of ritual and custom to the gods of commercialism? Sometimes, though, there are no other options; ingredients may be scarce or the chaos of party-planning may necessitate a little corner-cutting in the interest of time. (And frankly, the more rigid guests will be none the wiser.)

My two cents: It's another one of those context things. In a perfect world, the only way to enjoy a steaming cup of winter-spice-infused wine is with a coat, wool hat, and mittens in a faux village constructed of wood paneling and holiday cheer. If we can't have that, any drink, handcrafted or machine-bottled, that can at least evoke that experience, is okay in this Yuletide reveler's book.

Week 51
Timeless Tiki

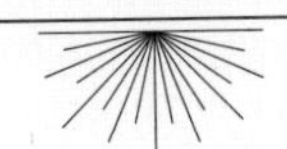

Winter is just beginning and summer seems but a concept you may or may not have imagined during a fever dream. At this point you're probably more inclined to drink a hot toddy, spiked coffee, or a big, boozy, warming beer like a barleywine or Russian Imperial stout. But why not, for just one week, try to remember what swimsuits and sunshine are like and embrace the tropical. And those of you in the less temperate parts of North America needn't stress about booking those midwinter jaunts to toastier climes. Summer is a state of mind one can tap into even when the ice and snow conspire to keep everyone indoors.

All the more reason to go out and declare, "Winter, you are not the boss of me!"

Some drinking experiences are more about context than ingredients (though the latter certainly is a critical component) and that's why you're going to find your nearest tiki bar (there are more of them than you realize, you just need to know where to look), embrace the faux-Polynesian tchotchkes and kitsch (the divey-er the better) and let the liquid calories be damned. It's time to consume an unnecessarily large glass, tiki-faced mug or, hell, even a coconut full of a decadent mixture of multiple juices and (mostly) rums with sundry fresh fruit slices and maybe a couple of toys protruding from it. And leave the irony at home. Tiki-ing is serious business and the bars are often tight and cramped, so there's no room for that hipster sense of superiority.

We're at least forty years removed from tiki culture's prime, but the scene has gradually been making a comeback of sorts; it goes hand-in-hand with the rockabilly underground, which enjoys a relatively small but devoted and growing following. Major national weekend gatherings—kind of a Comic-Con for the tiki set—have been outgrowing their venues in Florida, Southern California, and Upstate New York as the concept attracts new followers.

"There are people who come from the United Kingdom, Australia, Japan,"[110] observes Nell Mellon, a longtime fixture of the scene and co-owner of the New York City tiki bar, Otto's Shrunken Head. "Americana for most people outside the United States is really a genre in and of itself, and tiki kind of gets lumped in with that Americana."

Internationally, therefore, tiki is interchangeable with Elvis and classic hot rods.

Most major metro markets will have at least one tiki-style establishment; sometimes it's in the form of an old-school 1960s- and 1970s-era Pan-Asian/Polynesian restaurant. You know, the places that have the flaming Pu-Pu Platter on the menu. During my North Jersey childhood, my parents took my brother and me at least monthly to a place called China Paradise, which fit that profile to a T. Sadly, long before I was old enough to drink, the place underwent a massive renovation/rebranding that essentially sterilized its decor, dumping the jade fountain and the hanging bamboo petrified blowfish in favor of bland inoffensiveness. I can't blame them really. The tiki heyday had passed and most of the bars and restaurants that had relied on the island aesthetic were closing. Many years later, I was happy to discover Chan's Dragon Inn, just a few miles off the George Washington Bridge in Ridgefield, NJ, retaining the visual splendor that China Paradise had abandoned, down to the Hawaiian-shirted waiters. It scares me when my wife and I are among maybe twelve other people there at 8:30 p.m. on a Saturday. I'd hate for the days to be numbered for one of the last vestiges of New Jersey endangered Polynesian scene.

Some seasonal, seaside meat market bars (very often on boardwalks) have tried to carry the tiki torch but have been little more than pale imitations reviled by the true devotees. Those are what I like to call TINOs: Tikis in Name Only. Putting up a couple of fake palm trees and the odd thatched awning and offering one or two fruit-based rum cocktails (but mostly bottles of Corona and shots of Jaegermeister) does not a tiki bar make.

SECRET SOCIETY

This is one of the rare cases where I can't give you an exact recommendation of what to drink. The thing is, most tiki bars worth their salt will have an extensive list of proprietary cocktails unlikely to be replicated by their peers. Sure, you'll always be able to find a Mai Tai or a Singapore Sling and it's fun to keep score and determine which establishment masters each of those, but there are so many other drinks to try that you'll never be able to get to them all in your lifetime.

There's also a very practical reason for so many variations and house exclusives—during the golden age of tiki, say from the 1950s through the early 1970s, there was something of a creative turf war occurring among the major early purveyors. Quite a bit of poaching reportedly was going on. If a drink was a hit at Don the Beachcomber's, you could bet that Trader Vic wanted to get his hands on the recipe. The only way to do that would be to lure the bartenders away, house secrets in tow.

As tiki lore has it, the owners would have to resort to peeling the labels from the bottles and clandestinely marking them as, simply, A, B, C, D, etc. The bartender would only know to mix, say, two parts A, with three parts D and one part B—you get the idea.

There are few cities in the contiguous forty-eight states (okay, let's throw in Alaska, too) that have the bona fide tiki scenes that Los Angeles has—arguably where the whole mainland tiki craze was born, in the form of original hotspot, Don the Beachcomber.

Today, even though the golden age of tikis has long since passed, there still are enough of them left to constitute an entire weekend bar crawl. And some of them have occupied the same spaces for more than five decades. The title of Most Iconic Tiki Bar in Los Angeles (and the rest of the country for that matter) goes to Tiki-Ti. The hole-in-the-wall establishment has sat at the same Sunset Boulevard address in Silver Lake since 1961, and time seems to have done little to pry it from its comfort zone. For one thing, people still smoke inside, when the rest of California (and much of the country) has been smoke-free since the turn of the millennium. It's not flipping the bird to the powers that be by brazenly flouting the law. Tiki-Ti is owner-operated; there are no employees other than the proprietor—second- and third-generation progeny of founder Ray Buhen, who, incidentally, cut his teeth at Don the Beachcomber before launching his own place—so it's not required to provide a cigarette-less environment.

Plastic toys, shrunken heads, and other island icons densely dangle from the ceiling, giving plenty of visuals for visitors to ponder while they make their way through the ninety-plus mixed drinks Tiki-Ti offers. Among those:

- UGA BOOGA: Myers Dark Rum (a lot of it) and a secret blend of tropical juices (they'll never tell you, so don't bother asking) garnished with pineapple and a maraschino cherry. It's a Tiki-Ti tradition for the crowd to chant "Uga Booga!" when a visitor orders one.
- RAY'S MISTAKE: Named for founder Buhen, it's the most popular attraction at Tiki-Ti. It includes a blend (again, a secret combo) of botanic liqueurs, passion fruit, gin, and Dark Corub rum. As the story goes, Buhen mixed the wrong syrups in a drink called an Anting Anting and the happy accident became a tiki institution
- JIM'S SPECIAL: One of the more recent inventions on Tiki-Ti's list, it was created in 2001 and made with Meyer's rum, Casadores tequila, passion fruit, and lime.

Other City of Angels favorites are Tonga Hut and Tiki-No, both in North Hollywood. Tiki-No is the least dive-like and offers service with a smile—sometimes a rarity in this genre. It doesn't make it any less authentic. Like anything else, it all depends on your mood at a given moment.

Before there's a collective explosion of all of the heads in the Bay Area, it must be stated that San Francisco comes in a close second for its tiki scene. Some might even argue that it boasts some more famous establishments than its Southern California sister, but since its best known is also as famous for its Polynesian-inspired food, the prize still goes to LA in terms of pure drinking joints. The Tonga Room, which was featured on Anthony Bourdain's *The Layover*, is located within the Fairmont San Francisco hotel and has been a Fog City fixture since the end of World War II.

The other big one is Smuggler's Cove, which combines the old Polynesian favorites with popular cocktails from pre-Castro Havana and other Caribbean classics.

On the opposite coast, New York City unsurprisingly hasn't typically been thought of as a tiki mecca and was pretty much devoid of the concept before Otto's set up shop in 2002 at the site of what was Barmacy, an apothecary-themed watering hole that was a fixture of the East Village after-dark scene in the 1990s.

The founding partners call Otto's "a new interpretation of the tiki bar," combining the usual South Pacific flavors and aesthetic trappings (especially the eponymous heads dangling near the entrance) with live bands and loungey DJs (this is Manhattan, after all). There's a decidedly punk rock vibe to the place that harkens a bit back to the grittier East Village of the 1970s when the Ramones, Patti Smith, and Richard Hell and the Voidoids ruled the scene. It should come as no surprise then that Otto's also has been featured on bad boy Bourdain's televisual itinerary (his 2010 holiday special, no less).

Signature Otto's house drinks, complete with umbrellas, fruit garnishes, and tiny plastic monkeys, include:

- OTTO'S OCTANE: Pineapple rum, coffee liqueur, and banana
- PATTY'S POISON: Seven exotic fruits and rum
- WICKED WILLIE: Passionfruit, pineapple, and "a surprising kick"
- NAUGHTY NELL: Named after the proprietor herself, it combines grape, citrus, and vodka
- SCURVY DOG: This one's definitely got a spicy kick; it blends house-infused cinnamon vodka and butterscotch
- PANG'S PUNCH: It glows in the dark! Don't worry, it's not actually radioactive; an immersed glow stick illuminates this blue rum punch (nice kick of coconut in it)

Otto's keeps up the mystique about its recipes, but not in the "guard-these-with-your-life" sort of way that the old schoolers like Don the Beachcomber and Ray Buhen did.

"We're not that secretive," Mellon admits. "If someone wants a recipe, I'm not going to handwrite it. If they're like, 'It's really good, what's in it?' I'll say 'Order another one and watch me.'"

Some tiki establishments don't even let customers do that. At the six-decades-old tiki mecca Mai-Kai in Fort Lauderdale—Florida's scene often gives California's a run for its money, by the way—customers can't even see the drinks being made. They're all mixed in a back kitchen by a veritable assembly line of bartenders who pass the finished concoction to sarong-clad waitresses. Mai-Kai is famous for its nightly Polynesian floor shows, as well as its "Mystery Bowl." As the waitress delivers the communal drink, she dances for and never breaks her fierce eye contact with he who ordered it, while a usually-male member of Mai-Kai's traditionally robed staff bangs a gong. Presentation is a key component of drinking adventurously, and few imbibing occasions can match such theatricality.

Wherever you may uncover a tiki hideaway from sea to shining sea, it's always advisable to try the house creations first (it's a sign of respect, after all). Beyond those, it's helpful to cultivate a short list of go-tos that are more or less standard across the vast majority of the genre (again, compare/contrast from bar to bar). You really can't go wrong with the following:

Mai Tai: I would wager that anyone not even remotely familiar with the tiki scene will have heard of this one. There are many, many variations, as the drink definitely has evolved over time. Trader Vic's original includes aged rum over shaved ice, lime juice, orange Curaçao liqueur, rock candy syrup, and orgeat syrup. Later versions have had as many as four types of rum and have added splashes of orange juice, pineapple juice, bitters, Triple sec, and/or grenadine.

Zombie: Here's another one that's practically a household name, as far as cocktails go (the Howells name-checked it on *Gilligan's Island*, for crying out loud). It's the invention of Don the Beach-comber himself, giving it roots at the dawn of tiki. The Zombie is usually, but not exclusively, served in a tall glass and contains a mix of light and dark rums, grenadine, brandy (usually apricot-based), and citrus juices (any combo of orange, lime, pineapple, etc.).

Singapore Sling: The Singapore Sling was created at the historic Raffles Hotel in Singapore near the turn of the twentieth century. It usually involves gin, brandy, cherry liqueur, pineapple juice, lime juice, bitters, and club soda. If you happen to be in Singapore, don't order one. They're strictly for tourists there, and I'm a strong proponent of drinking like a local. (But if you must, you can get an obscenely overpriced one at Raffles). But at stateside tiki bars, the Sling is fair game.

Navy Grog: Another innovation of the Beachcombing One, the sailor-centric concoction usually includes three kinds of rum (dark, light, and a wild card) and a complex comingling of multiple tropical juices, usually orange, pineapple, guava, and/or lime. It's common for the ice to be crushed and compressed into snow-cone-like density.

The Scorpion: This stinging arachnid's origins can be traced back to a tiny Honolulu bar called The Hut; it was later adapted and popularized at California's Trader Vic's. Recipes vary wildly, but usually fuse orange and lemon juices, orgeat syrup (known for its sweet almond flavor), light rum, and brandy (some versions have included a half dozen other ingredients as well).

Suffering Bastard: Considering that this one is usually two parts light rum and two parts gin, it's likely you'd live up to its name if you had more than one or two. It also commonly includes ginger ale, lime juice, and bitters, almost making it a tiki/Prohibition-era hybrid of sorts.

For most tiki mavens, it's nearly as much about the drinking vessel (and assorted accoutrements), as it is about the liquid inside it. It's therefore not uncommon for a loyalist's home bar to rival that of the South Pacific–inspired watering holes throughout the country. Most places will let visitors take their house-specific mugs home for a nominal surcharge.

"It's escapism in its purest, simplest form," Mellon says of the scene. "It's a made-up culture."

What are you waiting for, then? Escape!

WEEK 52

RINGING IN THE NEW, ALSATION STYLE

CREMANT D'ALSACE

As we approach the year's end, it's time to ask a question that's so obvious, they turned it into a song: What are you doing New Year's Eve? If you're like the tens of millions of other revelers, either dancing the night away at a criminally overpriced club where the cover charge approaches four figures, or enjoying a quiet evening at home, struggling to keep your eyes open until the ball drops, it's likely you'll be drinking some form of Champagne. Ah, but chances are it may not actually be Champagne proper, as it's not from the eponymous region that boasts arguably the most prominent AOC in all of France. That hasn't stopped drinkers from genericizing the term. "Don't forget to grab a bottle of sparkling white wine," doesn't quite roll off the tongue the same way as specifying the most famous type does.

That's been both a blessing and a curse for makers of bubbly outside of Champagne. Consumers, especially those on the west side of the Atlantic who don't fall into the "connoisseur" category, often will buy on price and tend not to care too much where the grapes are grown. White (or sometimes pink)? Check. Carbonated? Check. The non-Champagne vintners benefit from this indifference/lack of knowledge/frugality on the part of the purchaser. But on the flip side, it does those same wine producers a disservice because many actually are producing some world-class sparklers in their own right, even if their A-list celebrity sibling is the one getting all of the attention.

The Alsace region, for instance, produces some of the finest wines in all of Europe, but usually gets overshadowed by the likes of Bourdeaux,

Burgundy, Rhone (especially its Cotes du Rhone appellation), the Loire Valley and, yes, Champagne.

Part of the reason it often has taken a backseat to many of those other French domains is that there have been times, historically, that Alsace wasn't even in France. It had been the rope in an ongoing tug of war between France and Germany and changed hands quite frequently. Germany annexed it at the end of the Franco-Prussian War in 1871, and France got it back as a condition of the Treaty of Versailles after World War I. (Germany continued to have designs on it and expected to get it back in a certain other conflict two decades later, but we all know how that turned out). Even the Alsatian dialect is of Germanic origin, though most Alsatians speak French. It's not uncommon to find Alsatians with French-given names and German-sounding surnames.

Alsace boasts fifty-three of its own AOCs, one of which, Crémant d'Alsace, often can give the stuff that's rightfully called Champagne a run for its money.[111]

First, about that AOC. Alsace doesn't have a claim on the word Cremant. But the full term, Cremant d'Alsace, is protected. Other AOCs include Crémant de Bourdeaux, Cremant de Bourgogne, Cremant de Loire and others. The word cremant itself is a generic term for non-Champagne bubblies that derives from crème, meaning "cream"; the robust carbonation gives the wine a certain creaminess.

Crémant d'Alsace represents nearly a quarter of Alsatian wine production and tends to be made from Pinot Blanc grapes.[112] It's not uncommon, however, to find some produced with Pinot Gris, Riesling, Chardonnay, or Pinot Noir varietals.

Incidentally if you're a staunch red wine person—like I am generally—and you plan to take a trip to Alsace, you'd better like Pinot Noir. It's likely the only Alsatian red you're going to find with any regularity throughout the region. Whites are far more prevalent. Again, as I've been drilling into everyone's heads since page one, this is all about getting out of your comfort zones. Whites are out of my comfort zone (and still are, for the most part), but Alsace did change my perception of some of them, especially when they're in bubbly form.

The aforementioned AOC, which is barely forty years old, helped a great deal from a quality-control perspective. In 1976, the government placed stringent guidelines on harvesting and production, which has helped keep Alsace on the map. [113]

Like any European viticultural region worth noting, Alsace certainly does attract its fair share of tourists. But, dare I say, parts of it are among the least touristy of such destinations. If visitor-friendly, hypercommercial wineries are your thing—you know, the sprawling establishments along the most traffic-heavy main roads in Napa and Sonoma—you'll find at least a few places where you'll feel right at home. But it's the wine makers on the opposite pole that offer the most charm. Dropping in for a tasting—especially in November, I might note—sometimes feels like you're participating in a home invasion. In a quaint, vineyard-enclosed village like Riquewhir, many of the "tasting rooms" are actually someone's residential dining room table. You might be tempted to move along before the proprietor opens the door (it's a house, after all, and there's knocking or ringing involved), but you won't get the chance. The enthusiastic vintner will beckon you inside. And this is old school, rural France, so don't expect there to be too much English fluency. If you're equally Français-challenged, just say "Crémant" and hope they have some (have a few backup, French-sounding grape varietals, just in case).

If that sounds too daunting (comfort zone, remember?), don't worry. You don't have to travel to western France to drink some really good Crémant d'Alsace. The staff at any slightly above-average neighborhood wine bar will at least have heard of it, even if they don't always have it on hand. (Pro Tip: Become a visible regular who's always generous with the gratuities. Chances are, they'll order it for you.) Same thing with retail shops, especially those that specialize in French labels. You might just impress and earn the respect of your friendly neighborhood wine merchant, and that's never a bad thing. There are now some five hundred producers crafting certified Crémant d'Alsace and, odds are, there's at least one making something you like.

A few good ones that won't break the bank—in the $18 to $25 range—include:

Gustave Lorentz Crémant d'Alsace Brut Blanc: Gustave Lorentz uses 100 percent pinot noir grapes for this dry Crémant. There's a subtle sour apple-ish tartness to it that complements the dryness well.

Allimant Laugner Crémant d'Alsace Brut Rosé: For those who like a little pinkish tint with their bubbles but don't want anything too sweet, there's Allimant Laugner's rosé. It's fairly fruit-forward with a decidedly dry finish. It's also pinot noir–based.

Domaine Mittnacht Freres Crémant d'Alsace Brut: Half of the grapes in Domaine Mittnacht's Crémant are of the Pinot Auxerrois varietal, while the other half is a combination of Riesling, Pinot Noir, and others. All of the complexity one would expect from such a dynamic marriage of grapes.

Now, hurry up. The clock is ticking and you don't want to be empty-handed at midnight when you toast the completion of your Year of Drinking Adventurously and toast the beginning of your next journey.

Epilogue
Consumption with Context

It's late January, and I'm in the city formerly known as Saigon, sitting with my wife on a pair of flimsy, foot-high, brightly colored plastic stools that look as though they'd just been liberated from a kindergarten classroom. We're huddled over an equally compact and rickety table in an open-air eatery waiting on some fresh garlic-rubbed cockles prepared on a crudely constructed grill on the sidewalk. It was the start of Tet, the Lunar New Year, which meant every fifteen minutes or so, a dragon-led procession of noise-making revelry would make its way down the thoroughfare.

The server brings us our beer, the local macro called 333 and he proceeds . . . to pour it . . . over ice!

We have about a millisecond to decide whether we wanted to be complete Western snobs, demand that we pour it ourselves, and dump out the ice cubes when the waiter's back is turned, or just go with the flow, shrug, and declare, "When in Ho Chi Minh City . . . "

As per our usual MO, we opted for the latter. And we wouldn't have had it any other way. On its own, the lager is subpar at best, even measured against the low bar set by mass-produced, adjunct-laden fizzy yellow beer coming from a multinational brewing behemoth. And drinking it warm—refrigeration's still something of a luxury in Vietnam—would not have improved it. But on the rocks? It just seemed right. Somehow the context made it one of the most memorable drinking experiences I've ever had. It's a fleeting moment, a meal among thousands of meals I've consumed, a beer among countless ones I've drunk—most I've since forgotten. But I'm remembering this watered-down, clumsily crafted light lager and writing about it now, several years later. It may have been far from a quality beverage, but it was no less an adventure.

Drinking, first and foremost, is a social fuel, powering the engine of conversation.

At the same time, what you're drinking should be part of the conversation. You not only have an extensive repertoire of beverage suggestions to get you through a fifty-two-week period, you've also got fifty-two potential topics to enliven your discussions. Everyone likes to be in the know and impress friends, casual acquaintances, and significant others—whether current or prospective—with a few anecdotes demystifying what's behind the bar. (But no one likes a pontificating pedant; don't be that person).

And while you're making yourself comfortable on the barstool, at the dinner table, or on a couch or armchair in a cozy nook nestled in the corner of a pub or club (or, yes, even a tiny, broken plastic stool in a Vietnam dive), remember to make yourself a little uncomfortable as well. There's now no excuse not to stray a little bit from the routine that's been your Linus blanket and order outside your safe zone.

It's likely that at least a few things you'll sip during your own Year of Drinking Adventurously will join the rotation of your most frequently consumed libations.

The more experienced imbibers among you who already had many of these in your stable hopefully get to experience them in an entirely new light—and maybe pour a few new ones into your glass in the process.

I'd like to think I've helped encourage more cross-consumption. There's no more beautiful sight than having a self-described wine drinker order a bourbon neat, or that Maker's Mark disciple order a black coffee stout. Keep blurring those category lines!

Before we part ways, I want to let you in on a little secret. This has been as much an adventure for me as I hope it's been for you. While I generally like to think I know my way around a pint glass, snifter, or tumbler, I actually had to nudge myself out of my own comfort zone for a number of the weeks of the year we've just spent together. In fact, my entire adult drinking life has been one long process of removing the training wheels. (Wheeled vehicles probably don't make for the most appropriate of analogies when talking about alcohol, but oh well.)

A bit of a mantra—well, at this point, more of a cliché—that's been circulating through the alcohol beverage industry for the past couple of decades is the notion that consumers have been "drinking less, but drinking better." As nauseating as it can be to hear that soundbite repeated over and over again every time a marketing rep is hawking a new brand, it's still anchored by truth. That's essentially what it is to drink adventurously—shacking up with quality after kicking quantity to the curb. And, despite its common definition, "quality" doesn't have to mean "delicious" 100 percent of the time. It just has to be memorable; it just has to make an impression on one extreme or the other. Utter revulsion could be one of those extremes (I'm looking at you, Fernet and Malört). But even then, hey, it's something to talk about! You may never again want to come within one hundred yards of it, but you'll be damned if you don't have a story to tell your friends while you're out trying something else. So, here's to all of the stories ahead, from all of the adventures you've yet to embrace, in all of the years that lay in front of you. Cheers, Kanpai, Prost, Na dzrovie, Slainte, and all that good stuff! It's a good time—and an adventure—in any language!

And, to keep the good times going a bit longer, don't forget to check out a few of the cocktail recipes in the back!

COCKTAILING ADVENTUROUSLY

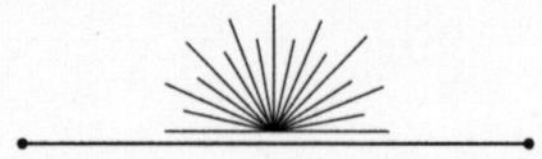

Many of the spirits personalities featured in The Year of Drinking Adventurously were generous enough to share a few cocktail recipes.

THE ROOT OF ALL EVIL

This particular recipe comes courtesy of St. George Spirits. It calls for the distillery's own Absinthe Verte, but if it's not available, you can substitute another absinthe in a pinch.

- 1 ounce St. George Absinthe Verte
- 2 ounces artisanal root beer

Pour absinthe into a rocks glass filled with ice, then top off with root beer. Gradually let *louche* (a process by which the gradual addition of water creates a haze) or stir gently until consistently cloudy.

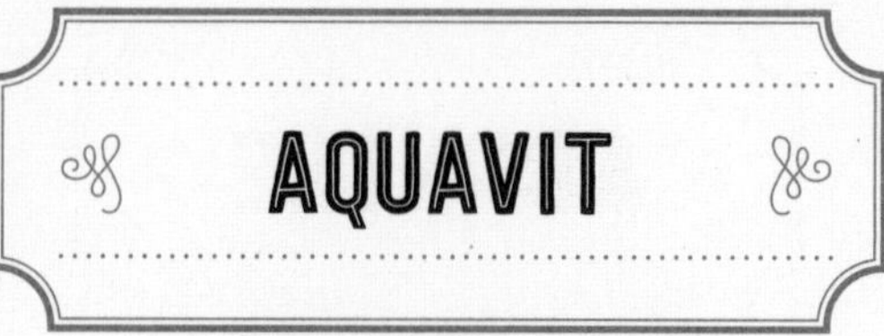

AQUAVIT

PEPPER SMASH

This sweet and tart (with a touch of savory) combo comes courtesy Portland's House Spirits Distillery, maker of Krogstad Festlig Aquavit.

- 2 ounces, Krogstad Festlig Aquavit
- ¾ ounces freshly squeezed lemon juice
- 2 slices, red bell pepper
- 12 leaves mint
- ¾ ounce clover honey syrup (Combine equal parts honey to heated water and sir until honey is dissolved and then let cool).

In a pint glass, add spirits and mixers. Muddle. Fill with ice and shake vigorously. Double fine strain into an ice-filled cocktail glass. Garnish with a thin red bell pepper slice and a large mint sprig.

BAIJIU

DRAGON'S CLAW

Bó Drake's, an East Asian barbecue restaurant in London, created this concoction with the always-challenging-to-mix baijiu. The Bó Drakes mixology team used the Shui Jing Fang brand for this drink. It's also a crossover drink for those curious about elderflower liqueur. Measurements use the metric system, which I've translated for us nonmetric folk.

- 40mL (about 1.4 ounces—let's call it an ounce and a half) Shui Jing Fang baijiu
- 20 mL (about 2/3 ounce) agave nectar
- 20 mL (about 2/3 ounce) elderflower cordial
- 3 dashes of hopped grapefruit bitters

Shake ingredients together and pour through a single strainer into an iced Boston glass. Garnish with grated lime peel, a slice of grapefruit, and a hibiscus flower.

BLOOD AND WATER

The team at CNS Imports offered up this baijiu and brandy combo.

- 2/3 ounce baijiu (Shui Jing Fang recommended)
- 1 ounce Luxardo cherry brandy
- 1 ounce fresh orange juice
- 1 ounce sweet vermouth

Shake hard with ice and double strain into a coupette glass; add a twist of orange zest and discard the peel.

BITTERS

OLD-FASHIONED

(BITTERS-FORWARD VERSION)

Tom Macy, resident mixologist at the Clover Club in Brooklyn, NY, amps up the bitterness quotient in his riff on the classic old-fashioned.

- 2 ounces rye whiskey (Macy recommends either Wild Turkey 101, Rittenhouse, or Russel's Reserve 6)
- 1 barspoon (1/2 teaspoon) 2:1 demerara syrup
- 2 dashes of Angostura bitters
- 1 dash Regan's orange bitters
- 1 small dash ("a few drops") Bitter Truth Jerry Thomas Decanter bitters

Stir and strain into rocks glass over one large cube; garnish with lemon and orange peels.

BLOODY MARY

"THE COCKTAIL SNOB," BEN PARÉ, SHARED THIS RECIPE FOR AN OFFBEAT BLOODY MARY.

SWEET AND SMOKY BLOODY MARY

- 2 ounces vodka of choice
- 3–4 dashes Worcestershire sauce
- 1 barspoon smoky black tea spice blend*
- 3–4 dashes Tabasco
- Juice of ½ lime
- Juice of ¼ lemon
- 1 barspoon olive or caper brine
- House-made San Marzano tomato juice**
- 1 heaping barspoon prepared horseradish (optional)

In a pint glass, combine all ingredients over ice, shake, and serve with garnish of choice (e.g., pickled veggies, olives, celery stalk, old bay rim, etc.)

*For the smoky black tea spice blend, in a spice grinder, combine equal parts black peppercorns and high-quality Lapsang souchong Chinese black tea.

**For the San Marzano tomato juice, strain the solids out of a jar of peeled whole DOP San Marzano tomatoes (DOP or Denominazione d'Origine Protetta is protected designation of origin certification). (Don't throw away the solids though; use them for something!) You may also elect to puree the tomatoes and their juices for a more flavorful juice base. Additionally, for a thicker and even more flavorful base, simmer the tomatoes in a saucepan until reduced by 1/3 (about 1.5 to 2 hours per 28-ounce can), transfer to a blender, blend, and cool completely before use. Keep in mind, with this juice base and anything else, you get out what you put in!

CAIPIRINHA

We can't talk about cachaça without offering a recipe for a Caipirinha. This one comes from the folks behind the Novo Fogo brand.

- 1-1/2 to 2 ounces silver cachaça
- Half a lime, sliced
- 1 heaping tablespoon of ultra fine sugar

Muddle the lime and sugar together. Add the cachaça and ice and shake. Pour everything, including the ice, into a rocks glass.

CUCUMBER JALAPEÑO CAIPIRHINA

For a spicy variation on Brazil's national cocktail, try this one, recommended by the team at Leblon.

- 2 ounces cachaça
- 2 thin slices English cucumber
- 1 lime wedge
- 1/4 inch slice jalapeño
- 3/4 ounce agave nectar

Muddle the jalapeño, lime, cucumber, and agave in a shaker. Fill the shaker with ice and add Leblon Cachaça. Shake well and serve in a rocks glass. Garnish with a cucumber wheel.

ANTIQUADO

Another Novo Fogo favorite, Antiquado is a Brazilian spin on the old-fashioned.

- 2 ounces Novo Fogo barrel-aged cachaça.
- 0.5 ounce cinnamon syrup
- 2 dashes of chocolate bitters
- Orange peel

Place the cinnamon syrup at the bottom of the glass. Nearly fill the glass with ice, then add cachaça and the bitters. Stir and fill the glass with ice. Squeeze orange peel over the glass and then drop it in.

RASPBERRY BRAMBLE

Here's another one from the good folks at St. George Spirits. It works well with the distillery's Terroir Gin.

- 2 ounces of St. George Terroir Gin
- 1/2 ounce of St. George Raspberry Liqueur
- 1/2 ounce fresh lemon juice
- 1/2 ounce simple syrup

Shake gin, lemon juice, and simple syrup with ice, then strain it into a tall glass filled with crushed ice. Drizzle the raspberry liqueur over the top and garnish with lemon.

MOONSHINE

OLE SMOKY CREATED A SIGNATURE COCKTAIL WITH OLE SMOKY CHARRED MOONSHINE, A SPIN ON THE OLD-FASHIONED CALLED, WHAT ELSE, THE NEW-FASHIONED:

THE NEW-FASHIONED

- Ole Smoky Charred Moonshine
- Sugar Cube
- Splash of water
- 2 dashes of bitters
- Orange and Ole Smoky Moonshine Cherries for garnish

To prepare, muddle the orange and Moonshine Cherries with water, bitters, and sugar and then pour in the Charred.

THE PISCO COCKTAILS ARE SOME ORIGINAL CREATIONS FROM MACCHU PISCO.

SALSA VERDE PISCO

- 2 ounces of pisco
- 2 ounces of muddled fresh cilantro
- Dash of habanero tincture
- 1 ounce of fresh lime
- 1 ounce of citrus syrup

Shake and strain over a salted rocks glass with ice. Garnish with a cilantro clover.

PERUVIAN INSPIRATION

Macchu Pisco recommends using its blended product, La Diablada, for this inspiring cocktail.

- 4.5 ounces of La Diablada pisco
- 3 ounces of lemon chamomile tea
- 1 teaspoon of honey
- 1 ounce of fresh lemon juice
- Dash of egg whites
- Sweet Peruvian potato chip (or other sweet potato chip)

Melt the honey with the tea and the lemon juice and let it sit in the refrigerator for a couple of hours. Add the pisco in a shaker with egg whites and tea mix and shake vigorously. Garnish with a honey-drizzled baked sweet Peruvian potato chip.

BESO PICANTE NO. 2

The creators of the brand, and essentially new spirit category, Solbeso, recommend this spicy concoction.

- 2 ounces Solbeso
- 3/4 ounce fresh lemon juice
- 3/4 ounce simple syrup
- 2 slices jalapeño

Muddle the jalapeño in a mixing tin or glass. Add all other ingredients, shake and strain into a double rocks glass over fresh ice. Garnish with a jalapeño slice.

NEW YORK'S OTTO'S SHRUNKEN HEAD WAS KIND ENOUGH TO SHARE THREE RECIPES; THESE ARE BEST ENJOYED IN TIKI-APPROPRIATE DRINKING VESSELS. THE FIRST IS THE HOUSE RECIPE FOR, PERHAPS, THE BEST-KNOWN TIKI DRINK THERE IS.

MAI TAI

- 1 ounce Myers rum
- 1 ounce Bacardi Gold rum
- 1 ounce Bacardi light rum
- 1/4 ounce orgeat
- Dash of Triple sec
- Splash of seltzer
- Slice of lime
- Maraschino cherry

Shake, strain into a glass with ice, and add a splash of seltzer. Garnish with a slice of lime, a cherry, tiny umbrellas, and more.

PINKY'S POTION

- 1-1/2 ounce Chairman's Reserve spiced rum
- 1-1/2 ounces Rumchata (or your own homemade horchata)
- Dash of St. Elizabeth All Spice Dram
- Seltzer
- Cinnamon stick
- Maraschino cherry

Shake, strain into a glass with ice, and top off with seltzer. Garnish with a cinnamon stick, cherry, umbrellas, and more.

SHRUNKEN HEAD

This one's a house specialty at Otto's.

- 1-1/2 ounces Myers rum
- 1/2 ounce Cruzan coconut rum
- 2 splashes of orange juice
- 7Up
- Orange wedge
- Maraschino cherry

Shake, strain into a glass with ice, and top off with 7Up. Garnish with the orange, cherry, umbrellas, and more.

NOTES

1. Fraser, Scott. Personal interview. 14 Jan. 2015.
2. McWilliam, Ian. Personal interview. 16 Jan. 2015.
3. Cant, Andy. Personal interview. 17 Jan. 2015.
4. Ibid.
5. Noe, Fred. Personal interview. 23 Sept. 2014.
6. Pickerell, David. Phone interview. 10 Dec. 2014.
7. de Kergommeaux, Davin. Phone interview. 26 Jan. 2015.
8. Ibid.
9. Buchanan, Rose Troup. "'Best whisky in the world' prize won by Japanese single malt for first time as Scottish distilleries lose out," *The Independent*, http://www.independent.co.uk/life-style/food-and-drink/news/best-whisky-in-the-world-prize-won-by-japanese-malt-for-first-time-as-scottish-distilleries-lose-out-9835583.html, 3 Nov. 2014.
10. Mountain, Jake. E-mail interview. 3 Feb. 2015.
11. Bennett, Magnus. "The Scottish Mother of Japanese Whisky," BBC.com, http://www.bbc.com/news/uk-scotland-scotland-business-30682239, 11 Jan. 2015.
12. Sterling, Justine. "You've Never Tasted Anything Like Baijiu," *The Huffington Post*, http://www.huffingtonpost.com/food-wine/youve-never-tasted-anythi_b_5500647.html, 17 June 2014.
13. Liu, Yuan. Personal interview. 14 Nov. 2014.
14. "Roggenbier," *German Beer Institute*. http://www.germanbeerinstitute.com/Roggenbier.html, 28 Jan. 2015.
15. Winters, Lance. Phone interview. 6 Nov. 2014.
16. Ibid.
17. Difford, Simon. "Distillation: Pot vs. Column," *Difford's Guide for Discerning Drinkers*, http://www.diffordsguide.com/magazine/2014-03-04/6/distillation, 4 March 2014.
18. Donelon, Heidi. Phone interview. 22 Jan. 2015
19. Sisson, Hugh. Phone interview. 13 Feb. 2015.
20. Graves, Jamie. E-mail interview. 26 May 2015.
21. Graves, Jamie. Personal interview. 19 May 2015.
22. Vuylsteke, Steve. Personal interview. 9 Sept. 2014.
23. Okada, Takahiro. Personal interview. 20 Oct. 2014
24. Lyman, Stephen. Personal interview. 12 May 2015

25. "Sho-chu, The Precious Spirit of Kyushu, Japan," *The Sho-Chu Project*, http://www.shochu-style.jp/, Retrieved Oct. 2014
26. Lyman, Stephen. "Shochu vs. Soju!" Kampai.US, Web, http://kampai.us/shochu-vs-soju/, 18 Oct. 2011 http://articles.latimes.com/2002/jun/27/news/wk-club27, 27 June 2002.
27. "Jinro tops the IWSR list of top 100 spirits brands," International Wine and Spirit Research, http://www.iwsr.co.uk/pages/news/press-releases/JinrotopstheIWSRslistofthetop100spiritsbrands.pdf, 15 July 2013.
28. Hall, Joshua. "Soju Makers Aim to Turn Fire Water Into Liquid Gold," *Wall Street Journal Online*, http://blogs.wsj.com/korearealtime/2014/10/17/soju-makers-aim-to-turn-fire-water-into-liquid-gold/, 17 Oct. 2014.
29. Gardiner, Ross. "How to Drink Soju Like the Koreans," *TheSavory.com*, http://www.thesavory.com/drink/how-drink-soju-koreans.html, 24 Feb. 2014.

30. "Notes from the Field: Botulism from Drinking Prison-Made Illicit Alcohol-Arizona, 2012," Centers for Disease Control and Prevention, http://www.cdc.gov/mmwr/preview/mmwrhtml/mm6205a3.htm?s_cid=mm6205a3_e, 8 Feb. 2013.
31. Pearson, Brian. Phone interview. 8 Jan. 2015.
32. Sachs, Monte. Phone interview. 12 Jan. 2015.
33. French, Douglas. Phone interview. 20 Jan. 2015.
34. Ibid.
35. Ibid.
36. Rogers, Felisa. "Seven Common Misconceptions about Tequila and Mezcal," *The People's Guide to Mexico*, Web, http://thepeoplesguidetomexico.com, 19 Dec. 2013.
37. Torgove, Mishi. Phone interview. 3 Feb. 2015.
38. Gilman, Nicholas. "Here's to Mexico's Roots," *Los Angeles Times online*, http://articles.latimes.com/2011/nov/10/food/la-fo-pulquerias-20111110, 10 Nov. 2011
39. Torgove, Mishi. Phone interview. 3 Feb. 2015.
40. *The Balance and Columbian Repository*, May 13, 1806, No. 19, Vol. V, page 146
41. AngosturaBitters.com
42. Sazerac.com/cocktail
43. Macy, Tom. Personal interview. 16 Sept. 2014.
44. Ludwig, Tobin. Personal interview. 19 Aug. 2014.
45. www.FernetBranca.com, Retrieved Aug. 2014
46. Cosentino, Chris. Phone interview. 6 Jan. 2015.
47. Macy, Tom. Personal interview. 16 Sept. 2014.

48. Tepper, Rachel. "St-Germain Elderflower Liquor Acquired by Bacardi, Plans to Go Global," *The Huffington Post*, Web, http://www.huffingtonpost.com/2013/01/08/st-germain-bacardi_n_2432472.html, 8 Jan. 2013.
49. Miller, Matthew. "Grey Goose Billionaire's Second Act." Forbes, Web, http://www.forbes.com/2004/09/10/cz_mm_0910goose.html, 10 Sept. 2004.
50. Paré, Ben. Personal interview. 9 Jan. 2015.
51. Yeldell, Cynthia. "Ground zero for whiskey: Law allows production of distilled spirits in state," *Knoxville News Sentinel*, Web, http://www.knoxnews.com/business/ground-zero-whiskey-law-allows-production-distille, 5 July 2009.
52. Baker, Joe. Phone interview. 23 Dec. 2014.
53. Koffel, Sean. Phone interview. 17 Dec. 2014.
54. Schuster, Amanda. "The National Spirit of Belgium, Now Available in the U.S.!" *The Alcohol Professor*, Web, https://www.alcoholprofessor.com/blog/2013/10/02/the-national-spirit-of-belgium-now-available-in-the-u-s/, Web, 2 Oct. 2013.
55. Raustiala, Kal. "The Imperial Cocktail." *Slate.com*, http://www.slate.com/articles/health_and_science/foreigners/2013/08/gin_and_tonic_kept_the_british_empire_healthy_the_drink_s_quinine_powder.html, 28 Aug. 2013.
56. "London Gin," *Gin & Vodka*, http://www.ginvodka.org/londongin/, Oct 2014.
57. Ibid.
58. Graham, Colleen. "A Basic Introduction to Gin," *About Food*, http://cocktails.about.com/od/spirits/p/gist_gin.htm, 2014.
59. Winters, Lance. Phone interview. 6 Nov. 2014.
60. Krogstad, Christian. Phone interview. 20 Nov. 2014.
61. Facquet, Brian. Personal interview. 19 May 2015.
62. Liem, Peter. Phone interview. 2 Feb. 2015.
63. Ibid.
64. Domecq, Beltran. E-mail interview. 9 Jan. 2015
65. "Canadian Wineries Will Say Goodbye to 'Port' and 'Sherry by December 31, 2013," Canadian Vintners Association, Web, http://www.canadianvintners.com/2013/08/21/canadian-wineries-to-cease-using-terms-port-and-sherry-by-december-31-2013/, 8 Aug. 2013.
66. Broadbent, Bartholomew. Phone interview. 31 Dec. 2014.
67. Ibid.
68. Ibid.
69. Ibid.
70. Burnichon, Manny. Phone interview. 18 Dec. 2014.
71. Ibid.
72. Asseline, Rebecca. Phone interview. 6 Jan. 2015.

73. Brooks, Jay. "Italy's Tre Fontane Approved as Newest Trappist Brewery," *Brookston Beer Bulletin*, Web, http://brookstonbeerbulletin.com/italys-tre-fontane-approved-as-newest-trappist-brewery/, 11 May 2015.
74. Webber, Chris. E-mail interview. 1 March 2014.
75. "History of Mead," *Beer100.com*, Web, http://www.beer100.com/history/meadhistory.htm, Retrieved Jan. 2015.
76. "Mead Styles," American Mead Makers Association website, http://www.meadmakers.org/styles.htm.
77. Faul, Michael. Personal interview. 8 May 2015.
78. Dahlhofer, Brad. Personal interview. 11 Sept. 2014.
79. Bartlett, Bob. Phone interview. 9 Jan. 2015.
80. Da Trindade-Asher, Melanie. Phone interview. 3 Jan. 2015.
81. Da Trindade-Asher, Elizabeth. Phone interview. 3 Jan. 2015.
82. Simonson, Robert. "The Pisco Wars," *The New York Times*, Web, http://dinersjournal.blogs.nytimes.com/2012/07/27/the-pisco-wars/, 27 July 2012.
83. Higbee, Thomas. Phone interview. 12 Feb. 2015.
84. Sullivan, Emmet. "The Power of Malört," *Chicago Magazine online*, http://www.chicagomag.com/Chicago-Magazine/April-2014/The-Power-of-Malort/, 27 March 2014.
85. Mechling, Sam. Personal interview. 5 Feb. 2015.
86. Berger, Patrick. Personal interview. 5 Feb. 2015.
87. Luttman, Steve. Phone interview. 29 Jan. 2015.
88. Torgove, Mishi. Phone interview. 3 Feb. 2015.
89. Ceñal, Reyes. E-mail interview. 12 Dec. 2014.
90. Ibid.
91. Pouliot, François. Phone interview. 10 Dec. 2014.
92. "Crafting a Modern Beverage Market," BeverageWorld.com, Webinar, 13 September 2013.
93. Bell, Darek. Phone interview. 28 Oct. 2014.
94. West, Nat. 7 Oct. 2014.
95. Paré, Ben. Personal interview. 3 Feb. 2015.
96. Penn, Alyson. "A Bar in Wisconsin Is Now Selling a Bloody Mary Garnished with an Entire Fried Chicken," *Business Insider*, http://www.businessinsider.com/chicken-fried-bloody-mary-in-milwaukee-2014-8, 11 Aug. 2014.
97. Cunningham, Reggie. Phone interview. 10 Jan. 2015
98. Roberts, John. Phone interview. 8 Jan. 2015.
99. Girard, Eric. Phone interview. 6 Jan. 2015.
100. Asagiri, Shigeharu. E-mail interview. 22 Dec. 2014.
101. Wilson, Sean Lilly. Phone interview. 18 Dec. 2014.
102. Crompton, Kevin. Phone interview. 12 Feb. 2015.

103. "Ginger Ale History." Ginger Ale Authority, Web, http://gingeraleauthority.com/ginger-ale-history/, Retrieved Nov. 2014.
104. Clark, Richard. Clark, Richard. Phone interview. 13 Feb. 2015.
105. Grier, Jacob, "Announcing Aquavit Week 2014," Web, www.aquavitweek .com, 14 Nov. 2014.
106. Aquavit." *Encyclopedia Britannica*, Web. Nov. 2014.
107."Regulation of the European Parliament and of the Council of 15 January 2008 on the Definition, Description, Presentation, Labelling and the Protection of Geographical Indications of Spirit Drinks," *Official Journal of the European Union*, p. 23 Oct. 2014.
108. Swahn, Håkan. Personal interview. 24 Nov. 2014.
109. Krogstad, Christian. Phone interview. 20 Nov. 2014.
110. Mellon, Nell. Personal interview. 2 Dec. 2014.
111. "AOC Crémant d'Alsace," Vins d'Alsace, http://www.vinsalsace.com/en/alsace-wines/appellations/aoc-cremant-d-alsace/aoc-cremant-d-alsace-art1211.html, 16 Dec. 2014.
112. Ibid.
113. Ibid.

OTHER RESOURCES

Bacardi Acquires St-Germain Liqueur." Bacardilimited.com/news/244, 8 Jan. 2013

Beckett, Fiona. "Wine: Give Madeira a Chance This Christmas." *The Guardian*, http://www.theguardian.com/lifeandstyle/2014/nov/22/madeira-christmas-fiona-beckett-wine, 22 Nov. 2014.

Bell, Darek. *Alt Whiskeys: Alternative Whiskey Recipes and Distilling Techniques for the Adventurous Craft Distiller*. Nashville: Corsair Artisan Distillery, 2012.

de Kergommeaux, Davin. *Canadian Whisky: The Portable Guide.* Toronto: McClelland & Stewart, 2012

Hindy, Steve. *The Craft Beer Revolution: How a Band of Microbrewers Is Transforming the World's Favorite Drink*. New York: Palgrave Macmillan Trade, 2014.

Mosher, Randy. *Tasting Beer: An Insider's Guide to the World's Greatest Drink*. New York: Storey Publishing, 2009.

Oliver, Garrett. *The Brewmaster's Table: Discover the Pleasures of Real Beer with Real Food.* New York: Ecco Press, 2003.

Spivak, Mark. *Iconic Spirits: An Intoxicating History*. Guilford, Connecticut: Globe Pequot, 2012.

"Tequila and Mezcal facts." http://tastings.com/spirits/tequila.html

"What is Pisco?" http://www.barsolpisco.eu/en/pisco.html

Wilson, Jason. "Becoming Fluent in Shochu, Japan's Answer to Vodka," *WashingtonPost.com*, http://www.washingtonpost.com/wp-dyn/content/article/2010/05/04/AR2010050401204.html, 5 May 2010.

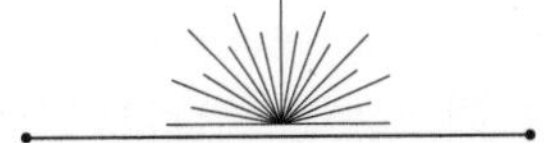

ACKNOWLEDGMENTS

Drinking adventurously should never be a solo journey and it certainly has not been one for me. There are so many people who've helped me on this adventure—too many to name, really—and their support has been invaluable.

First, I'd like to express my gratitude to everyone at Turner Publishing for embracing my concept, as well as my writing style, and agreeing to unleash it onto the world. I'd especially like to thank Todd Bottorff for his enthusiasm toward my work and my subject. I knew from our first conversation—which centered a great deal on tequila—that *The Year of Drinking Adventurously* was in very expert hands. He's also got a knack for hiring extremely talented, patient, and accommodating people—particularly Caroline Davidson, Stephanie Beard, Katherine Rowley, Jon O'Neal, Maddie Cothren, and Kelsey Reiman.

Additionally, I want to give a shout-out to Diane Gedymin, the initial editor on this project who acquired it for Turner and made this whole thing happen.

I'd also like to thank my agent (I've always wanted to say that), John Willig, who believed in my potential as a writer and in my ideas from the get-go. He's been a tireless advocate for my work, as well as my most trusted advisor, helping me navigate through the intricacies of the publishing world. I look forward to our continued partnership on future liquid literature titles.

And I wouldn't even have an agent if it hadn't been for Michi Kanno, who introduced me to John in the first place, after a fortuitous meeting at a beverage trade show.

And speaking of beverages, there are so many people who work (and play) in the drinking world to whom I'd also like to raise a glass:

—Beer, wine, and spirits editors who allow my bylines to appear in their fine publications, including Erika Rietz, William Tish, and my frequent comrade-in-consumption, sounding board, and all-around advice-giver, John Holl.

—Beverage Worlders past and present, especially Andrea Foote for introducing me to this crazy and wonderful industry, Jennifer Kirby,

Andrew Kaplan, Michelle Villas, Rosanna Bulian, Lisa Adams, Erin Fiden, and Kevin Francella.

—Industry folks who are always giving me something to write about, including, but not limited to, Darek Bell, Bartholomew Broadbent, Julia Herz, Dave Pickerell, Yuan Liu, Steaven Chen, Jeremy Cowan, Manny Burnichon, Davin de Kergommeaux, Steve Hindy, Ben Paré, Nell Mellon, Heidi Donelon, Jennie Hatton, and Chris Cosentino. A hearty "kanpai!" goes out to Takahiro Okada, Yuji Naito, Goichi Hirano, Noriyuki Yamashita, and Stephen Lyman for enhancing my shochu experience, and to Jamie Graves for the continuing saké education. Similarly, "ganbei!" to Steaven Chen, Yuan Liu, and Hakkasan Los Angeles for putting baijiu into my tipple rotation. And "slainte!" to the Cardhu, Tomatin, and Glenfarclas distilleries in Scotland. On the Kentucky side of things, a tip of the derby to Jessica Dillree of the Louisville Convention and Visitors Bureau.

—Those with whom I've shared many a drink and, whether they realize it or not, have helped in ways large and small shape the content of this book, including, in no particular order, Thomas and Amanda Cioletti, Jim and Lisa Flynn, Jeff and Joanna Bauman, Karen Auerbach, Jenny and Erik Roth, Alena Kerins, Will Salas, John Kleinchester, Natasha Bahrs, Carrie Havranek, April Darcy, Leila Hamdan, Bill Rooney, Geoff and Jennifer Clark, Sarah and Giancarlo Annese, Don Tse, and Christopher Shepard.

And, of course, cheers to my family. To my mom and dad, Clarissa and Jim Cioletti, for not disowning me when I decided to pursue writing professionally—and writing about alcohol, at that. To my grandmother, Marie Cioletti, the most badass, no-nonsense octogenarian on the planet. To my incredibly adventurous in-laws, Marty and Temple Moore, who share and very frequently indulge my passion for travel and fine drink.

I've naturally saved the best for last. To Craige Moore, the love of my life and a more patient and supportive wife than a guy like me deserves. Without you this book would not have happened. You'll always be my number one drinking buddy and my favorite adventure.

ABOUT THE AUTHOR

Jeff Cioletti's tenure in liquid literacy has exposed him to some of the best libations the world has to offer and given him access to the producers and purveyors of such fine refreshments. He combines his love of drink with a passion for travel, and one usually involves the other. As editor-at-large of Beverage World magazine and founder of *The Drinkable Globe* (DrinkableGlobe.com), Jeff continues to explore the planet, one drink at a time. When he's not writing about or traveling for beverages, he's making films about them. He is the writer, producer, and director of the feature film *Beerituality*, a comedy set in the world of craft beer. The film is available for on-demand streaming and download at Amazon.com. Jeff has offered his beverage-related insights in interviews with CNN International, Fox Business News, CNBC, NPR, BBC World, BBC Radio, Associated Press, the *New York Post*, *Financial Times*, WCBS-TV, *Bloomberg BusinessWeek*, *Investors Business Daily*, *Advertising Age*, and many other media outlets.

ABOUT THE AUTHOR